STUDIES IN NATIONAL POLICY

Pricing
of
Military
Procurements

BY

JOHN PERRY MILLER

NEW HAVEN

Yale University Press

LONDON · GEOFFREY CUMBERLEGE · OXFORD UNIVERSITY PRESS

1949

To D. M. M.

PREFACE

THE present study presents an analysis of the purchasing policies of the armed services with particular attention to matters of price. It may appear strange that the pricing aspects of military purchasing has been selected for special treatment. Clearly we are but little concerned with dollars when considering matters vital to the defense of the nation. But the prices of military goods both in war and peace have an importance which far transcends their immediate effects upon the federal budget. In our society the price system is a delicate mechanism which serves several functions. It provides the stimulus for the continuous allocation of our economic resources to the production of those goods we need most; it provides an important incentive to individuals and firms to produce efficiently; and it provides the rewards to individuals and groups for the efforts and resources which they devote to production. The type of purchasing and pricing policies followed by the services will determine in large part the effectiveness with which the price system performs these functions.

Of course the price system as an instrument for allocating resources plays a lesser role in times of war than in times of peace. In wartime production and material controls must play a vital part. But this study shows that price played a very vital role in the allocation of resources during World War II and that proper pricing by the armed services and industry may make a real contribution to economic mobilization in any major war. Appropriate pricing may not only facilitate the allocation of our scarce resources to the most vital uses, but it may also serve as an important incentive to efficiency in production. Conversely, inappropriate pricing of military goods may put a premium on the waste of manpower and materials. A waste of resources in military production may reduce the volume of materials and manpower which can be made available to the fighting forces and the speed with which the fighting forces can be mobilized. Pricing policies are, then, an important element in economic mobilization and therefore of considerable importance to military strategy.

Poor pricing is not the only cause of inefficiency and waste in the use of our resources. Deficiencies in the systems for determining military requirements, inadequate inventory procedures, and insistence by the services on unnecessarily rigid specifications for military goods are equally important if not more important sources of economic waste in times of war. These problems deserve serious attention. Likewise the labor policies pursued by the government, unions, and management have a tremendous impact on industrial efficiency. Any impartial observer will admit that there is room for improvement upon the labor policies pursued during World War II. Finally, the effects of our tax policies on individual and group incentives deserve careful consideration. Although I have given only passing attention to these problems, I do not mean to minimize their importance. More effective policies and procedures in these related areas could do much to increase industrial efficiency and thereby reduce the impact of military procurement upon our economy. They would, thereby, facilitate the purchasing and pricing problems of the services materially.

I hope this study will prove useful to students of price control and fiscal policy as well as to those interested in the immediate problem of military procurement. Although much has been written about wartime control of the prices of basic war materials and of consumers' goods, the prices of military goods have received little attention. But any study of wartime price policy is incomplete which ignores this important part of the wartime economy. Likewise, with government expenditures playing an increasingly important part in our national economy even apart from military crisis, it is important that students of fiscal policy consider the effects of government purchasing on the structure and functioning of our markets. This is particularly true in view of proposals to use fiscal policy as an instrument for affecting the level of economic activity.

I wish to express my gratitude to the Social Science Research Council for the grant of a Demobilization Award in 1946–1947 which made the research on this volume possible and to the Carnegie Corporation which has made publication possible by a grant through the National Policy Committee at Yale University.

I am indebted to many individuals for stimulus and aid in the writing of this monograph. Among these are the many colleagues with whom it was my privilege to work in the armed services during World War II. They deserve great credit for the energy and resourcefulness which they brought to bear upon these problems. I am also indebted for most helpful criticisms and suggestions to the members of the Seminar of the National Policy Committee at Yale University and to the participants in the Conference on Pricing of Military Procurements held by the committee in New York on June 23, 1948. Chapter XV lists these participants and provides a report of the discussion at this conference prepared by Mr. Henry E. Hansen of the National Industrial Conference Board.

I wish also to acknowledge the detailed comments on an early draft by the following: Professors Challis A. Hall, Jr., Kent T. Healy, Harold D. Lasswell, Max F. Millikan, and Eugene V. Rostow of Yale University; Mr. W. Browne Baker, Vice-President, South Texas Commercial National Bank; Mr. William Sheffield Cowles, Wood, Walker and Company, New York; Mr. Vincent deP. Goubeau, Director of Materials, Victor Division, RCA; Mr. Henry E. Hansen, National Industrial Conference Board; Lt. Cdr. Joseph L. Howard, SC, USN; Mr. Harry Howell, UNRRA; Mr. Harris Kempner, Galveston, Texas; Mr. John A. Moffitt, President, Connecticut Hard Rubber Company; Dr. William H. Moore, Assistant to the Assistant Secretary of the Navy; Dr. Eugene E. Oakes, Economist to the Joint Committee on Internal Revenue Taxation, U.S. Congress.

I am also indebted to the following for the opportunity to discuss many points involved: Mr. Mark E. Andrews, Assistant Secretary of the Navy; Rear Admirals Morton I. Ring and James D. Boyle, Office of Naval Material, USN; Brigadier General E. M. Brannon, Assistant Judge Advocate General, USA; Colonel Phillips W. Smith, USAF; Dr. Gustav Seidler, General Staff, USA; Mr. E. P. McGuire, President, The Linder Coy, Cleveland; Dr. Andrew J. Kress, Georgetown University.

I wish also to acknowledge the able assistance of Dr. Phyllis Wallace and Miss Hazel Golenbock, who served as my research assistants; of Donald T. Dorsey who helped with the proofs; of Miss Theodora Pniewski and Miss Ruth Ericson, who did much of the typing of the several drafts. Miss Ericson also prepared the charts. I am particularly grateful to my wife who prepared the index and at many points exercised a stern editorial hand.

Acknowledgement is made also to the editors of the *Harvard Business Review* for permission to use portions of my article entitled "Military Procurement in Peacetime," published therein in the Summer Issue, 1947; to Harcourt, Brace and Company, Inc., for permission to quote from *Arsenal of Democracy* by Donald Nelson; to Rinehart and Company, Inc., for permission to quote from *The Impact of War*, by Pendleton Herring; and to the President and Fellows of Harvard University for permission to quote from "How Government Buys: An Appraisal," by A. M. Freiberg, *Public Policy*, 1942.

JOHN PERRY MILLER

Silliman College, Yale University
September 1, 1948

CONTENTS

CHARTS

TABLES

APPENDICES

ABBREVIATIONS

AAF   Army Air Forces.

APR   Army Procurement Regulations.

ASF   Army Service Forces (Successor to SOS).

CPA   Civilian Production Administration.

CPPC   Cost-plus-percentage-of-cost.

CPFF   Cost-plus-fixed-fee.

DPC   Defense Plant Corporation.

F.R.   Federal Register.

GMPR   General Maximum Price Regulation.

GOCO   Government-owned-contractor-operated.

NDAC   National Defense Advisory Commission.

NPD   Navy Procurement Directives.

OPA   Office of Price Administration.

OPM   Office of Production Management.

OP&M   Office of Procurement and Material (Navy Department).

P.&C.   Purchases and Contracts Branch (War Department prior to March 1942).

RFC   Reconstruction Finance Corporation.

RR   Renegotiation Regulations.

SOS   Services of Supply (Superseded by ASF).

WLB   War Labor Board.

WPB   War Production Board.

I

THE PROBLEM

Introduction

SUCCESS in modern warfare has come to depend increasingly on efficient mobilization of economic resources. Since a nation's military strategy is limited by its economic potential, the success of its military operations depends upon the careful coordination of its military strategy with its programs of economic mobilization. If we become involved in another major war, the efficiency with which we mobilize our manpower, productive facilities, and natural resources will without doubt be decisive in determining the outcome.[1]

The threat of atomic warfare has already compelled changes in military strategy and may shorten if not eliminate the period available for mobilization after the outbreak of hostilities.[2] We are apparently entering an era in which a high degree of economic mobilization for the support of our military forces will be an important and continuing element of our international strategy especially during these years of precarious peace. But even though the nature and timing of economic mobilization may change, it will still be critical. It may be that the initial attacks in atomic warfare will be decisive, but this only emphasizes the importance of our mobilization efforts in advance of the outbreak of hostilities. If, however, defenses are developed which render the initial attack in such a war indecisive, efficient logistic support for our armed forces after the

1. Hanson W. Baldwin, *The Price of Power* (1948), chap. xi.
2. The recommendations of the President's Air Policy Committee were based on the assumption that if we are attacked before January 1, 1953 we shall still be able to follow our traditional course of mobilizing our armed forces and industry after war begins, but that after that date we shall need a military force in being capable of resisting atomic attacks without delay. See President's Air Policy Committee, *Survival in the Air Age: A Report by the President's Air Policy Committee* (Jan. 1, 1948).

outbreak of war may become even more important than in the past because of the probable effectiveness of such attacks in disrupting our economy.

In the foreseeable future we apparently face the problem of maintaining a large military establishment as an instrument of national policy in a world of international tension and crisis. This poses the unprecedented problem of making large and continuing military procurements in a peacetime economy which already shows signs of chronic hyper-employment and inflation. Can we solve these problems while maintaining our democratic traditions and thereby avoid the danger, so characteristic of our modern world, of drifting into a "garrison state"? [3]

The primary purpose of economic mobilization is to provide the manpower necessary to our armed forces and the logistic support of these forces. Military logistics involves three main functions: the determination of requirements, procurement of material, and distribution of this material to the places where it may be most effectively used. Clearly these three components are interdependent, and there are compelling reasons for urging that they should be more closely coordinated than they have been in the past. It is worth while, however, to isolate the procurement function for special study since military procurement is the point at which the logistic program impinges most directly upon the national economy. Such a study is facilitated by the fact that in the United States the procurement function is and has been organizationally separate from the other aspects of both logistics and economic mobilization.

Procurement itself has several facets: drafting of specifications, selection of sources, determination of prices and other contractual arrangements (including financing and provision of government-furnished equipment or facilities), expediting, inspection, and finally payment and audit of accounts. The

3. For a discussion of the implications of the drift to garrison states in the modern world see Harold D. Lasswell, *The Analysis of Political Behaviour: An Empirical Approach* (1947), pp. 146–157.

focus of the present study is upon the selection of sources and the determination of prices and other contractual arrangements. These may be referred to as the purchasing functions of procurement. Because procurement is the point at which the logistic program impinges most directly on the economy, a study of these aspects of procurement throws light on many difficult problems faced by our democratic society in supporting its military establishment. The critical importance of these problems was reflected during the early part of each of the two World Wars in the controversies as to whether the purchasing functions of procurement should be the administrative responsibility of the services or of a civilian agency responsible for industrial mobilization.

In focusing this study upon the purchasing functions of procurement I do not wish to minimize the importance of the other parts of logistics. Effective purchasing methods are not enough even to insure effective mobilization. Rigorous control over requirements and over storage and distribution, for example, play an important part. Failure to effect adequate control over requirements and over the storage and distribution of materials, as in the past, will be important sources of waste and inefficiency. Moreover, by accentuating the scarcities of labor and materials such failures will magnify the need for various economic controls and complicate their administration.

Policy Objectives

The objectives of military procurement policy are several. The overriding economic objective is to insure to the services the necessary goods of the quality and kind at the time and place required for the defense of our vital national interests. This objective is paramount whether in time of peace, in time of crisis such as the present, or in time of war. Ways must be found to allocate to the production of military goods those resources of manpower and materials which are necessary to supply the services' needs. Moreover, ways must be found to

provide incentives to efficient production so that the services'
needs may be supplied with the least possible burden upon the
civilian economy. This is particularly true in time of crisis or
war, but it is likewise important in time of peace. Inefficient
production which involves a waste of manpower or resources
means either a lesser supply of goods to the services or more
serious inroads upon supplies to the civilian economy. The
first may endanger the success of military operations directly,
while the latter may have the same result through its effects
upon civilian morale.

Military procurement policy must also be formulated with
consideration for other socio-political objectives. It is important that the services conduct their operations, including
procurement, so as to promote unity of purpose within the
nation. Maximum and expeditious production of military
goods as well as the success of military and international strategy depend upon such unity. In our democratic society the
military establishment has long been subject to suspicion. We
have resisted all tendencies of military groups to increase their
influence and to dominate our political and economic institutions. The history of the Thirties and of our mobilization
efforts before Pearl Harbor stands as a striking lesson of the
effects upon our international diplomacy, economic mobilization, and military operations of an atmosphere of mutual
suspicion and distrust between the various groups within our
society such as labor, agriculture, business, and the military.[4]

A second socio-political objective of economic mobilization is to preserve and strengthen our democratic institutions
by insuring respect for the individual, wide-spread sharing of
economic and political power, and a decentralization of
decision-making as against centralized planning. A society in
crisis or in war is seriously tempted and in fact to some extent
forced to make inroads upon these institutions. Political and
economic power becomes increasingly centralized. The free-

4. United States Bureau of the Budget, *The United States at War: Development and Administration of the War Program by the Federal Government*
(1947), "Historical Records on War Administration," No. 1, prepared under the
auspices of the Committee of Records of War Administration, *passim*.

dom of individuals becomes circumscribed. Institutions for decentralized decision-making, such as our market economy, are subjected to centralized controls. In times of crisis and above all in times of war many of these inroads upon our democratic institutions are inevitable. But in the interest of our long-run aspirations it is important that we seek to devise means of effecting our over-all objectives while making the least possible inroad upon our democratic institutions. Where the same production objective can be accomplished by alternative methods, it is important that we should choose those methods which will impair our democratic institutions the least, will provide the greatest respect for the initiative and preference of the individual, and provide for the greatest possible decentralization of decision-making. In this way we may help to preserve our democratic heritage.

Moreover, ours is a society in which we are still in the process of achieving some of our most cherished ideals. All will agree that our tradition of respecting the political, social, and economic equality of individuals without regard to race, color, or creed has as yet been imperfectly realized. Likewise in the field of business we have long striven to provide increased opportunity for small and independent enterprises which can compete effectively. In some ways a crisis or war economy makes it easier to proceed toward the further realization of some of these social and political objectives upon which there is general consensus. Such an opportunity should not be allowed to pass unheeded. This is not an invitation for all and sundry to seek to further their individual objectives. It is suggested rather that where the conditions of crisis or war facilitate the further realization of long-run aspirations upon which we are agreed the opportunity should not be missed.

Policy Objectives and the Price System

What is the relation between these objectives and purchasing policy on military procurement? It may seem strange that considerations of price and of related business arrangements should be thought matters of serious consequence in dealing with the grim realities of crisis and war. It is clearly the consensus of opinion in Western civilizations that considerations of price or budgetary cost should not be allowed to delay or in any way interfere with the defense of a nation's vital interests. Nevertheless, in any economy such as ours based on private property and freedom of contract in which we rely upon market forces in large part to organize production and determine individuals' shares in the national income and wealth, consideration of the prices paid on military contracts will continue to be matters of public concern. The price system has an important place among the institutions which may further these objectives.[5]

Functions of the Price System in Peace. In the United States we depend in large part upon individual and corporate enterprise working through competitive markets to organize our economic life. In this system of free competitive enterprise the price system, meaning thereby our system of prices, wages, interest, rents, and profits, plays a very important part. This system provides a decentralized mechanism which serves three main functions. First, it allocates our limited economic resources as between the various alternative uses to which they may be put. Our economic system has been founded on the assumption that for the most part in any given state of the arts and sciences the type of commodities produced should depend upon the desires of consumers, limited only by the willingness of others to produce these items in freely competitive markets. Consequently we depend upon the incentives of greater or lesser rewards provided by the price system to induce individuals and firms to redirect their energies from time to time away from the production of goods which are in lesser demand to the production of those which are in greater demand. In short, through the price system we determine what

5. For a discussion of the functions and limits of the price system in modern democratic societies see Lionel Robbins, *The Economic Problem in Peace and War* (1947); Arthur C. Pigou, *Income: An Introduction to Economics* (1946); Frank H. Knight, *The Economic Organization* (1933); Henry C. Simons, *Economic Policy for a Free Society* (1948).

goods are produced and in what quantities they are produced. It also determines how they are produced and by whom. The success with which the price system accomplishes this depends upon many things including the extent to which we preserve markets which are truly competitive and free from monopolistic or restrictive policies. Its success is also affected by our tax policies, labor policies, the attitudes and motives of individuals, and many other factors which affect the incentives or opportunities of individuals and business enterprises to adapt themselves to economic change.

A second function of the price system is to provide individuals and business enterprises with an important incentive to efficiency.[6] It must be recognized, of course, that monetary rewards are by no means the sole incentives which induce people to make their contribution to production and that we have been slow in recognizing many of these other motives.[7] It may be assumed, however, that the prospect of financial rewards is still an important type of incentive even in times of crisis or war. The effectiveness with which price incentives are used in contemporary United States varies from one part of the economy to another. It depends among other things upon the motives and training of individuals, internal management techniques, the incidence of tax policy, and upon the existence and importance of other non-financial incentives such as power, prestige, activity, or security. While it must be recognized that price incentives are by no means the whole answer to efficient production, in our democratic society we must still depend upon such incentives to a large extent. Even in Soviet Russia wage incentives play an important part.[8] It is therefore important that where such a policy is consistent with other objectives we shape our institutions so as to provide in-

6. For an interesting discussion by a war contractor of the role of financial incentives in promoting efficiency see James F. Lincoln, *Lincoln's Incentive System* (1946).

7. Wilbert E. Moore, *Industrial Relations and the Social Order* (1947), chap. xvi; T. N. Whitehead, *Leadership in a Free Society* (1937), chap. ix; Chester I. Barnard, *The Functions of the Executive* (1938), chap. xi.

8. Abram Bergson, *The Structure of Soviet Wages: A Study in Socialist Economics* (1944), pp. 195-197, 203-204 and *passim*.

centives for efficient production and above all so as to avoid positive incentives to inefficiency.

The third function of our price system is to provide the disposable income or "take home" pay of individuals in the form of wages, salaries, rents, interest, or profit. Clearly it is not the price system alone which determines our individual disposable incomes. Tax policy takes its toll and is consciously used to change the distribution of income and wealth as between individuals. But it remains true that the principal claims which we have as individuals to participate in the joint annual produce of the nation arise from the income received through the price system for our individual efforts or for the use of the resources we have accumulated.

It is my basic assumption that in line with the objectives stated above we wish to preserve and strengthen our freely competitive economy and to continue to use the price system as a vigorous and effective instrument for organizing our economic life. I shall argue that the purchasing policy of the services in peacetime can and should be devised so as to insure to the services their necessary supplies, while at the same time furthering rather than hindering the operations of the competitive price system. The analysis and recommendations presented below for peacetime procurement by the armed services are designed to accomplish this. This will necessitate substantial changes in the traditional procedures for peacetime purchasing and the adaptation to government conditions of many purchasing methods which have long since proved their effectiveness in industry.[9] The adoption of more business-like purchasing policies by the armed services in peacetime will not only further the objective of preserving and strengthening our competitive price system but will also serve to insure that the services acquire in advance the personnel and skills required for effective procurement in war.

If the price system is to serve in peacetime as a means for

9. For discussion of industrial purchasing practices see Howard T. Lewis, *Industrial Purchasing* (1933) and *Procurement: Principles and Cases* (1948); National Industrial Conference Board, *Purchasing for Industry*, "Studies in Business Policy," No. 33 (1948).

organizing our economic resources, we must insure a structure of markets which will promote competition and we must pursue monetary and fiscal policies which will avoid chronic tendencies toward unemployment on the one hand and inflation on the other. Chronic unemployment in the Thirties gave rise to many restrictive policies which are inconsistent with a vigorous and progressive economy.[10] Failure to pursue fiscal and monetary policies which will avoid the opposite danger of inflation will certainly lead to the adoption of other restrictive policies which are equally undesirable.

Price System in War. In times of war the overriding objective of economic policy is the mobilization of resources to insure maximum and expeditious production. At such times it is clear that we cannot rely upon the price system to organize our economic resources to the same extent as in peace. Other controls are necessary for both economic and political reasons. It is questionable whether in such circumstances and in the absence of other controls the price system can act with sufficient precision or rapidity to divert resources from peacetime uses to military needs.[11] This is true even if we assume the most spartan monetary and fiscal policies compatible with expeditious mobilization. Moreover, if we are to be realistic in our planning, we must recognize that it is very improbable that we shall adopt such spartan monetary and fiscal policies. We need only note the timidity with which we used monetary and fiscal controls in World War II despite the urging of many in high repute to realize the need to plan for the worst while hoping for the best.[12] Our very success in direct control of prices by OPA, a success beyond the expectations of most experts, has doubtlessly strengthened our tendency to turn to this type of control and diverted our attention from the possibilities of monetary and fiscal policy. But this only underlines

10. Allan G. B. Fisher, *The Clash of Progress and Security* (1935), esp. chap. iii.
11. See Arthur C. Pigou, *The Political Economy of War* (1941); Robbins, *op. cit.*, chap. ii; Seymour E. Harris, *Inflation and the American Economy* (1945), chap. i.
12. For example see John Maynard Keynes, *How to Pay for the War* (1940); also Bureau of the Budget, *op. cit.*, chap. ix.

the importance of pressing in time of war for more rigorous monetary and fiscal policies so that the inflationary dangers may be minimized.

Granted that the price system alone is not adequate in war to do the job of mobilization, it is clear that various direct controls of production will be required, such as limitation orders on the production of unnecessary civilian goods, priorities, and other schemes for the control of basic materials. Likewise direct controls of manpower, wages, rents, and prices will be necessary.

Despite the need for such controls the price system will not be a completely passive factor. Economic mobilization on the scale required by modern warfare requires the use of all available devices of social organization including the price system. Even in war price policy is a potent instrument which, if not used consciously to facilitate economic mobilization, may obstruct it. The price system operated by the forces of the freely competitive market will certainly not exist, but *a* price system probably will, if only as a device to determine individuals' rewards. It is perhaps needless to point out that except under conditions of seige we are likely to depend primarily upon the price system, even in wartime, to provide individuals with their claims to share in the current flow of goods and services available for consumption and in future claims against the wealth of the country arising from accumulated savings.

But the potentialities of a wartime price system to aid in the allocation of resources and in the provision of incentives for efficiency should not be minimized. The use of the wartime price system for these purposes will serve the important objective of decentralized decision-making and the sharing of power. If the production and material controls are not to become so detailed as to be cumbersome, they must be confined to general controls of the use of materials such as limitation orders on the production of unnecessary goods and priorities. But while such controls may shake resources loose from the civilian economy, they do not insure that specific resources released from civilian uses will be devoted to military production. It is important that wherever possible the price system should work in such a way as to facilitate the diversion of these resources to particular contracts rather than to militate against it. Otherwise it will be necessary to rely heavily upon issuing a multitude of individual orders to particular firms. Of course, in the event of atomic warfare within our own borders it may be necessary to rely increasingly upon orders directed at individuals rather than upon the price system, but this should be avoided if possible.

The price system may also serve even in war as one device to encourage efficiency in the use of labor and materials. Such efficiency is a major objective of wartime national policy because of its direct relation to the striking power of the armed forces. It is true, of course, that effective appeals may be made during war to patriotism, pride of achievement, and other motives to encourage efficient production. But financial incentives are by no means unimportant. It is generally recognized that contract prices may be so low and contractual arrangements so rigorous as to discourage contractors from production. It is equally true that prices may be so high and contractual arrangements may be of such a nature as to encourage waste and inefficiency. It is important that we avoid contractual and price arrangements which put a premium on inefficiency and that we seek to devise arrangements and arrive at prices which will provide positive incentives to individuals to exert their best efforts and to conserve labor and materials in producing the goods for war.

Under wartime conditions prices paid for military goods take on additional importance because of their relation to the general program of economic stabilization, *i.e.*, stabilization of prices, wages, and profits. Although economic stabilization is designed in part to facilitate maximum and expeditious production directly, it has an equally important role in a democratic society as a device for securing the whole-hearted cooperation of the various economic, political, and social groups whose immediate interests and long-run aspirations find themselves in conflict with one another or with the overall objectives of the economic mobilization for war.

Problems of wartime administration are not simply problems of the mechanics and procedures of government. The objectives of government, even in time of war, are often in warm dispute and the building of administrative mechanisms must proceed with great urgency in an atmosphere of conflict about what the objectives should be. . . . In the American democracy, a government, no matter how wise its judgment may be, cannot for long execute its will arbitrarily against the opposition of substantial blocs of opinion. It must educate, placate, temporize, and act boldly as conditions require.[13]

It is inevitable that economic mobilization for a major war should have far-reaching effects on the economic, political, and social positions of various groups. It is likewise inevitable that each of these groups should try to minimize the burdens of war upon itself and seek to protect or even improve its strategic position in line with its long-run aspirations. With the approach of World War II agriculture, recalling its years of depression between the wars, saw its opportunity to gain parity prices or better.[14] Labor saw an opportunity to push forward the gains which it had made during the Thirties. Industry wished to avoid disturbing customary business practices wherever possible. Moreover, it was being asked to make large capital commitments and to divert its energies from customary markets to new and perhaps ephemoral ones. In doing this it wished to avoid the inevitable risks by shifting them to others or to be well compensated for assuming them.[15] The proponents of small business saw in the war effort an opportunity to secure for such firms a more secure position in the economy. On the other hand, they were fearful that the concentration of prime contracts with large firms might have the long-run consequence of making their position less se-

13. *Ibid.*, p. 3.
14. For discussion of agricultural policy in the early period of the war see John D. Black, *Parity, Parity, Parity* (1942).
15. See below, Chap. VIII.

cure.[16] This led to efforts to spread contracts among smaller firms even though a price differential in favor of such firms might be necessary. These will serve as examples of some of the major interests at conflict in the mobilization program. These conflicts were aggravated by the fact that until Pearl Harbor there was no general consensus as to the objectives of the United States in the world crisis or the probability of our entering the war.

The economic stabilization program was an important device for reconciling many of these conflicts and molding together these various groups into that unity of purpose so necessary to victory. It is clear that in some cases the terms of stabilization were determined by the relative strategic position or political power of the groups at interest rather than by the interests of the nation at large. This is one of the prices of democracy.

In this conflict it was inevitable that the question of the profits of war contractors should be given important consideration. Proposals for the draft of manpower into military service and the control of wages led inevitably to proposals for the draft of industry and for the control of profits.[17] Consequently the policies for pricing military procurements were influenced not only by the economic considerations outlined above but also by the political necessity of controlling the extremes of excessive profits. This complicated seriously the problem of using price as an incentive device. The services were faced with the problem of developing methods of pricing which would facilitate production and at the same time provide profits which were compatible with political and social stability.

In the case of foreign purchases as well, procurement often assumed non-economic objectives of both a military and political nature. In the purchase of many strategic materials the

16. Smaller War Plants Corporation, *Economic Concentration and World War II*, Report to the Special Committee of the United States Senate to Study Problems of American Small Business, Senate Doc. No. 206, 79th Cong., 2d Sess. (1946), pp. vii–viii.

17. See below, pp. 39–43.

dominant consideration was their immediate importance to our production program. But an important, though secondary, consideration was to make such purchases so as to foster friendly diplomatic relations with the countries involved and thereby strengthen the unity of purpose with our allies and with the neutrals. This meant adapting purchasing policies to the desires of the dominant political forces in these countries. Other purchases abroad were made solely for the purpose of maintaining friendly diplomatic relations with little concern for our needs for the particular item. Where purchases of strategic materials were made to prevent their coming into the hands of the Axis powers, tactical considerations of economic warfare were dominant. In the case of local purchases to supply our forces stationed abroad the dominant objective was acquisition of necessary materials. Concessions were usually made, however, to the general domestic stabilization programs of our allies. We have not been so sensitive to the impact of volume purchases on the economies of occupied countries. Such considerations have usually had to wait upon the development of a general stabilization program out of the chaos following defeat.

The price system can then continue to serve important functions even in wartime. Although the price system itself may be controlled and the role of price may be less than in peacetime, the proper functioning of this system becomes a major consideration of policy for both economic and sociopolitical reasons. Since it is clear that the various objectives to be accomplished through the price system may in some respects conflict, the problem of working out effective purchasing policies is one of developing the best possible compromise. It must be recognized that it is not easy to devise a synthetic substitute for genuine competition. When this is complicated by other political and social objectives, the problem becomes even more difficult. The compromise will inevitably be less than the ideal from the point of view of any one objective. The analysis and recommendations below for wartime procurement by the armed services are made on the assumption that we shall and should rely significantly upon a price system even in a major war to serve a multiplicity of economic and socio-political objectives.

Price System in a Crisis Society. There is a state of society midway between one at war and one at peace which we may refer to as a "crisis society." By this is meant a society in which continuing international tension requires a continuing high level of economic mobilization to support the military establishment. This appears to be a characteristic of the years immediately ahead. In a crisis society the problems of supplying the armed services with their necessary supplies is in many respects more difficult than in either peace or war. Since the procurement program in such a society will generally be larger than in normal peacetime, the effects of such a program upon the economy are likely to be so great as to threaten the development of serious scarcities and inflation in the absence of rigorous monetary and fiscal policies. Moreover, procurement in a crisis society may be more difficult than in time of war because of understandable reluctance to impose rigorous controls over production, manpower, and prices and because of the lesser effectiveness of appeals to patriotism, prestige, and pride of accomplishment.

The problem of formulating purchasing policies in such times of crisis is particularly difficult. Continuing crisis may prove a serious threat to the persistence of our democratic institutions unless ways can be found to mobilize our resources with the minimum centralization of power and direct controls. We face a serious danger in such a society of relying so heavily upon centralized and detailed controls that we destroy our democratic institutions, stifle individual initiative, centralize economic and political power, and enhance to an unnecessary and undesirable extent the power of the military. It is especially important that we make every effort in a crisis society to devise means which, while insuring the necessary military establishment, will at the same time preserve our democratic institutions.

This is particularly important in the field of procurement,

which is the point where a military program impinges most directly upon our economy. If we are to preserve the unity of purpose necessary for a firm international policy, we must make a choice. We must invoke either rigorous monetary and fiscal policies or direct controls of prices, wages, and production, or of course, some blend of the two approaches. The alternative is economic instability which will be disruptive of national unity.

We demonstrated during World War II that direct control of prices, wages, and production can be effective far beyond the expectations of most experts. There are signs that we are coming to think too much in terms of the use of these devices in our crisis economy and are giving too little attention to the possibilities of using monetary and fiscal devices to minimize the tendencies to inflation and the development of scarcities. It is time that we gave more attention to monetary and fiscal devices including the much neglected devices of compulsory savings and incentive saving schemes as instruments for control in our crisis society in place of direct controls over prices, wages, and production.[18] There are those who fear that rigorous use of monetary and fiscal policies may precipitate disastrous deflation and unemployment. This is a real danger in some circumstances. But so long as our society shows signs of continuing international crisis it is probable that our foreign exports and military expenditure programs, together with the large backlog of private investment in plant and equipment and in consumers' durable goods, will supply sufficient effective demand to make the dangers of invoking rigorous monetary and fiscal policies slight. Consequently the analysis and recommendations below for procurement in a society of crisis are made on the assumption that in order to preserve our democratic institutions, individual initiative, and the decentralization of decision-making we shall rely heavily upon indirect controls through monetary and fiscal policies rather than upon direct controls to promote economic stability.

18. For discussion of some of the problems involved see Albert G. Hart, *Money Debt and Economic Activity* (1948), part v.

II

PURCHASE REQUIREMENTS IN WORLD WAR II

THE impact of war mobilization upon the national economy depends upon many factors including the availability of unemployed or unused resources, the system of economic controls adopted, and above all upon the total requirements of goods necessary to satisfy the needs of the nation's armed forces and of its allies. These requirements will depend upon the nation's strategic plans.

In the event of a major crisis or war the efficient use and allocation of scarce resources to a multiplicity of ends becomes a critical issue of national policy. A nation must decide the extent to which its resources can be mobilized to increase its production by drawing additional resources and labor into production and by increasing their efficiency. It must also allocate its mobilized resources between its military establishment, its civilian economy, and its commitments to its allies and to the neutrals. In addition it must determine the proportion of the resources to be allocated to each branch of the military establishment and to the production of alternative items for the supply of these branches. Failure to mobilize adequately or to make rational allocation of resources to the various claimants may jeopardize victory and will in any event lead to unnecessary waste of labor and materials and unnecessary expenditures.

Requirements

The accurate estimate of minimum requirements for the armed services in accordance with strategic plans is of critical importance to military success. There are two aspects of the problem of military requirements both of which demand careful attention: (1) determining requirements of end products to implement strategic plans and (2) determining requirements of labor, basic materials, and productive facilities necessary to produce these end products within the allotted time. The determination of end products provides the starting point of the purchase function and is therefore of particular significance to this study. A determination of the requirements of labor, materials, and facilities and a comparison of these requirements with available resources is necessary to determine the feasibility of the strategic plans or the need to develop new resources or to shake resources loose from the civilian economy.

An overestimate of requirements either in terms of end products or in terms of labor, materials, and facilities may jeopardize victory through leading to unnecessarily cautious strategic plans. It will most certainly lead to waste of resources through the production of unnecessary goods, building of unnecessary facilities, and recruiting and training of unnecessary labor forces. It will also magnify the need for controls over the economy. An underestimate of requirements may likewise jeopardize military operations. It may mean production plans which have to be abandoned or delayed and this in turn may necessitate revision of strategic plans. Such revisions in procurement plans will inevitably lead to confusion and waste. Finally, failure to estimate requirements realistically will by exposing the ineptitude of the military and civilian mobilization agencies create suspicion and disunity at a time when unity of purpose is especially necessary.

The determination of purchase requirements of end products starts with the basic strategic plans. In peacetime or times of crisis these depend upon what types of military preparedness seem most likely to reduce the possibilities of the outbreak of war and upon an estimate of when and where military action may be necessary. After the outbreak of a war requirements depend upon constantly changing military strategy and tactics. It should be noted that so long as the enemy has initiative the strategic plans must necessarily be in constant flux. But even after a nation has acquired the initiative in warfare itself, its strategy will be subject to continuous change when it faces unexpected resistances as in the case of the Battle of the Bulge in the fall of 1944 or when it seeks to exploit unexpected advantages as in the case of the by-passing of Truk in the spring of 1944.[1]

But requirements of end products depend on several factors other than strategic plans. They depend upon whether products can be devised with sufficient flexibility to be adapted to several alternative operational plans without unduly limiting operational effectiveness. They depend likewise upon the rate at which specific strategic plans can be translated into precise schedules for the purchase of new goods and the cancellation of contracts for other goods no longer needed. They depend finally upon the realism of estimates of rates of utilization and upon the efficiency of the systems of distribution and inventory control.

If the impact of procurement upon the economy is to be minimized and waste of labor and materials is to be avoided, it is necessary that requirements of end products be scrutinized regularly, that estimates of rates of utilization be realistic, and that efficient systems of inventory controls, transportation, and distribution be developed. It is equally important that requirements in terms of end products be translated quickly and accurately into requirements in terms of labor, materials, and facilities so that the feasibility of procurement programs can be determined. This means also that there must be a detailed and up-to-date inventory of our potential in terms of labor, materials, and facilities so that the requirements programs can be matched against our potential.

It is not the purpose of this book to discuss ways and means of accomplishing these ends, but it should be emphasized that the successful solution of these problems with a minimum of waste of resources will contribute substantially to minimizing the impact of procurement upon the economy and to an increase in the striking power of the armed forces.

1. Duncan S. Ballantine, *U.S. Naval Logistics in the Second World War* (1947), pp. 171-172.

The controversy over requirements during World War II between WPB (and its predecessors), the armed services, and other groups indicates the extent to which many major mobilization decisions depend upon the accurate determination of minimum requirements.[2] Prior to Pearl Harbor the military requirements both in terms of end products and in terms of labor, materials, and facilities were uncertain. Moreover, there was much controversy as to whether resources and facilities were adequate. By the spring of 1942 it was discovered that the uncoordinated procurements of the armed services plus the international commitments made by the President called for war expenditures which would have taken 75 per cent of the national product in December, 1943.[3] This, it was argued by WPB, was too large. 1942 was a year of constant struggle by the parties at interest to determine the over-all division of our economic potential between the civilian economy, our international commitments, and the various claimants within the armed services.[4] One reason for this was our failure to develop our strategic plans. The major strategy for the war was still under discussion until August, 1942, when the invasion of Africa was determined upon. Plans for invading Northern Europe did not become firm commitments until May, 1943. Until that time we were manufacturing munitions for the shelf, "for equipping armies and squadrons, and not for special operations the strength and date of which could be forecast even by the chiefs of staff." [5] But equally important as causes of this controversy was failure to develop adequate techniques for determining requirements and feasibility and failure to clarify the question of who should have ultimate responsibility for determining requirements.

Whether the determination of requirements is a military or

2. Civilian Production Administration, *Industrial Mobilization for War: History of the War Production Board and Predecessor Agencies 1940–1945* (1947), "Historical Records on War Administration, War Production Board," General Study No. 1, pp. 91–92, 121–140, 273–292.

3. *Ibid.*, p. 285.

4. *Ibid.*, chap. iv. See also War Production Board, *Wartime Production Achievements and the Reconversion Outlook* (Oct. 9, 1945), pp. 10–13.

5. Bureau of the Budget, *The United States at War*, p. 131.

civilian responsibility is an issue which has been hotly debated. It has been argued vigorously that the military which is responsible for the success or failure of military operations must be responsible for determining what items it must have, in what volume, and at what time. It has been argued with equal vigor that in a major war the basic determination of the amounts of our economic potential to be mobilized and allocated to the military establishment as against the civilian economy and international commitments is a problem to be determined at the highest policy level with due consideration of various domestic interests and of the nation's international diplomacy.

I believe that our wartime experience as well as disinterested analysis of the problem indicate that the decision as to the over-all allocation of resources between the various claimants is clearly one for the highest level decision after debate by the various groups at interest. The military is one claimant whose opinion must and will be respected, but it has no monopoly of insight into the problems of public opinion, domestic politics, or international diplomacy. The military must be prepared to submit alternative budgets of requirements depending upon major decisions as to the over-all mobilization and allocation of resources together with a statement of what these alternative budgets will mean in terms of striking power and military strategy. The basic decision as between a more or less effective and speedy conclusion of military operations, greater or lesser sacrifice on the domestic front, and greater or lesser aid to our allies and the neutrals is a problem to be thrashed out by a group widely representative of the interests of the nation. Within the over-all limits of resources allocated to the military services, it should be their prerogative to determine the specific bill of goods to be procured.

Magnitude of Military Purchases in World War II

The importance of economic mobilization to the prosecution of modern war is perhaps best indicated by the fact that

Chart I

Expenditures for War Activities *
Quarterly
July 1940–June 1946

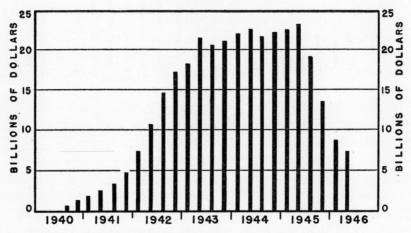

* Does not include net outlays of government corporations.

Source: United States Treasury, *Bulletin*. See Table IX in Appendix A for detailed data.

Chart II

War Supply Contracts Awarded
Quarterly
April 1940–December 1944

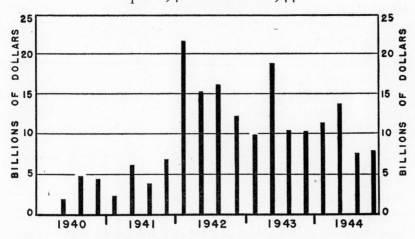

Source: War Production Board. See Appendix B for details and explanation of the basic data.

Chart III

War Facility Projects
Quarterly
April 1940–December 1944

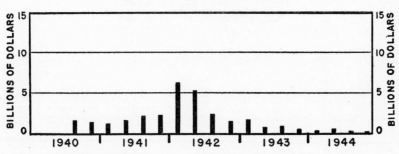

Source: War Production Board. See Appendix B for details and explanation of basic data.

in the United States during the years 1943 and 1944 about 42 per cent of the gross national product, *i.e.*, 42 per cent of the gross volume of goods and services produced, was devoted to federal war purposes. This compares with 1.4 per cent for 1939. In dollar terms this represented an increase from $1.3 billion in 1939 to $88.6 billion in 1944.[6] In the latter year over $60 billion represented purchases from business, while most of the remainder was compensation of employees.[7] Other major belligerents showed similar degrees of economic mobilization during the recent war. In 1944 Great Britain was devoting 51 per cent of its gross national product to war purposes;[8] Canada devoted 51 per cent;[9] Japan devoted 51 per cent.[10]

The actual magnitude of federal government expenditures is indicated in Chart I. From July 1, 1940 to June 30, 1946 the federal government spent directly $330 billion which was classified as expenditures for war activities. In addition there were net outlays of some $8.9 billion by various government corporations and credit agencies concerned with the war effort.[11] Of this total of $339 billion, some $290.9 billion was spent by the War and Navy Departments. Not all these expenditures were for goods. Some represented pay and travel expenses for the armed forces. But $184 billion was expended on munitions, including ships and aircraft but excluding food and clothing, and $30.8 billion was spent by the government or its agencies on construction and war plants.[12]

These represent the actual expenditures. The magnitude and timing of contracts placed or other commitments is equally significant in analyzing the impact of a military pro-

6. United States Department of Commerce, *Survey of Current Business*, July, 1948, p. 16, Table 2.

7. *Ibid.*, p. 18, Table 9.

8. Combined Production and Resources Board, *The Impact of the War on Civilian Consumption in the United Kingdom, the United States and Canada* (1945), p. 141.

9. *Ibid.*, p. 147.

10. The United States Strategic Bombing Survey, *The Effects of Strategic Bombing on Japan's War Economy* (1946), p. 16.

11. United States Bureau of the Budget, *The Budget of the United States Government for the Fiscal Year 1947*, p. 1378.

12. *Loc. cit.*

gram on the industrial economy. Since it is the placing of a contract, or its anticipation, which leads industry to plan its acquisition of materials and labor and to schedule its production, the impact of procurement on commodity and labor markets will precede actual government expenditures by a substantial period. The trend of contracts for both supplies and facilities from April, 1940 through December, 1944 is indicated by Charts II and III. These figures understate substantially the total of awards because they exclude awards having a value of less than $50,000 and all awards for foodstuffs and food processing.[13] These data will serve, however, to indicate roughly the trend in contract commitments for the bulk of military items and facilities. It will be noted that the peak in contract awards came in the first quarter of 1942, immediately after Pearl Harbor. This was the period of feverish activity when many contracts were placed without adequate consideration of price and many other awards were made in the form of unpriced letters of intent. It was this flood of procurements which precipitated the controversy between WPB and the services over requirements in 1942. Only in the case of ships and communications equipment did the awards of any subsequent quarter exceed those of the first quarter of 1942 in dollar value.

Equally interesting is the tendency of supply awards to be heavy in the second quarter of each calendar year. This is clearly a reflection of the desire of the services to commit funds before the end of the fiscal year, at which time many appropriations lapsed. A third factor of interest is the rapid fall in the volume of contracts for facilities after the second quarter of 1942. As was to be expected, facility contracts fell off much more rapidly than supply contracts.

Finally, comparison of Charts I and II indicates that the trend of contract awards and expenditures differed materially. While awards reached their peak in the first quarter of 1942 and tended to fall off thereafter, expenditures increased quar-

13. See Appendix B for detailed statement of the meaning of this series and its limitations.

terly until the first quarter of 1944, when they leveled off at about $23 billion per quarter, at which level they remained until V-J Day.

Even more impressive than the over-all figures of the procurement program was the impact of the program on specific industries. When President Roosevelt appeared before Congress on May 16, 1940 to call for an aircraft industry with an annual capacity of 50,000 planes a year and an air force of 50,000 military and naval planes, we were producing military planes at a maximum yearly rate of between 5,400 and 6,000 planes per year. The President's goal called for an eight- or ninefold increase in the production rate of an industry the capacity of which was already seriously taxed.[14] Likewise, when in June and July of 1940 the President requested expansion of naval vessels and facilities to provide a two-ocean Navy, Congress made authorizations which called for a 70 per cent increase in the size of the fleet at a total cost of about $4 billion.[15] This required a substantial increase in the capacity of our shipyards. On June 30, 1940, when the industry was already greatly expanded from its interwar low, there were 138 naval vessels under construction, 68 of them in private yards and 70 in Navy yards. One year later there were 697 naval vessels under construction, 603 of which were under construction in some 73 private yards and 94 in Navy yards.[16] These are only two examples, which could be multiplied many times over, of the impact of our military procurement programs on specific industries.

14. J. Carlyle Sitterson, *Aircraft Production Policies under the National Defense Advisory Commission and Office of Production Management: May 1940 to December 1941* (1946), "Historical Reports on War Administration: War Production Board," Special Study No. 21, pp. 2–3.

15. Charles H. Coleman, *Shipbuilding Activities of the National Defense Advisory Commission and Office of Production Management: July 1940 to December 1941* (1945), "Historical Reports on War Administration: War Production Board," Special Study No. 18, p. 9.

16. *Ibid.*, p. 92.

III

PEACETIME PROCUREMENT TECHNIQUES
BEFORE 1939

THE problems faced by the services in purchasing their requirements cannot be fully appreciated without an understanding of the competitive bid system of purchase which in the past has been the predominant method of peacetime purchase by all agencies of the federal government. While many exceptions have been made to the formal system, especially for the services in time of emergency or war, the restrictions and ritual of the system developed in peacetime have frequently interfered with the use of buying methods which have long since proven their effectiveness in industry. Moreover, the continued use of the system in time of peace has meant that when the time came to abandon the system in time of war the services were not trained or equipped to use the more effective and exacting purchasing methods which the occasion demanded.

Traditional Competitive Bid System

Until the enactment of the Armed Services Procurement Act of 1947 [1] the customary peacetime method of purchase by the services as well as by other agencies of the federal government has been by public advertisement for competitive sealed bids.[2] The basic statutory authority for this system stems from legislation passed in 1861 and is generally referred

1. Pub. Law No. 413, 80th Cong., 2d Sess.
2. For a brief summary of the development of the federal procurement organization and procedures see Clifton E. Mack, *Federal Procurement: A Manual for the Information of Federal Purchasing Officers,* United States Treasury Department (1934); R. J. Monteith and A. S. Burack, *Methods and Procedures in Federal Purchasing* (1933). For an evaluation of some aspects of federal procurement see Clem C. Linnenberg and Dana M. Barbour, *Government Purchasing: An Economic Commentary* (1940), TNEC Monograph No. 19.

to as section 3709 of the Revised Statutes.[3] This legislation provides that, except where public exigency requires immediate delivery, purchases shall be made by advance public advertising for sealed bids and public opening of the bids received. This provision has been interpreted as requiring award to the lowest responsible bidder who meets the advertised specifications.[4] In appropriate cases all bids may be rejected and new bids solicited by advertisement. Before World War II, standard forms for the advertisements and ensuing contracts were prescribed by the Procurement Division of the Treasury Department and were mandatory upon all purchasing agents of the federal government.[5]

There were several statutory exceptions to the rule of competitive bidding, but they were rather narrowly limited. Where the public exigency required immediate delivery or performance, purchases might be made "in the manner in which such articles are usually bought and sold, or such services engaged, between individuals." [6] Exceptions were also made for purchases of small value ranging from $25 to $500 depending upon the department or agency involved.[7] Other exceptions for the purchase of particular types of materials had been made from time to time, several of which applied specifically to the armed services. Two of the major exceptions applicable to the services were the Air Corps Act of 1926 providing special procedures for procurement of aircraft [8] and the Educational Order Act of 1938.[9] While the services have recently been granted powers to depart from the traditional

3. R.S. 3709 (41 U.S.C. 5) applies to all departments of the government. R.S. 3718 (34 U.S.C. 561) established the formal system of advertisement and award to the lowest bidder for the purchase of provisions for the Navy Department alone.

4. 5 Comp. Gen. 330 (Jan. 28, 1926).

5. See 41 Code of Federal Regulations, sec. 11.3. These standard forms were authorized by section 1 of Executive Order No. 6166 (June, 1933).

6. 41 U.S.C. 5.

7. 41 U.S.C. 6.

8. 44 Stat. 784, as amended by the acts of March 3, 1927 (44 Stat. 1380) and of March 5, 1940 (54 Stat. 45).

9. 50 U.S.C. 91–94. There were many other exceptions applicable to the services covering supplies purchased outside the United States, medical supplies, some foods, secret contracts, service contracts, etc.

system at their discretion in a series of important cases,[10] the traditional system still applies to most purchasing activities by agencies of the federal government.

Government purchases are surrounded by many special requirements, such as limitations on hours of work and wages paid to employees working on government contracts,[11] regulations designed to foster domestic production and the use of domestic materials,[12] and the filing of performance bonds. Disbursements by government agents on government contracts are subject to post-audit by the General Accounting Office to insure conformance with the terms of the contract.[13] On cost-plus-fixed-fee contracts and similar contracts the expenditures of the contractor are likewise subject to this post-audit. Contractors' expenditures are frequently disallowed.

The policies of the Comptroller General and the General Accounting Office have had a pervasive effect on purchasing policies and procedures of all federal agencies. Plans for wartime procurement were drafted in light of the Comptroller General's interpretations and of the responsibilities of contracting officers and industry to abide thereby. While the General Accounting Office has without doubt done much to insure care and honesty upon the part of federal purchasing agencies and industry, the rulings of the Comptroller General have often interfered with expeditious and efficient purchasing practices.

Advantages of Competitive Bid System

This system of purchase by public advertisement for competitive sealed bids is deeply embedded in the American governmental tradition. It purports to have a twofold purpose: (1) minimizing the administrative discretion of the contract-

10. See below, pp. 227–229, for recent legislation affecting peacetime procurement by the armed services.

11. 41 U.S.C. 35–45 (Walsh-Healy Act) and 40 U.S.C. 276a–276a(b) (Bacon-Davis Act).

12. 41 U.S.C. 10, 10a, 10b ("Buy American" Act).

13. 31 U.S.C. 71. See also Harvey C. Mansfield, *The Comptroller General: A Study in the Law and Practice of Financial Administration* (1939), pp. 93–94.

ing officer in the selection of sources of supply and (2) protecting the government financially by developing competition on price. The system has the merit of making the purchasing function a routine matter which leaves little discretion to public officials once requirements and the specifications of the items to be purchased are determined. It minimizes the opportunity for favoritism, affords an equal opportunity to all qualified suppliers to participate in government contracts, reduces pressures upon Congressmen and public officials from unsuccessful suppliers, and makes the least possible demand upon the talents of government purchasing officers. Furthermore, in peacetime markets which are actively competitive, it should result in the government being treated about the same as private industry, due allowance being made for the cost and inconvenience involved in dealing with the government.[14]

Presuppositions of Competitive Bid System

To be successful, however, this system presupposes certain conditions:

(1) that the government is concerned solely with performance of the item purchased and its price and is prepared to purchase from any responsible supplier;

(2) that there are rigid specifications or that there is sufficient time to develop such specifications before the selection of source;

(3) that specifications may be publicized;

(4) that specifications are honestly drawn in terms of technical requirements and not specially tailored for the purpose of limiting the number of eligible sources;

(5) that there are several alternative sources of supply which are in active competition with one another for government contracts and are willing to price competitively.

14. For a discussion of the many reasons, legal, political, and administrative, which make governments "poor customers" see Albert M. Freiberg, "How Government Buys: An Appraisal," *Public Policy*, eds. C. J. Friedrich and E. S. Mason, II (1941), 262–288.

Clearly many procurements by the services do not satisfy these conditions.[15] In the case of secret contracts, it is clear that the formal system of public advertisement for competitive sealed bids cannot be used. In the case of research and development contracts, it it equally clear that the formal system is not usable. Experience with the Air Corps Act of 1926 is conclusive in this regard.[16] Talent capable of undertaking scientific research and the engineering of new weapons cannot be secured by public advertisement and sealed bids. Since confidence in the ingenuity and know-how of particular individuals will be the overriding consideration in such procurement, administrative discretion in the selection of the contractor is imperative.

There are other cases where specifications cannot be sufficiently explicit to insure adequate quality. This is true of many perishable foodstuffs, which are best purchased after visual inspection and at current wholesale prices since it is generally impossible for a supplier to guarantee a given quantity and quality at a designated place at some future date. Likewise, in the case of some medical supplies, the only adequate assurance of quality appears to be the general reputation of the supplier.

In the case of many proprietary or trade-mark items, purchase by the formal competitive bid system is a mere form, lacking in substance. Ideally, under the competitive bid system, specifications are drawn so that substitute items which are equally acceptable can compete. Often, however, the

15. For a more elaborate discussion of the inadequacies of the formal competitive bid system for military procurement in peacetime see the author's article, "Military Procurement in Peacetime," *Harvard Business Review*, XXV (Summer, 1947), 444–462.

16. For a discussion of the difficulties involved from 1926 to 1939 in purchase of aircraft see Production and Purchases Division, ASF, *Purchasing Policies and Practices: Production and Purchasing Division*, ASF (no date), pp. 17–27. This volume is on file with the Historical Division, Department of the Army. See also statement by Maj. Gen. E. M. Powers, Assistant Chief of Air Staff, USA, in the United States House of Representatives, Hearings before the Subcommittee of the Committee on Armed Services on H.R. 1366, 80th Cong., 1st Sess., *A Bill to Facilitate Procurement of Supplies and Services by the War and Navy Departments, and for Other Purposes* (1947), pp. 532–550.

specifications become unnecessarily restrictive. Moreover, for some proprietary items and items controlled by patents there are no close substitutes. Finally, even when there are adequate substitutes for proprietary items as in the case of a truck or a gasoline engine, the technical requirement for uniformity of items and interchangeability of parts may make it imperative, after an initial purchase, that additions, replacements, and spare parts be of the same proprietary type as the initial purchase.[17] There were times during the recent war when the survival of isolated groups of men lacking inventories of spare parts depended upon their ability to "cannibalize" their mechanical equipment, a possibility which depended in turn upon standardization and interchangeability of parts.[18]

In all the above-mentioned cases some method had to be found even in peacetime to procure without being bound by the limitations of the formal competitive bid system. In some cases specific legislative exemptions were granted.[19] In many cases, however, the services were forced in peacetime, until recently, to go through the forms of soliciting bids by public advertisement, even though various devices, such as restrictive specifications, were found to circumvent the system in spirit while conforming to its ritual. As one commentator has remarked, all too often "the appearance of honesty becomes of paramount importance." [20]

17. The purchase of proprietary items may be minimized by drafting appropriate specifications. However, the cost of an item built to specially tailored specifications may be substantially greater than the cost of a proprietary substitute produced in large quantities for sale in civilian markets. Where either item would perform satisfactorily, the procurement officer must consider the over-all, long-run cost of using the proprietary item as against the other, including in his calculation such factors as the effects of restricting the available sources on the price of future orders and the relative costs of inventory.

18. United States House of Representatives, Hearings before the Subcommittee of the Committee on Armed Services on H.R. 1366, 80th Cong., 1st Sess., *A Bill to Facilitate Procurement of Supplies and Services by the War and Navy Departments and for Other Purposes*, p. 475; United States Senate, Hearings before the Committee on Armed Services on H.R. 1366, 80th Cong., 1st Sess., *Armed Services Procurement Act of 1947* (1947), p. 2.

19. For example, exceptions had been made for proprietary articles where competition was impracticable (31 Stat. 905), horses and mules (45 Stat. 245), medical supplies (27 Stat. 485), certain secret contracts (10 U.S.C. 1199), and for certain foodstuffs (28 Stat. 658, 34 U.S.C. 569, 34 U.S.C. 577, 34 U.S.C. 578).

20. Freiberg, *op. cit.*, p. 288.

Conflicts of Competitive Bid System with
Efficient Purchasing Methods

Moreover, the system often prevents the use of effective purchasing methods which have long since proved their usefulness to industrial purchasing departments. As one commentator has noted, ". . . a system which insures honesty often robs the buyer of so much discretion that he has no chance to be efficient." [21] There are several ways in which the system may conflict with efficient purchasing. In the first place the system tends to encourage a rigid separation of the function of drafting specifications from the function of purchase. Specifications are drafted by highly trained technical personnel, too often without consultation with purchasing personnel or consideration of market conditions. Moreover, these specifications become stabilized and inflexible. In many cases, however, the functional requirements of the government could be satisfied by any of several products of different design. An astute buyer, unencumbered by the formalities of traditional government purchasing, would take advantage of competition between sources using different designs, materials, or processes. Change in technology, in the relative costs of different materials and processes, and in the market conditions of various sources of supply will change the competitive picture for many items. Purchase by the traditional competitive bid system tends to prevent the government from developing such competition. The services maintain highly trained technical personnel responsible for design, but the purchasing function becomes too routine. This separation of function, together with the atrophy of the purchasing function in peacetime, is one of the unfortunate consequences of the formal competitive bid system which interferes seriously with the efficiency of peacetime procurement.

There are several conditions where it is questionable whether the ritual of the competitive bid system will insure the least possible cost to the services. The first of these involves

21. *Loc. cit.*

repeat production contracts on specialized military items where there are high starting costs. For example, an initial production contract for a new jet propulsion engine may require large initial starting costs in the nature of rearrangement of plant, tooling, training of personnel, developing new sources of materials, etc., for which the contractor will presumably be reimbursed on the initial contract but which will not have to be repeated in the case of subsequent orders. This gives the holder of the initial contract a distinct cost advantage on subsequent bids. Moreover, any supplier bidding on such a contract for the first time will face elements of uncertainty and risk which he will reflect in a contingency allowance but which an experienced contractor will no longer have to consider. Consequently the initial supplier has a range within which he may bid, bound on the low side by his minimum supply price, which reflects his absence of starting costs and his lesser degree of uncertainty, and on the high side by his estimate of rivals' bids. If the initial supplier is as efficient as his potential rivals and these rivals correctly estimate their own costs, the initial supplier stands a good chance of being successful on repeat proposals. If the award is made under the formal competitive bid system, however, there is no assurance that the successful bid will reflect these lower starting costs and lesser risks. In similar circumstances an industrial purchaser would not submit to the ritual of the sealed bid system. It is probable, however, that in such circumstances government contractors have frequently obtained limited protected positions as a result of successive contracts. It may well be good economy and good military strategy to place successive contracts with a particular source. But, in the interests of efficiency in production and of economy in the expenditure of public funds, the services should have the authority in such cases to attempt to negotiate prices which reflect these lower costs and risks where it appears that formal competitive bidding will not do so.

A second class of procurements where economic considerations may dictate the use of negotiated contracts comprise procurements in markets where the government does not always reap the benefit of active price competition. These include situations where there are uniform bids or where there are collusive arrangements for the rotation of the position of low bidder.[22] In some such markets the prices to industry and government alike are subject to monopolistic controls. In other markets, characterized by imperfect price leadership or imperfect compliance with uniform published prices, it appears that the government is often quoted the published price by all parties while comparable sales to private industry are made at more or less of a discount, depending upon the state of the market and the bargaining strength of the parties involved. In some cases this disadvantage is evidently due to a failure of the government to distinguish in its purchasing between large and small purchases. But in other cases it appears that the government's purchasing procedures, particularly the publicity incident to the opening of bids, puts the government at a distinct price disadvantage in buying compared with industrial purchasers, who often receive secret concessions or specially advantageous long-term contracts.

Considerable evidence has been presented showing that in the 1930's the federal government was frequently at a disadvantage in the buying of such items as steel products, cement, and rubber tires.[23] Moreover, identical bidding was reported as being so common at times that "the conclusion seems inescapable that something is wrong" on such varied items as condensed and evaporated milk, salt, ammunition and related products, compressed and liquified gases, refined petroleum products, motor-vehicle bodies and parts, and electrical machinery and supplies.[24] These are all items which will bulk large in peacetime military procurement. It is significant that this list is based upon a study covering the period from July,

22. Particular attention is given to this problem in Linnenberg and Barbour, *op. cit.*, chap. iv.
23. *Ibid.*, pp. 36–38.
24. *Ibid.*, pp. 33–35.

1937 to May, 1939, a period during which the incentives to price competition were greater than we are likely to see on the average for some period to come.

The previous discussion of situations where the government does not obtain the results of competition has referred particularly to peacetime procurement of standard commercial articles or other items common to our civilian and military economies where publicity of the price or collusive devices put the government at a disadvantage. Even in the case of certain specialized military items, however, the conditions surrounding government procurement are such that the impact on prices may be substantially greater than purchases of a similar magnitude and type by business. For example, when a major shipbuilding program is undertaken, it is normally preceded by public debate and specific Congressional appropriations. The Navy comes to the market committed to purchase a fairly specific bill of goods. There is little likelihood that it will be deterred by price considerations so long as its appropriations last or the political climate is favorable for their increase. Such programs are frequently sizable in comparison with available capacity and other current orders. Potential suppliers are few. Finally, there is often an urgency in placing the contracts, dictated by general diplomatic strategy or by the exigencies of domestic politics. It is not surprising that price competition is not always active where only a few bidders are faced with a known and almost completely inelastic demand and each recognizes the over-all advantages of estimating costs liberally. An example of this is to be found in the much discussed shipbuilding program of 1933.[25] In such conditions formal competitive bidding is no substitute for selection of source and determination of price by informed negotiation in the manner of private business.

All too often under the preceding conditions it has been the policy of the services to procure by the formal competitive bid

25. United States Senate, Special Committee on Investigation of the Munitions Industry, Senate Report No. 944, Part 1, *Munitions Industry: Naval Shipbuilding,* 74th Cong., 1st Sess. (1935), *passim.*

system regardless of the cost. Even where such procedure was not technically required by existing legislation, it could be easily rationalized. Regardless of the effects upon prices or upon the economy, purchase according to the formal system had the appearance of honesty and relieved procurement officers of formal responsibility for selecting sources.

Conclusion

Prior to 1939 the formal competitive bid system had become a well-established institution for peacetime purchasing. Although it was far from ideal, the services had learned to live with it. It was clear, however, that in many cases the system was ill adapted to the purchase of military requirements. Moreover, the system often discouraged or even prevented the adoption of purchasing methods which had long proved their efficiency in leading industrial concerns. Where military or technical considerations made it necessary, statutory exemptions had been granted or administrative dodges had been developed. Those responsible for military procurement showed little if any concern with those situations where compliance with the system might foster monopolistic practices or result in additional costs to the government. While there was a widely prevailing though by no means unanimous opinion that the system was not adaptable to wartime conditions, it was only after extensive experience with the negotiated contract under wartime conditions that serious proposals were entertained to overhaul the peacetime procurement system.[26]

26. See below, Chap. XIV.

IV

PROCUREMENT PLANNING BEFORE WORLD WAR II

Lessons of World War I

EXPERIENCE during World War I made it clear that peace-time procedures of purchasing were inadequate in time of war. During that war competition between the various purchasing agencies of the government and between the government and the civilian economy was to a large extent responsible for the inflation of prices of raw materials, wages, and finished goods. Although the services shifted to the negotiation of prices on many items, particularly specialized military items, the competitive bid procedure continued to predominate in the purchase of many standard quartermaster items throughout the war.[1]

The war experience demonstrated the need for several broad changes in the wartime purchasing policies of the services. It was obvious that in wartime all government purchases should be cleared through some central agency in order to eliminate the waste and competition for goods and services to which decentralized and uncoordinated purchasing had given rise in World War I. Moreover, it was clear that contracts should be placed and priced on some other basis than the peacetime system of competitive bidding. Finally, it was generally agreed that the cost-plus-percentage-of-cost (CPPC) method of contracting should be eliminated since it provided industry with a positive incentive to be wasteful and inefficient in the use of labor and materials.[2] Although there were delays in putting these lessons into effect after the beginning of the

1. J. Franklin Crowell, *Government War Contracts* (1920), p. 21.
2. See testimony of Bernard Baruch before the War Policies Commission, House Doc. No. 163, 72d Cong., 1st Sess. (1931), pp. 30–72. Also Charles O. Hardy, *Wartime Control of Prices* (1940), pp. 5–6, 14, 58–67.

emergency in 1939, it is fair to say that these were guiding principles in most planning between the wars and in operations after the advent of the crisis.

Discussion Between the Wars

In the interwar years, which one student refers to as "The Decades of Divided Purposes," [3] there was considerable public discussion of the problems of industrial mobilization. In retrospect, however, this discussion appears to have had little effect on operations in the recent war. The discussion was to a large extent focused on the problem of "profiteering." As the record of World War I became known, many turned in their disillusion to an attack upon the war millionaires and the so-called "merchants of death." The thesis became popular that our entry into World War I had been engineered by those who stood to gain financially from war. Many argued that a future war could be avoided if we devised means "to take the profit out of war." Others, including the veterans' organizations, urged the need to plan for equalizing the burdens of war and for drafting capital as well as labor. It was in this atmosphere [4] and in response to such pressures that Congress established the War Policies Commission in 1930 ". . . to study and consider amending the Constitution of the United States to provide that private property may be taken by Congress for public use during war and methods of equalizing the burdens and to remove the profits of war, together with a study of policies to be pursued in event of war." [5] Perhaps the most significant contributions of this Commission were the testimony given by Bernard Baruch, particularly his proposal for a general price-freeze, and the presentation to the public for

3. Pendleton Herring, *The Impact of War* (1941), chap. viii.
4. For a picture of the atmosphere of the era and a very prevalent interpretation of the relation of business interests to war see Charles A. and Mary R. Beard, *America in Midpassage* (1939), I, chap. ix.
5. Pub. Res. No. 98, 71st Cong. (June 27, 1930). For the report of the commission see House Doc. No. 163 (1931), No. 264 (1932), and No. 271 (1932), 72d Cong., 1st Sess.

the first time of the War Department's plans for industrial mobilization.[6]

Three years later in 1934 the Senate established the so-called "Nye Committee" to investigate the munitions industry, review the findings of the War Policies Commission, and inquire into the desirability of creating a government monopoly in respect to the manufacture of munitions.[7] The hearings and recommendations of this committee were highly publicized. Senator Nye used the committee to further his argument that war was caused by the machinations of those who stood to gain financially therefrom. He proposed as a remedy the establishment of a government monopoly of all munitions manufacture. But the establishment of the committee also served to stimulate a large number of proposals for eliminating profiteering on the assumption that private industry would supply the bulk of munitions in peace and war. During the twenty-three-year period between the wars approximately 200 bills and resolutions dealing with the limitation of war profits were considered by Congress.[8] The principal focus of this public discussion was on ways and means of limiting profiteering by general price controls and taxation. Although price control is an obvious aid to controlling the prices and profits on military procurements, it is clearly insufficient unless extended to cover specialized military equipment. Moreover, the difficulties of so extending it are great. But consideration of the purchasing methods of the armed services and the pricing of military goods was clearly secondary in the discussions of this period. The War Department alone appears to have considered these matters in its industrial mobilization plans.

6. The Industrial Mobilization Plan was prepared in accordance with section 5a of the National Defense Act of 1920 (41 Stat. 764–765), which charged the Assistant Secretary of War with the ". . . supervision of the procurement of all military supplies and other business of the War Department pertaining thereto and the assurance of adequate provision for the mobilization of material and industrial organizations essential to war-time needs."

7. Senate Res. No. 206, 73d Cong., 2d Sess. (April 12, 1934).

8. H. Struve Hensel and Richard G. McClung, "Profit Limitation Controls Prior to the Present War," *Law and Contemporary Problems,* X (Autumn, 1943), 199.

The Industrial Mobilization Plan

In presenting the industrial mobilization plan to the War Policies Commission in 1931 General MacArthur, then Chief-of-Staff, gave the most extensive public statement of the War Department's plans for wartime procurement which appeared between the wars.[9] He insisted upon the necessity for decentralized procurement by the technical services. In order to avoid the evils of competitive bidding he proposed that procurements be made on the basis of allocation, *i.e.*, "the assignment of a definite list of facilities to each procurement agency to supply its needs." Such an allocation of private industrial facilities was to be arranged in advance. In the case of specialized equipment on which manufacturers had no prior production experience, he proposed that educational orders for a limited quantity be placed in peacetime without advertising. In wartime "prices will be determined by negotiations, controlled by the knowledge obtained in peacetime planning, of the items that make up costs and by all information that can be collected by the Government." [10]

General MacArthur also stated that to avoid the evils incident to many types of contracts used in World War I the War Department had prepared various contract forms "which would be adaptable to use in the unsettled economic and industrial conditions of war; which would, so far as possible, relieve the contractors of the perplexing hazards of wartime production; which would facilitate prompt payment and early final settlements; which would avoid the evils accompanying the cost-plus contracts; which would be self-settling in the event that the necessities of the Government required termination before completion; and which would protect adequately the Government and contractor, and contribute to speedy and early production." [11] To accomplish this the War Department proposed the following practices:

9. House Doc. No. 163, 72d Cong., 1st Sess. (1931), pp. 354–386. For a copy of the industrial mobilization plan, see *ibid.*, pp. 395–470.

10. *Ibid.*, p. 364.

11. *Ibid.*, pp. 365–366.

That for commercial supplies and for relatively simple construction the ordinary peace-time contract forms be used, and that these be modified to meet war conditions. The most important changes relate to clauses providing for settlement in event of termination before completion, and to provisions respecting increased costs of labor and material, when such increases are authorized by Federal authority.

That for large construction projects and for the procurement of non-commercial items, the adjusted compensation contract be used. In this form the contracting parties agree in advance upon tentative cost schedules which are revised from time to time as more accurate information becomes available. The Government audits all accounts as they arise and pays all approved costs of performance. In the end it also pays the contractor an amount as nearly as practicable equal to a fair rental for that part of his plant involved in the contract. Under present conditions the department believes a fair rental should approximate a rate of 6 per cent per annum on the estimated value of the part of the plant involved. If the contractor has performed the job at a cost less than the revised estimate of costs, the Government pays him a small added compensation. If actual cost exceeds the estimate, his profit is reduced. Temptation to pad costs is removed.[12]

General MacArthur acknowledged that the adjusted compensation contract ". . . contemplated inspection and auditing, detailed and complete, but not pernicious, throughout performance."[13] By use of this procurement system he believed that "profiteering based on Army contracts is thus eliminated and profits are kept within reasonable limits. . . . Army purchases, in the event of a future war, will not be, as they have been in past wars, one of the principal causes for profiteering and for the useless and unnecessary piling up of burdensome war debts."[14]

There were several interesting features of these War Department plans. First, they assumed that the government

12. *Ibid.*, p. 366. For detailed discussion and copies of these contract forms and of others subsequently approved see United States Senate, Hearings before the Special Committee Investigating the Munitions Industry, Part 15, 73d Cong., 2d Sess., *Munitions Industry* (1935), pp. 3619–3642.

13. House Doc. No. 163, 72d Cong., 1st Sess. (1931), p. 366.

14. *Ibid.*, pp. 366–367.

would have sufficient knowledge of costs and would exercise
sufficient ingenuity in its negotiations to set prices for many
commercial supplies and for relatively simple construction
which would be free from unreasonable profits. Second, they
assumed that it would be feasible on all other items to determine costs of production periodically on an individual contract
basis including therein a fair rental on the estimated value of
plant used in the performance of the contract. The valuation
and accounting problems involved in these proposals in addition to the problem of auditing costs of materials and labor
would, of course, have been tremendous. Finally, there was
a clear recognition of the need for government authorization
of increased costs of labor and materials, which implied a wide-
spread and effective system of controls of wages and of the
prices of materials.

These points became clear in the investigations of the Nye
Committee which pointed out that the industrial mobilization
plan was founded on certain assumptions which made the
elimination of the evil of profiteering difficult. "Among them
are that victory and its prerequisite, increased production,
are the primary object of a nation at war to which all other
aims are subsidiary, that any controls undertaken in war should
not be so drastic as to cause any change in normal economic
conditions, and that a major part of the planning effort should
be devoted to effecting a smooth functioning of the procurement machine rather than profit limitation." [15]

Commenting directly on the procurement plans of the War
Department the Nye Committee made many prophetic remarks. It noted that the proposals relied to a large extent upon
accounting determination of costs and valuations which ". . .
are extremely difficult to determine. To a large extent the
Government must rely upon industry for information. In
the pressure of wartime, these accounting items are inevitably
determined on a basis advantageous to industry." [16] The com-

15. United States Senate, Special Committee on Investigation of the Munitions
Industry, Senate Report No. 944, Part 4, *Munitions Industry*, 74th Cong., 2d
Sess. (1936), p. 2.
16. *Ibid.*, p. 3.

mittee noted that despite fifteen years of planning the services
had practically none of the requisite information. "The Navy
Department does not know what it costs private shipbuilders
to construct naval vessels. It has no information on their
profits. The War Department is no better off." [17] Concerning the nature of wartime controls the committee said that "because of the necessity for flexibility, the character of war
regulation is largely determined by negotiation between
Government officials and industry. Industry inevitably has the
upper hand in these negotiations because of its superior information and the existence of a seller's market in war." [18] Finally,
the committee concluded that "there are two reasons for believing that even theoretically full powers to eliminate profiteering actually would not be used for this purpose. (1) Industry, through its control over production, can strike against
the Government which is, in fact, in no position to com-
mandeer any industry or plant, and thus force compliance with
its wishes in regard to prices and contracts. (2) The control
agencies must necessarily be administered by men who are
industrially trained and presumably sympathetic to private
industry's contentions." [19]

This analysis of the War Department's procurement plans
was perhaps the most significant contribution of the Nye
Committee. It was truly prophetic of many problems faced in
World War II. It is most unfortunate that the challenge of this
part of the committee's work was not met by those in responsible positions. As it was, the more sensational charges sponsored by Senator Nye to the effect that the United States had
been led into war at the instigation of war profiteers took the
head-lines while the more substantial lessons of the investigation languished.[20] The services had been accused of not having
the cost and other information requisite to do its job. This was
still true when the war broke out. Moreover, they did not
have adequate plans for getting such information. The prac-

17. *Ibid.,* p. 30.
18. *Ibid.,* p. 3.
19. *Loc. cit.*
20. Herring, *op. cit.,* p. 200.

tical result of the Nye investigation seems to have been to induce increasing timidity upon the part of the services in their planning for industrial mobilization. In its successive revisions the industrial mobilization plan became shorter, more platitudinous, and increasingly evasive on critical issues. "In a literal sense this document shrank from criticism." [21]

A published industrial mobilization plan should serve to provide leadership and guidance to various groups at interest and to goad the legislative and executive branches of the government into a resolution of any conflicts in these interests. The discussions of the 1930's did not accomplish this. Although the earlier editions of the industrial mobilization plan had indicated that effective price control was a prerequisite for effective procurement, the 1939 edition could only say, "Control of prices in war *may* be required . . ." [22] Congressional authority for the placing of educational orders was not forthcoming until 1938 and then in only limited amounts.[23] On the critical issue of the suspension of competitive bidding and the use of negotiation the War Department seems to have been in a state of indecision. General MacArthur's proposals to use a system of allocations and the preparations of the War Department to implement these plans implied the immediate switch to negotiation upon the outbreak of war. There appears to have been considerable question, however, as to whether public opinion or Congress would countenance negotiated contracts.[24]

It is not surprising in the light of this vacillation that when war came the industrial mobilization plan was sidetracked.[25] There have been many explanations for this including the fact that war did not come with the suddenness on which the plan was predicated, the need to move slowly because of the iso-

---

21. *Ibid.*, p. 203.
22. Senate Doc. No. 134, 76th Cong., 2d Sess. (1939), p. 4. Present author's italics.
23. Pub. Law No. 639, 75th Cong., 3d Sess. (June 16, 1938).
24. See Army Industrial College, *Plans for Industrial Mobilization 1920–1939* (1945), "Study of Experience in Industrial Mobilization in World War II," pp. 50–53.
25. See *ibid.*, pp. 74–85. Herring, *op. cit.*, pp. 207–210.

lationist sentiment, the inclination of the Commander-in-Chief to hold the reins, and the pressures of New Deal groups in the administration to hold the military and business groups in check.[26] These were all important. But even more significant is the fact that on many matters including allocation of orders, negotiation of prices, price control, and profit limitation the industrial mobilization plan was no plan at all. The planners had neither given leadership to the conflicting groups at interest nor adapted themselves to the tune of the times. It appears to have been true of the period between the wars that ". . . soldiers are neither political theorists nor social philosophers." [27] The armed services have often been accused of failing to adapt their military strategy to innovations in science and technology. It appears that between the wars they were even less prone to adapt their mobilization plans to innovations in the facts and theories of our economic, social, and political life. In the field of purchasing policies mobilization planning showed great timidity induced without a doubt by excessive fear of the Comptroller General and of a public opinion aroused by the spectre of profiteering.

26. Bureau of the Budget, *The United States at War*, pp. 23–24.
27. Herring, *op. cit.*, p. 203.

V

ESTABLISHING PROCUREMENT RESPONSIBILITY:
1939–1942

ONE of the outstanding lessons of World War I was the need for coordination by some central group of the decentralized purchase operations of various federal procurement agencies. This did not mean centralized procurement operations, but rather coordination of the decentralized operations with respect to major policies and procedures. The industrial mobilization plan had provided for this through its provision for the establishment in the event of war of a War Resources Administration.[1] In the interim the Army and Navy Munitions Board was supposed to perform such coordination. Unfortunately it had accomplished little by 1939.

With the approach of war and the establishment of a succession of civilian agencies concerned with the mobilization of industry, the whole question of the policies and procedures to be followed in procurement became critical. What were the appropriate relations between the services and the various civilian organizations with respect to procurement? Should the responsibility for the award and administration of contracts be with the services in whom statutory responsibility had always resided? Or should some civilian agency responsible for industrial mobilization also have the responsibility for the award and administration of contracts? Should procurement be centralized in one organization or should it be decentralized? Should procurement be centralized geographically in Washington? To what extent should the conventional procedures of competitive bidding be retained? What alternatives might take their place? What should be the responsibili-

1. *Industrial Mobilization Plan: Revision of 1939,* Senate Doc. No. 134, 76th Cong., 2d Sess. (1939).

ties of the civilian price control agencies over prices of goods
for the armed services? These were problems which it took
almost three years to settle.[2]

Civilian Control of Procurement Policies and Procedures

In anticipation of war in Europe the President on August 9, 1939 appointed a War Resources Board for the purpose of "advising with the Army and Navy Munitions Board on policies pertaining to the mobilization of the economic resources of the country in the event of a war emergency." [3] It was generally supposed that in the event of an emergency this board would become an executive agency of the government with powers similar to the War Industries Board of World War I. As it turned out, the board after making its report in October, 1939 was allowed to expire.[4]

With the fall of France the administration was moved to more effective action. On May 29, 1940 the Council of National Defense, a Cabinet committee existing by virtue of an act in 1916,[5] established with the approval of the President an Advisory Commission of seven members.[6] Their assignments of responsibilities were as follows: William S. Knudsen, industrial production; Edward R. Stettinius, Jr., industrial materials; Sidney Hillman, labor; Chester C. Davis, agriculture; Ralph Budd, transportation; Leon Henderson, price stabilization; Harriet Elliott, consumers' interests. This was the beginning of the civilian command responsible for industrial mobilization during the war.

The National Defense Advisory Commission (NDAC) was a purely advisory body which dealt with the Cabinet

2. The official story of the struggles to solve these problems has been told in CPA, *Industrial Mobilization for War, passim.*

3. *The New York Times,* Aug. 10, 1939, pp. 1–2.

4. For a discussion of the nature of this report and some interesting comments on the vicissitudes of this board see Army Industrial College, *Plans for Industrial Mobilization 1920–1939* (1945), "Study of Experience in Industrial Mobilization in World War II," pp. 66–74.

5. 39 Stat. 649, sec. 2 (Aug. 29, 1916).

6. See 5 F.R. 2114 (June, 1940), establishing the general composition of the Advisory Commission and 5 F.R. 2381 (June, 1940), appointing the members.

Council of National Defense through the President or through his administrative assistant.[7] It was clearly thought that the work of the advisors on production, materials, and labor would be of principal immediate significance and that the other advisors would be concerned primarily with long-run planning.[8] The commission had the threefold task of helping to expedite the immediate problem of rearmament, synthesizing the views of the various groups at interest in the defense program, and laying the groundwork for subsequent administrative agencies which would be responsible for various phases of mobilization. Knudsen, as production advisor, was ". . . charged with the general duty of coordination of the activities of private industry with those of the War and Navy Departments to the end that the plant capacity in the industries will be so expanded as to produce the volume of military and naval materials and equipment which will be required . . ." [9]

The placing of contracts by the services was soon recognized as one of the most important day-to-day operating problems calling for the attention of the NDAC. From the beginning the NDAC recognized that the services alone had statutory authority to award contracts.[10] On June 6, however, the President directed the War and Navy Departments to submit to the Advisory Commission all proposed contracts for $500,000 or more for its approval prior to award.[11] If the

7. United States House of Representatives, Hearings before a Subcommittee on Appropriations, 76th Cong., 3d Sess., *Second Supplemental National Defense Appropriation Bill for 1941* (1940), p. 233.

8. See testimony of W. H. McReynolds, Administrative Assistant to the President, *ibid.* (June 3, 1940), p. 20.

9. See above, note 7.

10. Civilian Production Administration, *Minutes of the Advisory Commission to the Council of National Defense* (1946), "Historical Reports on War Administration, War Production Board," Doc. Pub. No. 1, p. 119. Donald Nelson states that at an early meeting of NDAC Mr. Baruch had warned him against ever assuming responsibility for signing the services' contracts. "This advice sank into and anchored itself in my mind, and I never deviated from it. Civilians who place Army and Navy orders are usually asking for more trouble than they can handle." Donald Nelson, *Arsenal of Democracy* (1946), p. 103.

11. On June 6, 1940 the President directed memoranda to the Secretaries of War and Navy stating, "In order that the program of industrial expansion in the preparedness field may be coordinated and expedited most effectively, I should like you to obtain the approval of Commissioner Knudsen of the Advisory Com-

NDAC found the proposals unsatisfactory, it could make its objections known to the initiating department or, if necessary, to the President. This constituted the chief sanction of the NDAC.

To facilitate even further the coordination of current procurement with the over-all mobilization program the President established on June 27, 1940 the Office for the Coordination of National Defense Purchases as a subordinate body to the Council of National Defense and appointed Donald Nelson as Coordinator.[12] Nelson's responsibilities included maintaining liaison between NDAC, the armed services, other government agencies, and private agencies ". . . to insure proper coordination of, and economy and efficiency in, purchases" for national defense. He was authorized to assign to the agency best qualified purchase responsibility for repetitive items common to several agencies with the limitation that the War and Navy Departments should make their own purchases subject to such coordination as might be required to establish priorities. Nelson was also responsible for coordinating research in procurement specifications and standardization, determining and keeping current estimates of requirements, and collecting statistics on purchases by the federal government.

From the beginning the responsibility of NDAC and the Coordinator for Defense Purchases for current procurement, limited though it was, played a very important part in the transition to war. Considerable pressure was brought to bear upon the services to alter specifications so that more sources of supply could be used, to time the placing of contracts so as to take advantage of off-season productive capacity and reduce the impact of growing demand by the services on the market, and to spread the placement of contracts.[13] By

---

mission to the Council of National Defense on all important contracts for purchase by your Department." (WPB, Historical Records Files).

12. 5 F.R. 2446–2447 (July, 1940).

13. Memorandum from A. C. C. Hill, Jr. to Mr. J. L. O'Brian, General Counsel of OPM, *Functions, Organization Procedures and Problems of Division of Purchases* (April 10, 1941) (WPB, Historical Records Files).

September of 1940 the NDAC was able to issue a statement of general principles governing the letting of contracts,[14] a forerunner of War Production Board Directive No. 2, which was to serve as the charter of the services after the outbreak of war.[15] This statement served as a prod to the services to make more effective use of their powers to place contracts by negotiation. Beyond this the NDAC was instrumental in developing various policies which had an indirect bearing on the pricing of military procurements such as accelerated amortization of defense facilities, financing of plant expansion, and financing of increases in working capital.[16]

The establishment of the Office of Production Management (OPM) in January, 1941 formalized somewhat the responsibilities and controls over procurement matters which had already developed without materially extending them.[17] Nelson, as Director of the Division of Purchases, was authorized to coordinate the placement of all major defense contracts; to review for clearance prior to award all proposals of the War and Navy Departments to purchase in an amount of $500,000 or more and such other purchases as involved "unusual procurement problems" or would have a substantial impact upon the market; and to review the procurement procedures, methods and policies, and specifications of various federal procurement agencies.[18] Again the key to civilian control lay in the clearance function on major contracts. On September 4, 1941, as the problem of conversion of industry became more acute, there was established in OPM a Division of Contract Distribution which was to formulate and promote programs for the wider distribution of the services' purchases

14. This document was sent to Congress by the President. See House Doc. No. 950, 76th Cong., 3d Sess. (1940).

15. See below, pp. 87–88, for discussion of the general principles established.

16. See below, Chap. VIII.

17. Executive Order No. 8629, Jan. 7, 1941, 6 F.R. 191. Prior to the issuance of the order Donald Nelson had protested that the powers proposed for the new organization were not sufficient stating ". . . apparently however, it is the intention of OPM to set up a Division of Purchases without the necessary authority delegated to it." Letter from D. Nelson to W. S. Knudsen, January 24, 1941 (WPB, Historical Records Files).

18. Regulation No. 2, 6 F.R. 1595–1596 (March, 1941).

by breaking up purchases into small units, promoting conversion of industry, promoting subcontracting, and assisting potential suppliers in various ways.[19] This represented one of many steps to spread contracts which had a major impact upon the services' procurement programs.

With the passage of the First War Powers Act on December 18, 1941 the President delegated to the War and Navy Departments and the Maritime Commission his broad discretionary powers to enter into negotiated contracts.[20] Although the formal relations between the services and the civilian command were not clarified until the establishment of the War Production Board (WPB) about three weeks later, the services were directed "to cooperate to the fullest possible degree with the Office of Production Management . . ."

The Executive Order establishing WPB gave the chairman of the board full powers over the procurement programs of the services.[21] He was authorized, among other things, to "exercise general direction over the war procurement and production program" and to "determine the policies, plans, procedures, and methods of the several Federal departments, establishments, and agencies in respect to war procurement and production, including purchasing, contracting, specifications, and construction; and including conversion, requisitioning, plant expansion, and the financing thereof." All federal

19. Executive Order No. 8891, 6 F.R. 4623 (Sept., 1941). This division superseded the Defense Contract Service which had been established with more limited responsibilities on July 29, 1941. See Regulation 9, 6 F.R. 3889 (August, 1941).

20. Executive Order No. 9001, Dec. 27, 1941, 6 F.R. 6787.

21. Executive Order No. 9024, Jan. 16, 1942, 7 F.R. 329. The board itself consisted of the Chairman appointed by the President, the Secretary of War, the Secretary of the Navy, the Federal Loan Administrator, the Director General and Associate Director General of the OPM, the Administrator of the Office of Price Administration, the Chairman of the Board of Economic Warfare, and the Special Assistant to the President supervising defense aid. The powers of the board were vested in the Chairman, who was instructed to act with the advice and assistance of the other members. A week later OPM was abolished and its functions transferred to WPB. The Director General of OPM, Mr. Knudsen, continued as a member of the board in his new capacity as Lieutenant General in Charge of Production for the War Department and the Associate Director General, Mr. Hillman, continued as a member in his new capacity as Director of the Labor Division of WPB. See Executive Order No. 9040, Jan. 24, 1942, 7 F.R. 527.

agencies were instructed to "comply with the policies, plans, methods, and procedures in respect to war procurement and production as determined by the Chairman . . ." Finally, the Army and Navy Munitions Board, now clearly a secondary organization, was instructed to report to the President through the chairman of WPB.

Responsibility of the chairman of WPB for "policies, plans, procedures, and methods" in the field of procurement was clear. This represents the high point in civilian responsibility for procurement matters. Although the authority of the chairman of WPB to assign purchase responsibility, to determine methods of awarding contracts, and to determine types of contracts was supreme, the basic responsibility of the services for the execution and administration of contracts was not impaired.

This power of the civilian command appears to have come too late for greatest effectiveness. WPB had complete responsibility over policies and procedures and through its clearance function was in a position to implement these powers. But with the outbreak of war speed in placing contracts became paramount. No sooner had WPB gained these powers than it became necessary to decentralize the clearance function in order to expedite the placing of contracts. As early as February 12, 1942 Douglas C. MacKeachie, Director of Purchases of WPB, outlined to the Truman Committee plans for delegation to the services of a substantial part of the clearance function.[22] WPB reserved the right to require clearance where it felt it was necessary and to exercise a post-clearance review in other cases. In order to insure that WPB's point of view prevailed in the placing of contracts, it arranged to place one of its men in each of the services to be responsible for the procurement policies of the service and to exercise the clearance function. Frank Folsom, who had formerly been Deputy Director of the Purchase Division of WPB, was made Assistant Chief in Charge of Procurement in the Office of Procurement and

22. See United States Senate, Hearings before Special Committee Investigating the National Defense Program, 77th Cong., 1st Sess. (1942), Part 10, p. 4051.

Material of the Navy and Albert Browning went to the Services of Supply (SOS) in the War Department.[23] The former remained a civilian, but Browning was commissioned as a Colonel and later raised to Brigadier General.

In explaining this arrangement to Congress Nelson made it clear that although these men were responsible to their chiefs in the Army and Navy, they were also responsible to him and had a right of appeal to him. "The supply services of the Army and the Navy report to me."[24] At the same time a Purchase Policy Committee was established consisting of the Director of Purchases of WPB and representatives of the War and Navy Departments and of other interested agencies to advise WPB on procurement policy matters.[25]

To clarify the relations between WPB and the services two letters were prepared, one signed jointly by Nelson and Patterson, Under Secretary of War, and the other by Nelson and Forrestal, Under Secretary of the Navy, each containing a statement of responsibilities of the WPB and the respective service. These were distributed widely to the staff of each of the agencies. The joint letter with the Army stated "The War Production Board gives general direction and supervision to the war supply system, formulates broad policies with respect to that system, makes the basic decisions on the allocation of resources to the various parts of the supply system in accordance with strategic directives and plans, makes provision for materials, services, tools, and facilities needed for the military effort and the civilian economy, and organizes industry for war production." The War Department "in accordance and compliance with the policies and directives of the War Production Board, carries on its supply functions of research, design, development, programming, purchase, production, storage, distribution, issue, maintenance, and salvage."[26]

23. See *ibid.*, Part 12, pp. 5227–5231, testimony of Donald Nelson.
24. *Ibid.*, p. 5230. For the official history of the development of the relations between WPB and the services see CPA, *Industrial Mobilization for War*, p. 212.
25. *Ibid.*, pp. 524–526.
26. WPB, General Administrative Order No. 2–23, reprinted in Hearings be-

The division between policy determination and administrative responsibility was clear. WPB was basically responsible for policy, and the Purchase Policy Committee served as a meeting ground for discussion of common problems prior to determination of policy by WPB. Folsom and Browning, as Nelson's representatives, were expected to see that WPB policies were implemented by the services. It was inevitable, however, that Folsom and Browning should come increasingly to represent the interests of the Navy and War Departments. Although they introduced substantial reform in the services' procurement systems, it is clear that from the spring of 1942 WPB exercised decreasing influence over the services in matters of procurement. It became increasingly divorced from operations. Although it possessed strong powers, it did not often exercise these powers in the face of strong objections from the services. Nelson has stated in retrospect, however, that he believes this decision to place his men in the services represented ". . . one of the best things I ever did as Chairman of WPB . . ." [27]

The Purchases Policy Committee, later renamed the Procurement Policy Board and expanded to include representatives of the Treasury, Maritime Commission, Office of Price Administration, and the Smaller War Plants Corporation, served as an important meeting ground. Its chairmanship was held at all times by the representative of the War or Navy Department, and it came to be dominated by the services' point of view. When its members could agree on policy recommendations, they were generally forthcoming from WPB. It is fair to say, however, that henceforth the WPB seldom exercised aggressively its power to modify the services' policies or to coordinate their policies and procedures where they could not agree. By the fall of 1942 the Procurement Policy Division of WPB, the successor to the Purchase Division,

fore Special Committee Investigating the National Defense Program, 77th Cong., 1st Sess., Part 12, pp. 5350–5353. This letter is reproduced in Nelson, *op. cit.*, pp. 372–376. For letter signed by Mr. Forrestal see WPB, General Administrative Order No. 2–33.

27. Nelson, *op. cit.*, pp. 369–370.

was rapidly declining in importance.[28] "Contract clearance [within WPB] no longer existed; the Services apparently were not interested in using the technical advice of the commodity advisors . . ."[29] WPB became increasingly concerned with the administration of the controlled materials plan and the services assumed increasing responsibility even on procurement policy matters. Centralized coordination of procurement policies and procedures was weakening. Procurement coordination was coordination by consent. This was perhaps inevitable. Many policies had been thrashed out in the previous period. From the spring of 1942 on it became a matter of refinement of procedures and an adaptation of policies to changes in the war mobilization cycle.

Procurement Organization of the Services

This is not the place to give a detailed description of the procurement organizations of the services and their changes during World War II. But a brief description is necessary if the major implications of Nelson's decision to leave procurement with the services are to be grasped.

Procurement in the War Department was to a large extent decentralized, both functionally and geographically, although there were variations in the degree of geographical decentralization between the various technical services.[30] Prior to the reorganization of the War Department in February, 1942, the chiefs of each of the eight Supply Arms and Services were responsible for the procurement of supplies for their respective organizations. In the exercise of their responsibilities they were subject to the general supervision of G-4 of

28. CPA, *Industrial Mobilization for War*, pp. 521–527.

29. WPB, Procurement Policy Division, *History of Procurement Policies of the War Production Board and Predecessor Agencies, 1940–1945*, p. 3. (WPB, Historical Records Files.)

30. For more detailed description of the War Department organization for procurement see Army Industrial College, *War Department Previous to 1942* (1946), "Study of Experience in Industrial Mobilization in World War II"; Services of Supply, *Annual Report*, 1942, pp. 4–8; Production and Purchases Division, ASF, *Purchasing Policies and Practices*, pp. 1–8, 52–93.

the War Department General Staff with respect to the determination of requirements and to storage and distribution of supplies once they were acquired. They were also subject to the general supervision of the Assistant Secretary (later the Under Secretary) with respect to procurement. His supervision was exercised by the issuance of Army Regulations, Procurement Directives, and Procurement Circulars and by a system of reports and review of procurement actions taken by the Supply Arms and Services. Moreover, certain contracts required approval by the Assistant Secretary prior to award.

The reorganization of the War Department announced on March 2, 1942 provided for three commands, the Ground Forces, the Air Forces, and the Services of Supply (SOS). The name of the latter was subsequently changed to the Army Service Forces (ASF).[31] Complete responsibility for procurement was vested in the Army Air Forces (AAF) and the Services of Supply, subject to the broad direction of the Under Secretary of War. The ASF, which had responsibility for procurement of all material except that peculiar to the AAF, was a highly decentralized purchase organization. All procurement was carried on by the seven technical services, which were the Quartermaster General, Ordnance, Engineers, Chemical Warfare Service, Signal Corps, Surgeon General, and Transportation. These were themselves decentralized to a greater or lesser extent geographically. The activities of the technical services were subject to the general supervision of the Purchases Division at Headquarters, ASF. The Purchases Division, which was a purely staff organization, exercised its supervision in several ways including the issuance of a new volume of Procurement Regulations, liaison with the technical services by personal visits to their field procurement offices, and regular reporting on purchasing matters. In some matters Headquarters, ASF, reserved final authority to itself. Thus, all proposed commitments by the technical services involving $5,000,000 or more had to be approved by Head-

31. War Department, Circular No. 59 (March 2, 1942).

quarters, ASF, before award. Moreover, the approval of Headquarters, ASF, was generally required before final actions were taken involving the use of mandatory procurement powers or the granting of contract relief. By these various devices an attempt was made to coordinate the purchasing policies of the various purchasing offices of ASF while maintaining decentralized responsibility for actual administration of procurement.

The provision for independent procurement by the Army Air Forces created a special problem of coordination. The AAF was directly responsible on procurement matters to the Under Secretary. In order to coordinate the procurement policies of the AAF and the ASF, the Under Secretary designated the Director of the Purchases Division, ASF, as the Under Secretary's Special Representative "in clearing, approving and taking other action in respect to Army Air Force contracts, change orders, supplemental agreements . . . to approve sales of Army Air Force equipment . . . and to approve new War Department Army Air Force contract forms and deviations from approved forms of Army Air Force contracts . . ." [32] By this device the responsibility for coordination of War Department purchasing policy was in effect placed upon the Director of the Purchases Division acting for the Under Secretary. "In the field of policy formulation and supervision, the experience of the Purchases Division with the Air Forces was exactly the same as that of the Army Service Forces." [33]

Navy procurement was organized on quite different lines.[34] It was at all times highly concentrated geographically. Between 80 and 90 per cent of all Navy contracts by dollar value were negotiated and awarded in Washington. Procurement responsibilities were divided between the Bureau of Supplies

32. APR, par. 107.7, Memorandum from the Under Secretary to Col. A. J. Browning, June 1, 1942.

33. Production and Purchases Division, ASF, *op. cit.*, p. 91.

34. For more detailed description of the Navy Department's organization for procurement see R. H. Connery, "Organizing the Navy's Industrial Mobilization," *Public Administration Review*, V (1945), 303–311.

and Accounts, the five technical bureaus (Aeronautics, Medicine and Surgery, Ordnance, Ships, and Yards and Docks), the Marine Corps, and the Coast Guard. The technical bureaus were responsible for procuring the technical goods required by the Chief of Naval Operations, but prior to December 13, 1942 the preparation, award, execution, and administration of most contracts were the responsibility of the Bureau of Supplies and Accounts. The technical bureaus were authorized to negotiate and administer contracts for only a limited number of items. This system has often been characterized as a centralized procurement system. It might more appropriately be characterized as a system of divided authority. It has the further disadvantage of exaggerating the separation of the functions of purchase and design. With the rush to place contracts after Pearl Harbor this division of responsibility led to much delay and confusion. Consequently, on December 13, 1942, the chiefs of the bureaus were authorized to determine, subject to the approval of the Under Secretary, which items they wished to purchase themselves and which items they wished to have purchased by the Bureau of Supplies and Accounts.[35] The effect of this directive was that the bureaus took over the execution and administration of contracts on most technical items. Division of authority on much procurement was eliminated and functional decentralization of purchase operations accomplished.

Coordination of procurement policies was accomplished through the Office of Procurement and Material (OP&M), a staff organization responsible to the Under Secretary (later the Assistant Secretary) of the Navy.[36] This office served in both a staff and operating capacity. Its control over procurement was exercised in several ways. It issued Navy Procurement Directives establishing general policies and procedures

35. NPR, pars. 10,101–10,106.
36. For discussion of the functions of the OP&M by its chief see Admiral S. M. Robinson, "Procurement and Production," *Public Administration Review*, V (1945), 317–322. See also United States House of Representatives, Committee on Naval Affairs, Report No. 2056, *Investigations of the Progress of the War Effort*, 78th Cong., 2d Sess. (1944), pp. 132–137.

applicable to all bureaus. A staff of negotiators, responsible to OP&M, was recruited and placed in each of the principal bureaus, except the Bureau of Supplies and Accounts and the Bureau of Yards and Docks in Washington. These negotiators, who were technically business advisors to the contracting officers in the bureaus, assisted the bureaus in their negotiations and in some bureaus they in effect took over the purchasing functions in their entirety except for the actual signing of contracts. They also served as an effective line of communication between the groups responsible for policy and operations. They carried top policy down to the operating level and brought problems experienced at the operating level up to the top for policy consideration. This group served then in a dual capacity, as an operating group and as a vehicle for propagating and testing policy. Another mechanism for coordinating procurement policy was the Procurement Legal Division. It was responsible to the Under Secretary and had representatives assigned to the chief of each of the bureaus with responsibility for all legal problems pertaining to procurement.[37]

Finally, all proposed commitments for more than $200,000 had to be approved prior to award by the Assistant Chief of OP&M in Charge of Procurement. A Contract Clearance Division was established in OP&M to advise the Assistant Chief on these matters. The Contract Clearance Division served along with the negotiating and legal staffs as an important device for effecting consistent policies and procedures in the bureaus. While the negotiating and legal staffs provided top level advice and assistance at the operating levels, the Contract Clearance Division provided a daily review of the operations of the bureaus and of OP&M staffs assigned to the bureaus.[38]

The procurement operations of the services were, then, highly decentralized. In both the War and Navy Departments purchasing was decentralized to the technical services or bureaus. In the War Department the procurement of the tech-

37. *Ibid.,* pp. 137–138.
38. An excellent analysis of the work of the Contract Clearance Division is to be found in Eugene E. Oakes, *History of the Contract Clearance Division.* This study is on file with the Navy Department.

nical services and to a less extent of the AAF was further decentralized geographically. But decentralized purchase operations were subject to central control on policy matters. Coordination of purchase policy within the War and Navy Departments was effected through two high level groups, the Purchases Division, Headquarters, ASF, and OP&M. These were essentially staff organizations, although OP&M also performed operating functions in cooperation with the bureaus. The execution and administration of contracts remained at all times the responsibility of the contracting officer of the cognizant technical group, *e.g.*, the Army Signal Corps, the Bureau of Ships, and the AAF.

Coordination of policy between the War and Navy Departments was effected through the close cooperation between the Purchases Division, ASF, and OP&M. There was continuous direct contact between these groups. The two key persons in these groups in 1942 were Albert Browning, Director of Purchases and Special Representative of the Under Secretary, and Frank Folsom, Assistant Chief of OP&M in Charge of Procurement. They were Donald Nelson's personal choices. These two, and their successors, acting together and through the Procurement Policy Board served increasingly as the central coordinating force on procurement after the spring of 1942. Coordination was by no means perfect either within or between the two departments. The effectiveness with which top policy was implemented varied as between various bureaus, services, and districts. The coordinating groups were essentially civilian organizations superimposed on well-established procurement organizations. Implementation of policy was the prerogative of the established organizations. Although newer coordinating groups had sufficient powers to make their views prevail, their effectiveness depended in large part not upon invoking their formal powers but rather upon their ability to aid, assist, and persuade the operating groups. On many issues when agreement could not be reached the various groups were left to go their own way. In spite of all the difficulties, the coordination of policy was surprisingly effective. Moreover, there was a surprising amount of coordination of policy effected through the cooperation of the various operating groups. This was particularly true in the case of the AAF and the Bureau of Aeronautics.

A system of decentralized purchasing of this type inevitably raises the problem of competition between the various operating units. The arguments for decentralized operations, however, are strong. It is clear that a procurement organization of the magnitude required by modern war must be decentralized both geographically and functionally if the organization is not to become unwieldy. It seems equally clear that in the case of technical items effective procurement requires close cooperation between the technical personnel responsible for specifications and purchase personnel.[39] The basic question is not one of centralization versus decentralization but rather of the particular type of decentralized operations under a centralized policy control. The decentralized operations in effect during World War II reflected two basic factors: the division of responsibility between the services for military operations and the particular division of responsibility for material between the technical services or bureaus within each service. As a result the same or similar items might be purchased by two or more bureaus or technical services. Even in the case of negotiated contracts this may lead to difficulties in as much as the seller can play off one purchasing officer against another. The purchasing officer is not in a position to know the total market situation for a particular item or a particular firm unless he keeps in very close touch with other groups which are buying the same item or dealing with the same contractor.

Despite many attempts to avoid competition by assigning procurement responsibility between the War and Navy Departments and between the technical services and bureaus within each department, there were many instances of this type of rivalry during the war.[40] Thus in the Navy in 1944

39. For exposition of this view see pp. 33 and 231.
40. This problem was dealt with at considerable length in a study undertaken by the War and Navy Departments in 1944. See Col. W. H. Draper, Jr. and

binoculars and cranes were bought by four different bureaus and radio tubes and watches were bought by three bureaus.[41] Petroleum products were bought by the Quartermaster, the AAF, and the Bureau of Supplies and Accounts.[42] Incendiary bombs were purchased by Army Ordnance, and the Chemical Warfare Service.[43] It should be pointed out, however, that much was accomplished during the war in the direction of establishing functionally centralized purchasing of common or similar items. From 1942 on most of the Navy's subsistence requirements were purchased by the Army [44] and from September, 1942 most lumber was purchased by a Central Procuring Agency established within the Construction Division of the Corps of Engineers.[45] Many other items were being purchased by one service for the other through arrangements which had been worked out between the operating groups.[46] Toward the end of the war arrangements were worked out for centralized purchasing of medical supplies and petroleum and for closer cooperation in the purchase of clothing and textiles.

The purchase of the same or similar items by two or more services is only part of the problem which is subsumed under the heading "competition in procurement." Rivalry in purchase of similar products is simply the limiting case of a more general phenomenon, rivalry for the use of a firm's facilities. Many firms can and do produce a wide variety of items for military use. Moreover, in many cases their facilities are rather easily transferable from one product to another if the profit prospects make the transfer attractive. In such cases rivalry between groups responsible for the purchase of quite different items may be just as damaging to good procurement as rivalry between purchasers of the same or similar items. Even when facilities are not easily transferable, the purchasing policies of

---

Capt. L. L. Strauss, *Coordination of Procurement between the War and Navy Departments,* 3 vols. (Feb., 1945).

41. *Op. cit.,* II, 59.
42. *Op. cit.,* II, 62 and III, 42.
43. *Op. cit.,* II, 62.
44. *Op. cit.,* III, 1–7.
45. *Op. cit.,* III, 8–16.
46. *Op. cit.,* II, 63–68.

one buying office may have substantial effects upon others, since firms dealing with several services or bureaus will inevitably try to induce all buyers to adopt the most favorable policies adopted by any.[47]

47. For discussion of policies designed to deal with this problem see below, Chap. XII.

VI

OPA'S RELATION TO THE PRICING OF MILITARY PROCUREMENTS

Determining the Price Administrator's Authority

PRIOR to Pearl Harbor little consideration appears to have been given to the relation between the proposed price controls and the prices on military procurements established by the services through contract.[1] This is probably explained in part by the failure of the services to anticipate that price controls would be administered by a different agency from that responsible for control of materials and production and that they themselves would not participate directly in this agency. Moreover, since the price controls imposed prior to Pearl Harbor covered basic materials primarily, they had not impinged to any great extent directly on the services' contracts. Finally, the services were still making the bulk of their purchases of price-controlled items in accordance with the peacetime system of competitive bidding, under which it might be assumed that all bids would conform to existing ceilings.

It was quite generally agreed that some type of price stabilization would be of great assistance to the procurement activi-

1. In presenting the industrial mobilization plan to the War Policies Commission in 1931, it was clear that General MacArthur, Chief of Staff, believed that the War Department would establish prices for "special supplies" and a civilian control agency would be responsible for prices for "general purchasing." See House Doc. No. 163, 72d Cong., 1st Sess., p. 372. The plan apparently solved this problem by providing for a Price Control Commission on which the services were to be represented. The Price Control Commission was to be a quasi-judicial body to establish policies and methods which were to be administered by other wartime administrative agencies. "Representation of interested Government agencies on this committee is intended to insure complete cooperation and the elimination of conflicting action." *Industrial Mobilization Plan* (1936), p. 16. The services were to be responsible for developing contract forms and procedures such as would provide among other things an effective stimulus to production, protect the interest of the government, and prevent the contractor from making unreasonable profit. This mobilization plan was, of course, never put into effect. In 1942 the Price Administrator was given responsibility for administering the program as well as for determining policies.

ties of the services although the nature and limits of such controls were not usually specified.[2] Prior to Pearl Harbor the Under Secretary of War had urged the passage of price stabilization legislation as an insurance of sustained morale on the part of civilian and military personnel, an aid to maximum production, and a prerequisite to effective procurement.[3] He emphasized that in the absence of price control procurement might be seriously retarded by speculative withholding of goods from the market, the interruption of production resulting from strikes provoked by the rising cost of living, and hesitancy on the part of business to make long-term forward commitments. Moreover, it was recognized that effective price control would make the enforcement of priority controls easier by limiting the financial gains to be had from violating them.[4]

In view of the decision by Congress to give policy and administrative responsibilities to a single Price Administrator, the question of the scope of his authority over prices on contracts entered into by the services was bound to arise. The resulting controversy had two stages: the first in which the Price Administrator won from Congress undisputed responsibility for all prices, and the second in which he delegated to the services a substantial part of his authority for prices of specialized military procurement.[5]

The first stage of the controversy was essentially concerned with the relative dangers of courting inflation through diffusion of responsibility for controlling prices and of delaying procurement through tying the hands of the procurement agencies in negotiating contracts. The bill drafted by the

2. Leon Henderson and Donald M. Nelson, "Prices, Profits and Government," *Harvard Business Review*, XIX (Summer, 1941), 390–391. United States House of Representatives, Hearings before Committee on Banking and Currency, 77th Cong., 1st Sess., *Price Control Bill* (1941), pp. 146–148.

3. Testimony of Under Secretary of War Robert P. Patterson, *ibid.*, pp. 1519–1523.

4. See statement of Bernard Baruch, *ibid.*, p. 992.

5. For much light on the history of the negotiations incident to this controversy the author is indebted to the excellent *History of the Liaison Relationship between the Navy Department and the Office of Price Administration* prepared by Lt. Cdr. Chester H. Clemens. This study is on file with the Navy Department.

House of Representatives in the fall of 1941 provided that a single Price Administrator should have complete authority over all prices and that any contractual arrangement of the services to pay a price higher than the ceiling price established by him, whether entered into before or after the effective date of the ceiling price, should be invalid and unenforceable.[6] On December 10, 1941 the Under Secretaries of War and of the Navy in a joint letter to the Chairman of the Senate Banking and Currency Committee protested that these provisions "will have the effect of taking away from the Services the present statutory powers of these Departments to make firm contracts." They recommended that the bill be amended to provide that no action of the Price Administrator should "affect any contract heretofore or hereafter entered into by the War or Navy Departments, or subcontracts thereunder, or purchases of materials, or supplies required for the performance of such contracts or subcontracts, unless the head of the respective Department shall have concurred in the adoption. . . ."[7]

In a letter to the Senate Banking and Currency Committee in reply to this request Mr. Henderson stated that "*we cannot let price considerations prevent our getting needed equipment. . . . the Price Administrator, like everyone else, is going to gear his program to the needs of the Army and Navy.*" He pointed out that in accordance with the President's wishes he had not in the past concerned himself with the prices of "tanks, cannon, armored vessels, bombers." He was concerned, however, with the prices of "hundreds of basic commodities and articles which are the very substance of the entire economy" such as metals, chemicals, fats and oils, fuel, machinery, textiles, lumber and building materials and which the services obtained directly or indirectly through subcontracts. "If the Army and Navy, and possibly other agencies, can pay higher prices and authorize their contractors and

6. H.R. 5990, 77th Cong., 1st Sess., sec. 206.
7. Letter from Robert P. Patterson and James V. Forrestal to Senator Robert F. Wagner, December 10, 1941.

sub-contractors to pay higher prices, then both the priorities program and the anti-inflation program are endangered." [8]

In a subsequent letter to the Senate Banking and Currency Committee the services insisted that the issue was essentially a choice between division of responsibility for procurement and division of responsibility for price. ". . . just as Mr. Henderson is confident he will not disturb our military program, we are even more confident that we will not disturb his economic program." The services expressed willingness to modify their former position and agreed that price regulations should apply to military procurements except in cases where the Secretary of War or of the Navy should certify in writing to the Price Administrator "that the exemption of such sale is essential to the defense of the United States against her enemies." [9] It is significant that at no point in the controversy was there any claim that existing price controls had in any way given trouble. Eventually the Secretaries of War and of the Navy appealed the issue jointly to the President, who turned down their appeal. "It is absolutely imperative that final authority [over prices] be vested in one person, and the Army and Navy must conform as well as everybody else." [10]

Delegation of Price Responsibilities to the Services

The principle of single responsibility for all prices was incorporated in the Emergency Price Control Act of 1942,[11]

8. Letter from Leon Henderson to Senator Prentiss M. Brown of the Senate Banking and Currency Committee, December 11, 1941.

9. Letter from Robert P. Patterson and James V. Forrestal to Senator Prentiss M. Brown dated December 16, 1941.

10. Memorandum from President Roosevelt to the Secretary of War and the Secretary of the Navy, December 20, 1941. In the Senate debate Senator Brown made it clear that the bill gave the Price Administrator responsibility for prices of military procurements. ". . . nothing in the bill would prevent the Administrator, as a theoretical matter, from fixing the prices of articles which the Government buys as under contract. But as a practical matter, since the general public is not concerned with the price of planes and tanks, it is not expected that the Administrator will exercise authority in such fields. By fixing the prices of the commodities which go to make up the articles the Government buys, the prices of these articles will be kept down." 88 Cong. Rec. 55-56.

11. 56 Stat. 29, sec. 201.

but it was another nine months before a *modus vivendi* was worked out by which the Price Administrator redelegated a substantial part of his responsibility over prices on military procurements to the services. At the time of the passage of the act the controlled items which were of immediate concern to the services were few. But as controls were extended more rapidly and particularly with the issuance of the General Maximum Price Regulation (GMPR) in April freezing most prices at their March level,[12] the second phase of the controversy began.

For several months OPA made a series of concessions to the services. At the time of the issuance of the General Maximum Price Regulation the services requested exemption of most items which they purchased directly and of their various parts and subassemblies.[13] The Office of Price Administration (OPA) recognized that the pricing standards of GMPR were not well tailored to deal with military equipment. Costs on such equipment are uncertain and frequently subject to change because of changing specifications and often abrupt changes in the rate of output. In view of its preoccupation with the tremendous task of promulgating, explaining, and perfecting GMPR, OPA decided "to exempt from price control for the time being all finished assemblies of combat items and the parts and subassemblies thereof, with the exception of those parts and subassemblies which were already under control." [14] This was accomplished by providing that the regulation should not apply to sales or deliveries of such goods and services to the government or to such transactions as might be specified subsequently by supplementary regulations.[15] Supplementary Regulation No. 4 originally issued on May 13, 1942 exempted a large group of military items such as aircraft, ammunition, artillery, bombs, projectiles, small arms, ships, boats, tor-

12. 7 F.R. 3153 (April, 1942).
13. ASF, *Annual Report*, 1943, p. 28. OPA, *Second Quarterly Report*, pp. 39–45.
14. *Ibid.,* p. 39.
15. 7 F.R. 3155, sec. 1499.10 (April, 1942).

pedoes, fire control, equipment, armed vehicles, and the component parts and subassemblies thereof.[16]

Emergency purchases,[17] secret contracts,[18] and developmental contracts [19] were likewise exempted by Supplementary Regulation No. 4 and by other regulations dealing with specific products including the very important regulation covering machinery products.[20] In order to relieve procurement officers of the civil and criminal penalties of the Emergency Price Control Act of 1942 in the event that they purchased at higher than ceiling prices, the war procurement agencies and their contracting and disbursing officers were specifically exempted from these penalties.[21] OPA concluded that it would be sufficient to have contractors selling to the procurement agencies liable in case ceiling prices were violated.[22] As another step to facilitate military procurement, Procedural Regulation No. 6 was issued July 1, 1942 providing a special

16. 7 F.R. 3724 (May, 1942). This Supplementary Regulation was revised and amended from time to time and subsequently incorporated into Supplementary Regulation No. 1 to the General Maximum Price Regulation on April 16, 1943. See 8 F.R. 4982.

17. "The exemption for 'emergency purchases' . . . was prompted by a frank recognition that agencies of the Government may be faced with emergency situations, requiring immediate delivery which can be accomplished by the seller only at substantially increased costs. The need may be so acute that the seller would not even have time to apply to the Office for an adjustment in his price." OPA, *Second Quarterly Report*, p. 43. An emergency purchase was generally defined as one where the service certified that it was "imperative" to secure the item and "it was impossible to secure, or unfair to require immediate delivery or performance at the applicable maximum price." See Maximum Price Regulation No. 136, section 23 (7 F.R. 5053, July, 1942) and Supplementary Regulation No. 4 to the General Maximum Price Regulation (7 F.R. 3724, May, 1942). In such cases the regulations usually called for filing with OPA a brief statement of the facts of the case subsequent to the purchase.

18. In the case of secret contracts it was only necessary for the services to advise OPA of the number or other identification of the contract.

19. A contract was generally deemed to be for a developmental product during the period required for stabilization of specifications by the purchaser or for the accumulation of sufficient production experience by the supplier to enable him to make a fair estimate of his costs. In these cases the service was required to certify in writing that the contract was experimental. OPA was empowered to make a finding after consultation with the appropriate agency that the period necessary for development had expired.

20. Maximum Price Regulation No. 136 (7 F.R. 5047, July, 1942).

21. Supplementary Order No. 7 (7 F.R. 5176, July, 1942).

22. OPA, *Second Quarterly Report*, p. 43.

procedure for the upward adjustment of prices in cases where anyone holding or proposing to hold a prime contract or sub-contract believed that an established maximum price "impedes or threatens to impede production of a commodity which is essential to the war program." [23] After filing an application for upward revision of his ceiling price with OPA the con-tractor was free to contract with the procurement agencies at any price up to the new ceiling which he had requested of OPA. If the application were denied by OPA in whole or in part, however, the contract price would be revised downward to the maximum price finally established. This regulation was designed to aid the services in situations where a ceiling price might not provide sufficient incentive to a particular pro-ducer because of his exceptionally high costs or low price ceiling.

Despite these various steps designed to facilitate the work of the procurement agencies, OPA was clearly moving fur-ther and further into the control of prices of military goods. "As of midsummer, 1942, 135 of the 200 specific maximum price regulations of OPA included some articles sold on prime contracts with the war procurement agencies or on sub-contracts thereunder. With the added coverage of the GMPR the following categories of products consumed by the Services and other war agencies and commodities entering into their production were subject to price control by OPA: basic ma-terials, such as the metals, lumber, building materials, textiles, rubber, chemicals, fuels; most quartermaster supplies—ap-parel and other textile items, drugs and pharmaceuticals, furni-ture, bedding, refrigerators, stoves, china, silverware, and other consumer durable articles, rubber and paper products; machinery; and a substantial range of parts and subassemblies of combat equipment and merchant ships. The principal area of exemption was finished combat equipment and ships and a large portion of the parts and subassemblies thereof." [24]

The services became increasingly concerned over this

23. 7 F.R. 5087 (July, 1942).
24. OPA, *Second Quarterly Report*, p. 44.

gradual extension of controls. The machinery regulation first issued in April but later postponed until July had made the services apprehensive. This regulation covered many items purchased by the services directly or indirectly such as gasoline, steam and diesel engines, including marine engines; mechanical and electrical instruments used in aircraft, ships, and laboratories; pumps and compressors; industrial and marine power boilers; chemical manufacturing machinery; construction equipment; nonagricultural tractors; and radio and radar equipment. On the other hand OPA became increasingly fearful that the rise in profits in the field of aircraft and military vehicles would provide a powerful incentive to wage demands which would be communicated throughout the economic system.[25] OPA announced as early as May that unstandardized military equipment would soon be brought under control,[26] and discussions were begun on proposed regulations covering aircraft and military vehicles.[27]

These proposed regulations were the occasion for reopening the controversy over the scope of OPA controls in the area of military goods. They represented an extension of OPA's activities beyond that which Senator Prentiss Brown had indicated probable when defending the proposed price-control legislation on the floor of Congress.[28] On July 23, 1942 the Under Secretary of War and the Under Secretary of the Navy, asserting that the proposed regulations were delaying production, requested the Price Administrator to exempt all war goods from price regulations.[29]

The crux of the issue in this second stage of the argument was whether price stabilization in the civilian goods area could be effective so long as the services were free to determine prices on military purchases themselves. OPA argued that the services lacked the techniques to control prices on

25. *Loc. cit.*
26. *The New York Times,* May 28, 1942, p. 25.
27. *The Wall Street Journal,* July 8, 1942, p. 5.
28. See above, p. 68, note 10.
29. Memorandum from Robert P. Patterson and James V. Forrestal to Leon Henderson, July 23, 1942.

military goods effectively and that unduly high prices in the military goods area would contribute materially to inflation of wages and eventually of prices of civilian goods. Such an outcome, it was agreed on both sides, would destroy the morale of civilian and military personnel alike and would interfere with the objective of maximum production.

The services' counter-arguments were fourfold. First, they argued that prices of war goods, unlike civilian prices, could not contribute to inflation directly, but only indirectly through increased distribution of profits and wages. The distribution of profits, they argued, would be controlled by renegotiation and taxes. Wages, they implied, should be brought under control by a separate government policy. Second, they maintained that the nature of military procurement was such as to make effective and workable control of prices by OPA impossible. Third, they argued that the uncertainty and divided authority over procurement incident to such controls by OPA would impede production and procurement. Finally, through better procurement and renegotiation and with the aid of new wage controls the services claimed they were equipped to control prices of military goods themselves.

After much discussion and the introduction of a bill in Congress which would grant such exemption [30] the Price Administrator finally acceded to the request of the services.[31] He did so with great reluctance, swayed perhaps by the consideration noted later by one of his assistants that "if we blunder in the civilian goods area, some civilians may be inconvenienced, but if we blunder in the war goods area, some American boys may be killed." [32] In spite of his reservations, the Price Adminis-

30. *The New York Times*, Aug. 14, 1942, p. 1.
31. *Ibid.*, Nov. 15, 1942, sec. III, p. 6.
32. Statement by Mr. J. Philip Wernette, the first War Goods Price Coordinator of OPA. See OPA, *A Manual of Price Control; Lecture Series, Delivered at the Training Program for Price of the Office of Price Administration* (1943), p. 95. Dr. J. K. Galbraith who was Deputy Administrator for Price has recently stated, "For some months prior to the agreement with the War and Navy Departments I had been growing increasingly uneasy about efforts to control the prices of war goods. I was influenced partly by the fear of the blood-spattered criticism we would experience did it ever appear that price controls were delaying the production of arms but I also had begun to doubt that control in this

trator agreed to refrain from further extension of maximum price control in the area of strictly military goods with the understanding that the services would use their powers as effectively as possible to control both prices and profits in the exempted area so as "to prevent unnecessary growth in the public debt, unnecessary expenditure of the public funds, and indirect inflationary effects on prices in the civilian goods area." [33] The services also agreed to furnish OPA with information on prices and procedures adequate to appraise the effects of their controls.[34]

The general position resulting from this agreement is best summarized by an OPA staff memorandum:

1. In general, the areas of OPA control and of exemptions are to remain as they were in September. That is, those military commodities, parts subassemblies, and materials that were subject to OPA control, remain subject, those that were exempted continue exempted.
2. Commodities then under the General Maximum Price Regulation may be brought under specific maximum price regulations. Military goods exempted from GMPR will not be brought under control, except in moving toward the line of demarcation.
3. Maximum prices then in effect may be changed.
4. A line of demarcation of authority is indicated. In general, the Office of Price Administration will refrain from further extension of price control over all sales of commodities which are in such form that they will be used only for military purposes, except the sale made by the manufacturer who is the first to put the commodity into such form. This is to be interpreted, in general, to mean only the first stage of processing, counting from the raw material up toward the finished product.

field had any close bearing on the problem of inflation. Mr. Henderson, although formally committed to the use of price controls in this area, had, I believe, more than passing sympathy for this view." "The Disequilibrium System," *American Economic Review*, XXXVII (June, 1947), 299, note 17. The threat of OPA controls over aircraft in the summer of 1942 is credited with helping to prevent substantial prospective wage increases in the Pacific Coast aircraft industry. T. J. Kinsella, *War Procurement and OPA*, "OPA Historical Study" (unpublished), pp. 29–30.

33. Letter from Leon Henderson to Robert P. Patterson and James V. Forrestal, September 16, 1942.

34. Letter from Robert P. Patterson and James V. Forrestal to Leon Henderson, October 13, 1942.

5. The line of demarcation is very similar to the status of control authority as of September. There is no general policy to move toward the line either way; any instance of such extension or diminution of OPA control is to be decided on its merits, after communication with the Services concerned.[35]

This general division of responsibility was maintained throughout the war. Although it proved impossible to work out a precise line of demarcation, changes in the respective responsibilities were worked out in individual cases as the need arose.[36] OPA estimated that at least 70 per cent of its maximum price regulations applied in some degree to war goods.[37] On the other hand it has been stated that more than 60 per cent by value of the War Department's prime contracts were exempt as a result of the agreement during the years 1943 and 1944.[38] Despite the development of black markets for some items purchased by the services, "the evidence indicates that violation of OPA ceiling prices by these agencies is negligible." [39] Many problems faced by the services in the area of controlled goods were handled by affording the services special treatment under the regulations. In some cases where the regulations had made it less profitable to sell to the services than to others, it was necessary to raise the prices on sales to the services so that they could compete. Likewise in the spring of 1945 textile procurement was threatened due to the fact that costs were rising more rapidly than ceiling prices could be adjusted. Consequently, textile procurements were exempted from control by an order which permitted the War Department to pay higher than ceiling prices in accordance with OPA standards.[40]

35. OPA Staff Memorandum from J. K. Galbraith re "Division of Authority over Prices between the Office of Price Administration and the Armed Services," Dec. 15, 1942.

36. ASF, *Annual Report*, 1943, p. 29. For general statement of the spirit in which OPA handled the problem see the statement by Wernette in OPA, *A Manual of Price Control*, pp. 90–99.

37. *Ibid.*, p. 94.

38. ASF, *Annual Report*, 1944, p. 119; 1945, p. 215.

39. OPA, *A Manual of Price Control*, p. 99.

40. 10 F.R. 2683 (March, 1945). ASF, *Annual Report*, 1945, p. 215.

Effectiveness of Arrangements

The price and wage stabilization programs of OPA and the War Labor Board (WLB) together with the arrangements worked out between the services and OPA did much to facilitate procurement and effective pricing of military goods. The over-all effect of the arrangements between the services and OPA was to place the services in a preferential position to bid for resources.[41] While the prices of civilian products were rigidly controlled, prices on major military items purchased on prime contracts were exempt from OPA controls. This meant that the services were in a position to make it financially advantageous for contractors to take military contracts. Likewise in the case of purchases by the services of goods subject to OPA controls the individual price adjustment procedure provided by Procedural Regulation No. 6 and many other special arrangements were designed to place the services in a preferential position. These arrangements working within the context of over-all production and material controls facilitated the diversion of resources to necessary military production with the minimum use of compulsory orders directed at specific contractors. Used injudiciously such arrangements might have disrupted production and material controls, but used judiciously they simplified the administration of such controls.

The arrangements effected with OPA also aided the services in the negotiation of reasonable prices on their prime contracts. The stabilization of wage rates by WLB, together with the stabilization of the prices of raw materials, semi-manufactured products, and numerous component parts facilitated contractors' production planning by stabilizing their costs. This made it easier for the services in cooperation with industry to estimate costs on prospective contracts and negotiate reasonable prices.

The contribution which OPA made by controlling prices

41. Galbraith, *American Economic Review*, XXXVII, 299.

on subcontract purchases of many basic materials, standard commercial items, and component parts was a substantial one. The services found it difficult at all times to control the prices paid for such items by prime contractors to subcontractors, sub-subcontractors, etc. In the case of CPFF contractors the services were sometimes able to scrutinize purchase prices on subcontracts. In other cases the services brought pressure directly on fixed-price contractors to negotiate reasonable prices on subcontracts. In still other cases the services proceeded against subcontractors directly to induce them to reform their price policies. But these attempts by the services to insure reasonable prices on subcontract purchases did not become effective until the war was well along, and at no time did they come close to covering the bulk of major subcontract purchases.[42] There is no doubt, therefore, that OPA made a substantial contribution in this field to the control of costs on military contracts. There was some tendency for OPA ceiling prices to become floors as well as ceilings even where the ceiling prices were unreasonably high in view of the large wartime volume. But it is unquestionably true that contractors' costs of materials and supplies were controlled much more effectively than they would have been if exempted from OPA controls. If wage stabilization had been instituted earlier and the success of price stabilization on materials and supplies had been foreseen, many of the prices negotiated by the services early in the war might have been more moderate.

There seems to be a consensus that these various arrangements with OPA were generally satisfactory to the services. No serious charges of delays or interference with production have been made. The most serious problems seem to have developed with reference to items bought by the Quartermaster, many of which were subject to OPA controls. However, the official history of the Quartermaster Corps concluded that "serious bottlenecks frequently arose, but in most cases, necessary relief was obtained without undue delay of essential

42. See below, pp. 189–191, for further discussion of the problem.

procurement." [43] One of the Navy's liaison officers has stated that "in no single case presented to the OPA Liaison Section during 1944 and 1945 did the Navy fail to obtain the goods in question nor was there a single case where use of the mandatory powers were necessary." [44] The Purchases Division, ASF, has stated that "ceiling prices have had a profound effect upon War Department Pricing. . . . The negotiating of firm prices, which in so many instances in World War I was impossible, because of the instability of raw material costs, has in this war been possible, as a result of the stabilization of the general price level. In addition to all the usual business advantages resulting from a stabilized level of prices, tremendous savings accrued to the benefit of the War Department . . . particularly at the lower level of the industrial processes where prices are beyond the control of the War Department." [45] Moreover, at the time of the extension of the Emergency Price Control Act in 1944, the Secretary of War and the Secretary of the Navy each testified that price control had benefited the services through sustaining the morale of military personnel, saving billions of dollars, and helping to insure full and uninterrupted production for military needs.[46]

Procedural Regulation No. 6 for adjusting prices of war contractors where a ceiling price was so low as to threaten production seems to have been administered to the general satisfaction of all. It should be noted that a contractor was entitled to more liberal relief on war goods under this procedure than he could receive under the corresponding procedures on

43. Harry B. Yoshpe, *Production Control in the Quartermaster Corps, 1939–1944* (1944), "Quartermaster Corps Historical Studies," No. 8, p. 71.

44. Lt. M. H. Blackshear, *Effect and Assistance of OPA Price Control on Navy Procurement*, p. 14. This study is on file with the Navy Department.

45. Production and Purchases Division, ASF, *Purchasing Policies and Practices*, pp. 219–220.

46. United States House of Representatives, Hearings before Committee on Banking and Currency, 78th Cong., 2d Sess., *Extension of the Emergency Price Control Act of 1942* (1944), pp. 875–879. See also statement of Frank Knox, Secretary of the Navy, to United States Senate, Hearings before Committee on Banking and Currency, 78th Cong., 2d Sess., *Extension of the Emergency Price Control Act of 1942* (1944), pp. 629–633.

civilian goods. The criteria for relief were briefly as follows: if the contractor's current over-all earnings before taxes exceeded 115 per cent of his base period average earnings, OPA would grant an adjustment calculated to cover his manufacturing costs with full factory overhead, but without allowance for selling, administrative, and general overhead expenses; if current over-all earnings before taxes were between 100 and 115 per cent of his base period average, OPA would grant an adjustment to cover total costs of manufacture and sale; and if current over-all earnings were less than his base period average, OPA would grant an adjustment covering total costs plus a reasonable profit.[47]

The War Department reported that in 1944 only about 85 suppliers encountered major price difficulties under OPA regulations which called for individual treatment under Procedural Regulation No. 6 or by other methods.[48] In 1945 only 75 suppliers sought relief.[49] In commenting upon the Navy's experience under the adjustment procedure one officer responsible for liaison with OPA stated, "It is perhaps accurate to say that although processing delays by OPA were inconvenient and annoying they did not significantly delay procurement."[50]

The Problem Reconsidered

It is appropriate to reconsider the merits of the Price Administrator's claims in 1942 concerning the indirect inflationary effects of uncontrolled military pricing and the inability of the services to exercise effective controls. Although the following chapters will throw light on these matters, several comments may be appropriate here. In the first place the Price Administrator was correct in arguing that renegotiation and excess profits taxation alone could not be effective in con-

47. Kinsella, *op. cit.*, p. 11.
48. ASF, *Annual Report*, 1944, p. 119.
49. *Ibid.*, 1945, p. 215.
50. Blackshear, *op. cit.*, p. 15.

trolling inflation since they were effective only in recouping profits arising from prices which had already risen.[51] They could be effective only if buttressed by control of wages and of basic material prices and by effective incentives to efficiency. So long as wages were not controlled OPA was clearly correct in stressing the possibility that unreasonable prices on military goods would induce inflation in the civilian economy. Such prices on military goods might well have produced an inflation of wages offered by government contractors and this wage inflation in the military goods area would surely have led to increased wages and prices in the civilian goods area. Reasonable control of prices of military goods, however, would have served as a deterrent to wage increases in the military goods area.

Clearly such indirect control of wages is not wise as a long-run measure in times of a major war, and in most cases it is not even wise as a stop-gap in the early periods of mobilization. Granted that wages were not under direct control in the summer of 1942, however, an attempt to prevent the indirect inflationary effects of poor pricing on military purchases might be justified.

By the fall of 1942 wages as well as prices and profits were under control.[52] Thereafter the crux of the matter lay in the question as to whether OPA or the services were better equipped to control prices so as to provide positive incentives to industry to conserve manpower and material.

The most effective way to promote efficient production was clearly through careful pricing by the services. OPA controls were not well designed for this purpose. In the case of aircraft and military vehicles OPA proposed formula pricing which would have required the contractor to compute his maximum price on the basis of (a) labor rates as of some base date, (b) material prices as of a base date or at current rates, and (c) the price-determining method actually used by him on the base date. This type of formula pricing might have

51. See below, Chap. XI.
52. Executive Order No. 9250, 7 F.R. 7871 (Oct., 1942).

acted as a deterrent to indirect inflation of wage rates and material prices. But it would not have provided an incentive to efficiency in the use of labor and material. Moreover, under the price-determining methods used by many manufacturers by which burden or overhead are figured as a percentage of material or labor cost, this formula would have failed to insure that prices to the services reflected the economies of mass production. Consequently, I believe that negotiation of prices by the services in such cases held forth greater promise both in inducing efficiency and in eliminating the excessive profits incident to increased volume than the proposed formulas of OPA.[53] OPA was never able to establish a general policy of lowering prices to limit profits resulting from the increased volume incident to the war. Moreover, to subject contractors to controls by both the OPA and the services would have involved industry in keeping duplicate records.

Although it appears that the final division of responsibility proved satisfactory to both OPA and the services and that OPA's argument for control of the prices of military goods were not very persuasive under the conditions prevailing in the fall of 1942, it is not intended to imply that the division of authority was in all respects ideal. As has been indicated the services were not conspicuously successful in their attempts to induce contractors to negotiate close prices on their purchases of many subcontract items. Although OPA ceilings were often the only protection against serious inflation of such prices, it was clear that in many cases OPA ceilings were unduly high since they were based on peacetime volume. The

53. A. J. Kress in a study for the Army Industrial College states that the services and OPA "found it quite possible to work together toward a common end." (Army Industrial College, *Contract Pricing: Principal Developments*, 1946, "Study of Experience in Industrial Mobilization in World War II," p. 49.) Also T. J. Kinsella has stated that "in view of the initial position of the agency [OPA] in using the selective type of control, had wage stabilization been achieved sooner in the war effort OPA's attempt to establish over-all procurement price controls would not have been justified. In no case would OPA price controls have eliminated the need for military renegotiation and repricing of contracts, for even under OPA ceilings efficient expanded productions would have required reduction in prices which only renegotiation and repricing by procurement officers would have achieved effectively." *Op. cit.*, p. 52.

objective of the services was to arrive at prices below OPA ceilings which reflected the increased wartime volume. The services would have been materially aided in such cases if OPA had been able to reprice downward on an industry-wide basis certain of these items. This, of course, raises the basic problem of the differences in the pricing standards which were applied by OPA and the services, about which more will be said below.[54]

54. See below, pp. 97–101.

VII

DEVELOPMENT OF PURCHASING POLICY:
WORLD WAR II

WITH the approach of the emergency in 1939 the services were with some limited exceptions committed to purchasing by the competitive bid system. This meant that the criterion both for selecting the sources for military production and for determining prices was the minimum price received as the result of public advertising for competitive sealed bids. As has been indicated in Chapter III this procedure is unduly restrictive even for peacetime. In a major war it is completely impossible. The industrial mobilization plans of the War Department had contemplated a shift to the negotiated contract. When the emergency came, however, the industrial mobilization plan was sidetracked.

It took about two and one half years to move from our prewar peacetime system to the thoroughgoing system of negotiated contracts which was finally adopted in the full tide of war. During this period the purchasing policies of the services went through a gradual evolution guided in large part by the group which Donald Nelson brought into WPB and later transferred to the services. These men brought their wide experience in industrial purchasing practices to bear upon the problems of military procurement. Their efforts supplemented by the efforts of many others including economists, lawyers, accountants, and representatives of other business groups gradually shaped a workable system of procurement. In part the gradual changes in policies reflected changes in the political environment. From 1939 until Pearl Harbor our national objectives were not clear. The reality of the threat of war and the part which we might take in it were uncertain. The administration moved cautiously toward mobilization. It was necessary to accommodate mobilization procedures to a series of conflicting purposes. In part the slow evolution of policy reflected adjustment to basic differences in the various phases of the procurement cycle and in the surrounding contexts of other controls. Until the middle of 1942 the dominant problem was that of converting resources to war but the tactics used to effect industrial conversion were quite different before Pearl Harbor when our purposes were still in doubt from what they were after Pearl Harbor when the issue of war was no longer in doubt. After 1942 the problem became primarily one of insuring the smooth flow of labor and materials to industry and the efficient use of these materials in production. By this time the accompanying controls of material flows, prices, wages, and manpower were approaching full development. It is not surprising, therefore, to find that purchasing and pricing policies were subject to a continuous evolution and that the functions served by price and the relative importance of price as an active instrument of control changed as mobilization progressed.

This chapter seeks to trace the transition to the negotiated contract and the development of pricing policies. It must be recognized, however, that there was a parallel concern by the Congress and the services with the profits received from military contracts as distinct from prices paid. At times the concern with profits and their control through taxation and renegotiation overshadowed the concern with the negotiation of reasonable initial prices. The development of policy with reference to profits is discussed below in Chapter XI. In our discussion of pricing, however, it must be recognized that taxation and renegotiation of profits were implicitly, if not explicitly, a part of any contract with the armed services. All attempts by the services to develop incentive prices on initial contracts were affected by the expectations as to the effects of taxation and renegotiation upon the final outcome.

Transition to the Negotiated Contract

The adoption of the negotiated contract in place of the contract awarded by formal competitive bidding represented the greatest single step in the development of procurement policies during the war. The transition, however, was made slowly and with evident reluctance. Mobilization plans were not clear concerning the extent to which competitive bidding should be abandoned. Moreover, to the extent that they called for use of the negotiated contract they contemplated extensive accounting checks which are not feasible in a major war.[1] In several instances, particularly aircraft procurement and educational orders, it had been recognized that even in peacetime the usual procedures of competitive bidding were inapplicable because of the need for selectivity in choosing suppliers.[2] But even in these cases the procedures adopted were to be considered more in the nature of selective competition than of selective negotiation. Little had been done to provide for the adoption of the business-like purchasing procedures which a major war requires.

With the approach of war Congress began to make specific legislative exceptions to the competitive bid statute in response to the requests of the services. In early 1939 the War Department requested changes in procurement legislation as it applied to the procurement of aircraft in order to avoid overloading a few firms, thereby endangering delivery, and in order to develop sufficient capacity for possible emergencies.[3] This was followed in March, 1940 with the passage of the Split Award Act which authorized the services when purchasing aircraft to divide an award among the three lowest

1. See above, pp. 41–42.
2. For discussion of the Army's experience with the Air Corps Act of 1926 see Production and Purchases Division, ASF, *Purchasing Policies and Practices*, pp. 17–27. For discussion of the Navy's experience see Deputy Chief of Naval Operations (Air), *Procurement of Naval Aircraft, 1907–1934*, XVII, "United States Naval Administration in World War II" (unpublished), pp. 294–366. For experience with educational orders see Industrial College of the Armed Forces, *Plant Surveys and Education Orders* (1947), "Study of Experience in Industrial Mobilization in World War II." In commenting on the Educational Order Act in 1939 a Senate Report stated that "the War Department considers it desirable to have competition among the bidders best qualified to produce the items concerned although competition is not required by the basic legislation." See Senate Report No. 80, 76th Cong., 1st Sess. (1939), p. 12.
3. United States House of Representatives, Hearings before the Military Affairs Committee, 76th Cong., 1st Sess., *An Adequate National Defense* (1939), pp. 11, 17, 22–23.

bidders where this was necessary in the interest of national defense.[4] In April, 1939 the Navy was authorized to enter into cost-plus-fixed-fee (CPFF) contracts without advertising for construction projects outside the continental limits of the United States at fees not to exceed ten per cent of the estimated cost.[5] Such contracts, however, were to be awarded only after negotiations with three or more reputable and qualified firms. The principal purpose of this act was to speed construction by making it possible to begin work without waiting for complete specifications and to alter specifications with a minimum of delay. It was also believed that negotiation would minimize the cost to the government since Navy Department experience showed that due to the inherent risks "it is impracticable to obtain competitive bids from reliable and experienced contractors on work at outlying stations except at exorbitant prices." [6] The use of negotiated CPFF contracts made it possible for the government to assume many of the risks. Again in July, 1939 the War Department was authorized to make certain purchases of secret aircraft parts and accessories without advertising provided it submitted its request for bids to three reputable concerns.[7]

Despite these exceptions it was clear in 1939 that the services and Congress alike were reluctant to abandon the traditional purchasing procedures except under conditions of great urgency. Only in the case of Navy construction contracts did considerations of price appear to influence the decision to adopt the negotiated contract.

With the increased tempo of the defense program after Dunkirk, the traditional restrictions on purchasing were eased further in the interest of speed. Through a series of Congressional acts in June and July, 1940 the War Department was given wide discretion to place all contracts by negotiation and the Navy was authorized to use negotiation in the purchase of

4. Pub. Law No. 426, 76th Cong., 3d Sess. (54 Stat. 45) extended by act of June 30, 1941 (55 Stat. 379).
5. Pub. Law No. 43, 76th Cong., 1st Sess., April 25, 1939 (53 Stat. 591).
6. House Report No. 76, 76th Cong., 1st Sess. (1939), p. 11.
7. Pub. Law No. 168, 76th Cong., 1st Sess., July 13, 1939 (53 Stat. 1000).

ships and aircraft.[8] The Treasury in turn was authorized to proceed without reference to Section 3709 in its purchases of strategic materials.[9] These various acts prohibited the use of cost-plus-percentage-of-cost (CPPC) contracts, but permitted the use of CPFF contracts. The fees of such contracts were generally limited by law to a maximum of six or seven per cent of the estimated costs.

This legislation was motivated primarily by a desire to speed up production by saving the time consumed in drafting and circulating specifications and to enable contractors to start scheduling production before completion of the formal contracts. It also enabled the services to make a more effective allocation of limited facilities. The Navy was particularly conscious of this when placing contracts for vessels. It wanted to save shipyards with large ways for battleships and give destroyer contracts to other firms incapable of constructing the larger ships.[10]

The NDAC from its inception favored the use of the negotiated contract because of its greater effectiveness in mobilizing industry. Within three months it had formulated a statement of principles to be used in the placement of contracts which urged that attention be given to such factors as speed, quality of product, price, impact on consumer, impact on labor, tendency toward geographical concentration, financial responsibilities of suppliers, congestion of transportation facilities, availability of power facilities, moral responsibilities of suppliers, and preference for firms with experience under educational orders. These principles were clearly not generally compatible with contract placement by competitive bidding. On this issue the NDAC stated:

8. Pub. Law No. 671, 76th Cong., 3d Sess., June 28, 1940 (54 Stat. 676); Naval Appropriation Act of 1941, June 11, 1940 (54 Stat. 297); Military Establishment Appropriation Act of 1941, June 3, 1940 (54 Stat. 352); National Defense Supplemental Appropriation Act, June 26, 1940, Title II (54 Stat. 603); Pub. Law No. 730, 76th Cong., 3d Sess., July 2, 1940 (54 Stat. 712).

9. National Defense Supplemental Appropriation Act, Title I, June 26, 1940 (54 Stat. 601).

10. United States Senate, Hearings before Committee on Naval Affairs, 76th Cong., 3d Sess., *To Expedite Naval Shipbuilding* (1940), p. 19.

The Commission recognizes that competitive bidding is the better procedure in certain types of industry and circumstances. However, it is often impossible to make sure that [the necessary principles] are followed when contracts are placed on the basis of price alone and are let to the lowest bidder. Therefore, in cases where competitive bidding will not fulfill the above stated need of national defense, the Commission recommends that the use of the negotiated contract be authorized where necessary in order that these objectives be obtained in making defense purchases.[11]

Despite this broad legislative authority and pressure from NDAC, the services were still generally reluctant to use the negotiated contract except in certain limited areas such as construction, aircraft, and naval vessels. This reluctance stemmed in part from a desire to be protected by the formalities of the traditional system from criticism by Congress and the public. Time and again from 1939 to Pearl Harbor representatives of the services when testifying before Congress were induced to reaffirm their allegiance to competitive bidding and their intention to make the maximum use of the traditional procedures. But this reluctance also stemmed from an inadequate understanding of the problems of the negotiated contract as an instrument to stimulate production as well as a consciousness of the lack of experienced personnel to do the job. The traditional purchasing methods of the services had failed to provide them with men who were trained and experienced in the techniques of effective purchasing by negotiation. It was only gradually and in large part as a result of pressures from Donald Nelson and others in WPB that the purchasing methods which had long since proved their value to industry were adopted by the services.

As a result, the transition to the negotiated contract prior to Pearl Harbor was made slowly. For the period July 1, 1940 to March 1, 1941 the War Department announced that 733,000 contracts out of a total of 739,000 were awarded by com-

11. House Doc. No. 950, 76th Cong., 3d Sess. (1940), p. 2.

petitive bidding.[12] Although these were by and large the smaller contracts, in dollar value the contracts awarded by competitive bidding represented twenty-seven per cent of all contracts. From July through December, 1941 the Navy awarded contracts valued at $575 million on a competitive bid basis out of total awards of $3,498 million.[13] As late as January, 1942 it appears that the Quartermaster Corps still contemplated extensive use of the traditional system since a representative of that service announced through the press that "it is the Army's intention to continue the use of the competitive bid system so long as we are able to meet our needs by this method." [14]

With passage of the First War Powers Act immediately after Pearl Harbor, Congress abandoned the last restrictions on the use of negotiation. This act gave the President authority which he redelegated to the services "to enter into contracts and into amendments or modifications of contracts heretofore or hereafter made and to make advance, progress and other payments thereon without regard to the provisions of law relating to the making, performance, amendment, or modification of contracts whenever he deems such action would facilitate the prosecution of the war." [15] The only limitations placed upon the services were that they should not use CPPC contracts and that they should observe existing statutory limits on fees for CPFF contracts, which fees were in general limited by law to a maximum of six or seven per cent of estimated costs.

It was not until the issuance of WPB Directive No. 2 on March 3, 1942 that the final transition was effected.[16] This directed the services to place all contracts by negotiation and

12. United States House of Representatives, Hearings before Subcommittee of Committee on Appropriations, 77th Cong., 1st Sess., *Military Establishment Appropriation Bill for 1942* (1941), p. 71.
13. Affidavit of H. S. Hensel, *U.S. v. Alexander Wool Combing Co.*, U.S. District Court for District of Massachusetts (Civil No. 4121), pp. 5–7.
14. *The New York Times*, Jan. 16, 1942, p. 31.
15. Pub. Law No. 354, 77th Cong., 1st Sess., Title II (55 Stat. 838–839).
16. 7 F.R. 1732 (March, 1942).

established certain criteria to be followed in the selection of sources. This directive, subject only to several revisions of the criteria for selecting sources, continued as the basis of procurement by the services until its repeal on October 5, 1945.[17]

As Donald Nelson has pointed out, one of the purposes of the directive was to counteract the natural tendency of contracting officers to play safe by placing contracts with the "industrial giants whose technical qualifications leave no room for doubt." [18] Such a procedure was not consistent with the rational use of limited technical facilities. If followed by one contracting officer, it might work, but when followed by all, it led to undue concentration of contracts with the large firms and unemployment among many small concerns.

The criteria formulated by WPB Directive No. 2 for the placing of contracts were three:

(i) Primary emphasis shall be upon securing delivery in the time required by the war program.

(ii) In so far as it will effectuate the policy set forth in subparagraph (i) above, such contracts shall be placed so as to conserve, for the more difficult war production problems, the facilities of concerns best able, by reason of engineering, managerial, and physical resources, to handle them. Accordingly, contracts for standard or other items which involve relatively simple production problems shall be placed with concerns, normally the smaller ones, which are less able to handle the more difficult war production problems.

(iii) Subject to the considerations stated in subparagraphs (i) and (ii), such contracts shall be placed with concerns needing to acquire the least amounts of additional machinery and equipment for performance of the contracts. Accordingly, as an essential part of each negotiation, procurement officials shall secure from prospective contractors statements listing all additional machinery and equipment which will be needed for performance of the contract.

The emphasis in placement of contracts at this time was upon speed of conversion and conservation of scarce and specialized resources. The problem was one of selecting sources

17. 10 F.R. 12630 (Oct., 1945).
18. Donald Nelson, *Arsenal of Democracy*, p. 369.

and scheduling production, not one of price. In fact, many commitments were made in these early months after Pearl Harbor by unpriced letters of intent or by contracts with maximum prices which it was clearly intended should be re-determined downward. The paramount issue at this time was conversion of resources so that there could be the greatest possible speed in the scheduling of production. The use of price as an instrument for awarding contracts and regulating production had to await the development of a basic pricing philosophy for negotiated contracts and the recruiting and training of a staff.

As the procurement program developed, the criteria to be used in placing contracts as listed in WPB Directive No. 2 underwent several changes. At all times the primary emphasis was placed upon securing deliveries and performance at the times required by the war program. By October, 1942 the major reconversions had been completed so that consideration of scarce and specialized facilities, which had had second place in the list of criteria, was moved down to fourth place and consideration of machinery and equipment, which had been in third place, was moved up into second place. Subject to considerations of delivery and performance and minimizing the need for new equipment and facilities, the services were instructed to avoid placing contracts where acute labor shortages were known to exist. After satisfying these first four criteria, contracts were to be so placed "as to spread production among as many firms as is reasonable and feasible." Price was the last consideration. The services were specifically directed to pay higher prices, if necessary, than would otherwise be needed to give effect to the first four factors. If all these five considerations were met, "contracts shall be so placed as to obtain the lowest price for the Government." [19] Price was creeping into the program as a budgetary consideration only.

By September, 1943 a revolution had been effected in the announced policy. WPB Directive No. 2 was again revised and price was given a more prominent place, not only as a

19. 7 F.R. 8179 (Oct., 1942).

budgetary matter but as an instrument of control. The two principal considerations were still requirements of delivery and avoidance of areas of labor shortage. Subject to these considerations the services were instructed to give "due weight" to some five factors "for the purpose of making the most effective utilization of the national resources." These five factors were: cost and efficiency; effective utilization of small plants; conservation of special abilities and resources; minimizing the need for new equipment and facilities; and worthwhile savings in use of transportation facilities. The section on cost and efficiency provided for "placement of war contracts so as to incur the lowest possible cost to the Government consistent with the economic use of man hours and raw materials. In so far as possible, contracts should provide the maximum incentive to the producer for the reduction of his costs." [20] The forces which had been at work to bring about this change in the emphasis on price will be discussed below.

Price as an Instrument of Control in Military Procurement

Prior to Pearl Harbor there had been no systematic overall policy concerning prices on military contracts. NDAC in its statement of principles had recognized that price should not be a dominant consideration in the selection of sources, although the continued use of the competitive bid system indicated that it still was so used in many cases. In the case of negotiated contracts, however, there was still no explicit theory of the part which price should play. But in view of the problems of inducing voluntary conversion of resources to defense purposes price had to be relied upon substantially as an incentive. Many contractors were still very reluctant to abandon their peacetime markets for military production, the future of which was so uncertain, even though several steps had been taken to reduce the risks of conversion which had the

20. 8 F.R. 12969 (Sept., 1943).

effect of limiting the size of price incentives necessary.[21] After Pearl Harbor the resistances to conversion were much less, but still there was no statement as to the role of price.

As originally issued WPB Directive No. 2 made no mention of price as a consideration in negotiating contracts. This is not surprising when it is recalled that the immediate problem was the conversion of resources and the greatest speed in scheduling production. Any degree of precision in estimating costs and controlling prices was impossible. Many contractors who were asked to produce items completely foreign to their past experience could not estimate costs with any reasonable degree of accuracy. Contractors who were already converted faced rapid changes in specifications and delivery schedules which were bound to have great effect on their costs. Moreover, there was considerable uncertainty still as to the course of wages and material prices. Even if costs could have been estimated with reasonable accuracy, neither the services nor industry had sufficient experienced manpower available to analyze these costs and negotiate prices with care. During the spring and summer of 1942 the services were concerned in price matters primarily with stabilizing their relations with OPA and with initiating renegotiation procedures which would clean up the past record.

There were several forces at work, however, which led the services to evolve a more systematic philosophy for pricing negotiated contracts. The first of these was the negotiations with OPA over the relative responsibilities of OPA and the services for pricing military goods. The second was the revelation by several Congressional committees of exorbitant profits on some contracts and the revival of interest in techniques of profit control.[22] This led, of course, to the development of renegotiation. Finally, the Planning Committee of WPB was also working in this direction. In April, 1942 Mr. R. W. Goldsmith had submitted a report to Mr. R. R. Nathan, Chairman of the Planning Committee, in which he protested the current

21. See below, Chap. VIII.
22. See below, pp. 170–171.

plans for renegotiation as likely to lead to "profit pruning" rather than "cost control" and recommended the establishment of a Board of Contract Review to implement a program of cost control.

Control over costs is essential to insure the most economic use of resources. It will increase in importance as the size of the program grows; as cost differentials widen with the increasing utilization of smaller suppliers and subcontracting; and as the effectiveness of the profit incentive is impaired by the spread of cost-plus and escalator clauses and the tightening of taxes on corporate profits. . . .

There are not enough engineers available in the country to check efficiency in the use of real resources in the thousands of plants and operations involved. The only practicable way of exercising a fair degree of current control over economy in the use of resources is to do as the businessman himself does, *i.e.*, to control costs as they are reported in contractors' accounts and by methods employed by progressive large enterprises, *i.e.*, by cost comparison and cost standards.[23]

Subsequently there were discussions between the Planning Committee of WPB and the Purchases Division, ASF. Nathan submitted plans for a program of cost control to Colonel Browning, Chief of the Purchases Division, stating that "from the viewpoint of the WPB, economy in the use of real resources (labor, materials and plant facilities) is the primary objective of contract negotiation and renegotiation." [24] He recommended among other things the use of target price contracts. Again on August 31, 1942 the WPB Planning Committee criticized the existing renegotiation boards and "recommended that a War Contracts Policy Board be organized within WPB to utilize contract negotiations to the fullest extent in encouraging efficiency in war production." [25]

That these pressures and suggestions bore fruit is indicated

23. Report from R. W. Goldsmith to R. R. Nathan, "Cost Control and Contract Negotiation," April 29, 1942 (WPB, Historical Records Files).

24. Memorandum from R. R. Nathan to Col. A. J. Browning, May 7, 1942 (WPB, Historical Records Files).

25. WPB Planning Committee, *Recommendation No. 14*, Aug. 31, 1942, p. 1 (WPB, Historical Records Files).

by the statement of purchasing policies resulting from a conference held by the War Department in late October, 1942 at Tryon, North Carolina. The Tryon Conference was called to reformulate and integrate War Department purchasing policy "in order to promote more efficient use of labor, materials and plant facilities, to limit profits to reasonable levels as a corollary of price and wage freezing and to prevent inflation." [26] The Statement of Purchase Policies resulting from this conference is very important. Much of the subsequent development of War Department policy can be traced to this statement. The general principles enunciated were as follows:

1. The War Department recognizes that it is essential that prices and costs of war equipment continue to be kept at the lowest possible levels:
   (a) In this way efficiency in production will be encouraged and manpower and materials conserved.
   (b) In addition, the OPA has now agreed to refrain from further extension of its price regulations in the military field.
2. Under war conditions administrative control is necessary to keep prices close enough to costs to exert pressure on them.
3. *Purchase* control, rather than the use of formulas and regulations, is the best and simplest method of price control.
4. Unstable and varying factors make such control difficult but it should be feasible to do it by the use of a number of different techniques approaching the problem from various aspects. As wages, material prices, and production schedules are now becoming more stable, and as production experience increases, the problem should become less difficult.

Some of the detailed recommendations as to policies and procedures were even more significant. Preference was expressed for the fixed-price contract "well negotiated on the basis of accurate cost experience and close estimates" as "the best method of purchase control." CPFF contracts were discouraged. It was recommended that the government assume so far as possible unpredictable risks and that, where a con-

26. For memorandum on the Tryon Conference see Army Industrial College, *Contract Pricing: Principal Developments,* pp. 137–146.

tractor will suffer "an actual loss" as a result of increased costs over which he has no control and which were not included in his price, he should be given relief under the First War Powers Act. The fixing of prices for short periods of time and up-and-down redetermination of prices were recommended as methods for obtaining close prices. It was suggested that price control be effected by "improved purchasing methods and by better information on prices, costs and purchasing methods." Compulsory orders, "while their use is not to be favored . . . should be used when a contractor refuses to contract at a fair price, after prolonged negotiations." Attention was also directed to the need for close prices on subcontracts. "The purchasing methods of important prime contractors and subcontractors should be studied by the Services to determine their adequacy for sound purchasing." It was stated that "the emphasis in renegotiation should be shifted as far as possible from recapture of past profits to repricing for future periods," and it was recommended that a start be made by exempting contracts from renegotiation in accordance with the discretionary provisions of the Renegotiation Act. Finally suggestions were made for recruiting and training personnel in purchasing policies and techniques.

Here was a broad program which was to dominate the evolution of the War Department's pricing policy throughout the rest of the war. Although there appears to be no similar document reflecting Navy Department policy, it is fair to say that on broad objectives and even on many details of procedure the two services developed their policies in general harmony.[27] The War Department policies were subsequently incorporated in appropriate directives and a manual on pricing issued which summarized War Department policies as follows:

To obtain all that is needed for war purposes, of the quality required and on time; to buy what is needed at close prices—*i.e.*, at prices neither high nor low enough to discourage increased production and operating efficiency but rather at fair and reasonable

27. For a statement of Navy Department policies see Vincent deP. Goubeau, "Pricing Policies in Navy Procurement," *Purchasing*, XVIII (May, 1945), 96–101.

prices calculated to encourage both; to reward the production and efficiency the War Department seeks to encourage by awarding contracts at prices which will enable efficient producers to earn reasonable and adequate profits; to permit efficient producers who have adopted a reasonable pricing policy and carried the risks incident to it to retain more of such profits in statutory renegotiation; to remove by appropriate contract provisions those risks of war production which are substantially out of line with those of peacetime production.[28]

Here was a philosophy of price as an instrument of control, an instrument to encourage and reward efficiency. Price had come into its own once more. This policy was clearly recognized by the President in his Budget Message for the fiscal year 1944 [29] and in his hold-the-line order in April, 1943.[30] Moreover, the amendments of the renegotiation act of January, 1944 had as one of their purposes the implementation of this policy. They gave broad discretionary powers to the services to grant exemptions from renegotiation where the Secretary of the cognizant department found that the initial contract provided adequately against excessive profits.[31]

Conflicting Profit Standards

Because of the services' desire to offer contractors financial incentives to take military contracts voluntarily, it was basic to the pricing policy of the services that an efficient firm should have the reasonable expectation of a profit on each contract and even on each item on a contract. This did not mean that each contract should be priced on a cost-plus-conventional-profit basis. It was their purpose to see that the price should

---

28. ASF Manual, M 601, *Pricing in War Contracts* (August, 1943), p. 2.

29. "The procurement program must achieve maximum production with minimum waste and with the speed essential in time of war. This is a controlling objective not only for the original negotiation of contracts but also for the renegotiation required by law. . . . The proper negotiation and renegotiation of contracts must strive to reconcile the avoidance of excessive profit with the maintenance of incentives to economical management." *Budget Message of the President* (Jan. 6, 1943), p. viii.

30. Executive Order No. 9328, 8 F.R. 4681 (April 8, 1943).

31. See below, pp. 185–186.

not be so low as to discourage willingness to produce nor so high as to encourage inefficiency. In arriving at such a price all relevant factors were to be considered including comparative prices and costs where available. If there were evidence that a particular concern was inefficient, in the sense that an aggressive management in similar circumstances could be expected to effect lower costs, its profit expectation might be low. If the firm were very efficient or its contributions and risks large, its profit expectation might be large. It should be emphasized that the policy was simply one of providing the expectation of a profit on each contract. It was not intended to guarantee a fair profit. The policy of profit averaging between contracts and items was to be avoided wherever data were available to price each contract and item on an individual basis. Such a policy was essential to the incentive pricing philosophy of the services. Moreover, for many purely military items there was no other standard for pricing individual contracts except estimated costs plus an estimated reasonable profit. This policy received further support from the desires of the technical services and bureaus to conserve their individual appropriations and to avoid absorbing one another's costs.

This pricing standard differed significantly from the standards used by OPA.[32] Considerations of costs and profits took a secondary place among OPA's pricing standards. The Emergency Price Control Act had provided that prices should be "generally fair and equitable." [33] OPA interpreted this to mean that prices should be prevented from rising so long as this was consistent with the effective prosecution of the war. In establishing ceiling prices, OPA used to a large extent various techniques for freezing prices or pricing formulas as of some base period. It was recognized that in certain circumstances upward adjustments were necessary, either for an

32. For discussion of these standards see OPA, *Problems in Price Control: Pricing Standards* (1947), "Historical Reports on War Administration: Office of Price Administration," Gen. Pub. No. 7, chaps. ii, iii, and ix; Seymour E. Harris, *Price and Related Controls in the United States* (1945), pp. 50–55 and chap. iv.

33. 56 Stat. 24.

industry, a product, or a firm. It was general policy to allow
an industry-wide upward adjustment if the industry, or at
least a majority of the industry, was not making dollar earnings at least as high as the average annual dollar earnings obtained in a representative peacetime period, usually 1936–
1939, adjusted for changes in net investment. In the case of a
multiproduct industry, an upward adjustment of prices on
a particular product would be granted only if the over-all
profits were inadequate as judged by the base period earnings
or if the price of the particular product was below out-of-
pocket costs. If prices did not cover out-of-pocket costs, a
price adjustment was allowed sufficient to cover such costs
only, without allowance for overhead or profit. In many cases,
however, where an item was essential to civilian or military
supply, more liberal adjustments were in fact allowed, particularly where there was danger that resources would otherwise be diverted to less essential uses.

The pricing standards of OPA, then, made no pretense of
providing a reasonable profit on each product or to each firm.
Profits were, for the most part, residual. Adjustments in prices
to an industry or firm might be made when over-all hardship
was experienced. In considering adjustments on individual
products the profit on the individual product was not an issue
unless the provision of a profit was essential to insure necessary
supplies.

The effect of the difference in profit policy between OPA
and the services was not as serious as might have been expected.
The arrangements between OPA and the services worked out
in 1942 released an important area of military goods from OPA
controls so that it was only in the limited areas in which controls by OPA and the services overlapped, such as food, textiles, clothing, and machinery, that direct conflict developed.
The Army Quartermaster Corps seems to have had the most
difficulty.[34] Moreover, the effect of the more stringent OPA
standards as applied to civilian goods was to aid the services by

34. Harry B. Yoshpe, *Production Control in the Quartermaster Corps*, pp. 68–
71.

stimulating diversion of resources from less essential civilian uses into the production of military goods.

But the policy differences did lead to considerable controversy in the early years of the war. OPA product standards, in their more rigorous form, appeared to violate the services' policy of insuring production by providing an incentive profit on each item. The services felt that if a contractor found his ceiling price unprofitable on an item which they needed, he might be reluctant to produce it no matter how favorable his over-all profit position. OPA, however, felt that a more liberal policy of adjusting prices to insure reasonable profits on each product would seriously weaken its program of price stabilization and be a move in the direction of cost-plus pricing which would encourage waste, inefficiency, and cost increases. It argued that where over-all profits were adequate but the prices on particular products did not provide incentives sufficient to insure necessary production, WPB or the services should invoke their mandatory powers to compel production. It maintained that price ceilings could not prevent a contractor from producing. "If a seller is *not able* to make the war item, the OPA maximum price has no relevance. If the seller is able to produce the material, the impediment lies only in his refusal to do so." [35]

On several occasions OPA requested the Procurement Policy Board to approve its standards of price adjustment.[36] The representatives of the War and Navy Departments demurred. A subcommittee was established to study the problem, but no tangible results were forthcoming. Individual contractors with hardship on contracts with the services were treated under Procedural Regulation No. 6, which provided more liberal standards of adjustment for military goods than the normal OPA adjustment procedures.[37] In the food and textile fields,

35. Procurement Policy Board, Document No. 87, p. 3.
36. See the letter from J. Philip Wernette, War Goods Price Coordinator, OPA, to the Procurement Policy Board April 14, 1943; Procurement Policy Board, Document No. 87; also Procurement Policy Board Minutes, August 25, 1943.
37. See above, pp. 70–71, 78–79.

where OPA ceilings were insufficient to provide supplies, the solution was in general a compromise between the invoking of WPB allocation powers and the upward adjustment of OPA prices.

One interesting commentary on the differences between the profit policies of the services and the OPA came to light during the reconversion period. At that time it became apparent that during the war many contractors had been able to prosper with the ceiling prices established by OPA on civilian business only because of the more liberal profit policy of the services on war goods.[38] In short, it appears that the services made a special contribution to the steadiness of the consumers' price index. An interesting procedure for administering consumer subsidies!

It should be pointed out that the services themselves made many exceptions to their basic policy of providing contractors a reasonable expectation of a fair profit on each contract. Many contractors did not have adequate accounting systems for estimating costs on individual products. In such cases the services were prepared to adopt a price policy which would insure a reasonable over-all profit without regard to the profit on the individual contract or item. Such a policy reduced the administrative problems of the contractor and the services to a minimum. This policy did, however, involve considerable risk for the contractor, since a shift in the composition of the services' purchases from high-profit to low-profit items might quickly put the contractor in the position of making a low profit or no profit at all.

Although these differences in basic pricing policies between the services and OPA generated much controversy early in the war, they were not serious. The area of conflict was lim-

38. See T. J. Kinsella, *War Procurement and OPA*, pp. 52–53. "As a final observation, not generally realized by OPA until the great demand for price increases by manufacturing industries after 'V-J' Day, it should be noted that the large areas of non-control in the military field and the relatively more liberal pricing policies followed by military agencies enabled most manufacturers to maintain their civilian output at ceiling prices. This contributed greatly to the stability of living costs during the war period and was, as a result, of prime importance in the maintenance of wage stability."

ited and tended to diminish as the spheres of effectiveness and responsibility of the two groups became clear. The solution by which more liberal standards were established for adjustments on military contracts gave the services the preferential position which was necessary to insure their supplies and did not interfere with OPA's program for stabilizing the cost of living. If there had been greater willingness on the part of WPB and the services to use their allocation powers and to invoke mandatory orders, some price concessions might have been avoided.

Use of Mandatory Powers

It is one thing to develop policies and procedures for arriving at acceptable prices on military contracts in wartime and quite another to insure the acceptance of such prices by industry. A basic objective of the whole program of economic mobilization was to effect mobilization with as little use of compulsory powers as possible. This was particularly true in the field of pricing of military contracts, where every effort was made to conclude contracts on a voluntary basis. Particular effort was made to devise policies and procedures which would not alienate business and care was taken to select personnel to administer these policies who would impress business as being reasonable and understanding. It was clear, however, that unwillingness of even a small minority of contractors to go along with established policies voluntarily could seriously jeopardize the program. Consequently, some compulsory pricing powers were necessary during the course of the war.

Congress supplied the services with five different sets of mandatory powers. Although the record indicates a general reluctance on the part of the services to use these mandatory powers and a systematic policy to keep authority to do so in the higher echelons, the mere existence of the powers no doubt facilitated procurement. Judicious use of these mandatory powers and threats to use them were an important element in the pricing policies of the services.

These five mandatory powers were as follows: (1) power to requisition personal property; [39] (2) mandatory orders to produce under the Selective Training and Service Act; [40] (3) repricing orders under Title VIII of the Revenue Act of 1943; [41] (4) priorities and allocation powers under Title III of the Second War Powers Act; [42] and (5) the power to audit records and compel the submission of information under Title XIII of the Second War Powers Act.[43] With these various powers the services were adequately equipped. Brief remarks concerning the use of each of these powers are given below.[44]

The requisitioning acts of 1940 and 1941 are not of principal importance to the present study. They are concerned with the change in ownership of existing goods, not with the production of new goods. The act of 1940 authorized the services to requisition property which had been acquired for export in those cases where export had been subsequently prohibited by the President and the property was found to be vital to the prosecution of the war. The act of 1941 provided similar authority in the case of all personal property where property was needed for the defense of the United States and could not be obtained on reasonable terms.

Section 9 of the Selective Training and Service Act of 1940 empowered the President to place a mandatory order through the Secretary of War or of the Navy requiring any person to

39. Act of October 10, 1940 (54 Stat. 1090), as amended by Act of July 2, 1942 (56 Stat. 467) and by Act of June 28, 1944 (58 Stat. 624; 59 U.S.C., App. 711–713); and Act of October 16, 1941 (55 Stat. 742), as amended by Act of March 27, 1942 (56 Stat. 181), by Act of June 30, 1943 (57 Stat. 271), and by Act of June 28, 1944 (58 Stat. 624; 50 U.S.C., App. 721–724).

40. Act of September 16, 1940 (54 Stat. 892; 50 U.S.C., App. 309).

41. Act of February 25, 1944 (58 Stat. 92; 50 U.S.C., App. 1192).

42. Act of March 27, 1942 (56 Stat. 177; 50 U.S.C., App. 633).

43. Act of March 27, 1942 (56 Stat. 185; 50 U.S.C., App. 643) and Executive Order 9127, April 10, 1942 (7 F.R. 2753).

44. The following discussion is based in large part on Procurement Policy Board, Doc. No. 140, *Report to Procurement Policy Board by Committee on Mandatory Action* (Oct., 1944) and Production and Purchases Division, ASF, *op. cit.*, pp. 350–408.

produce any product of the type which he usually produced or was capable of producing. A reasonable price was to be established by the Secretary. Failure to comply with the order subjected the person to imprisonment and fine. Moreover, in the event of non-compliance the Army or Navy might take over and operate the producer's plant. Up to March, 1945 the War Department had issued some 25 mandatory orders.[45] Fifteen of these were served by the Quartermaster Corps, 7 on producers of boneless beef and 6 on manufacturers of field jackets. The Army Air Forces served 7 orders because of disputes as to price and, in all but one of the cases, the order was later superseded by a voluntary contract. Three orders were served upon various riparian owners at the request of the Secretary of the Interior requiring them to divert water needed by the Phelps Dodge Corporation to operate a copper plant built by the Defense Plant Corporation. The Secretary of Interior is reported to have believed that determination of compensation under this procedure would cause less difficulty for the Indian tribes involved and be less of a reflection on their patriotism than determination by a condemnation proceeding.

Of the 22 orders served, excluding the 3 orders served at the request of the Interior Department, 14 were served because of the refusal of contractors to accept war business and 8 were served because of a dispute as to price. All but 4 of these orders were complied with. According to an official study of the War Department which was based on the information available up to March 15, 1945, 11 of the orders including the above 4 orders which were not complied with, the 6 field jacket orders and 1 rice order, "probably could have been avoided by proper consideration of the facts, or proper negotiations or both. Nine of the orders (including the rice and 1 field jacket order, the balance being Air Force orders) were superseded by voluntary contracts. Three of the field jacket orders could have been superseded by voluntary con-

45. *Ibid.*, pp. 380–383. Apparently the Navy Department issued only two or three orders under Section 9 of the Selective Training and Service Act.

tracts but the Quartermaster General refused to supersede them." [46]

Title VIII of the Revenue Act of 1943 authorized the Secretary of War or Navy to issue an order establishing fair and reasonable prices for future deliveries in the event he was unable to negotiate voluntarily fair and reasonable prices. Although several preliminary notices were issued, only one mandatory pricing order was issued. This was issued jointly by the War and Navy Departments against the Lord Manufacturing Company, a manufacturer of rubber engine and instrument mounts used in aircraft. According to figures released by the services the company's sales had increased from an average of $238,000 in the years 1936–1939 to about $29,000,000 in 1943. Profits before taxes were alleged to have been about 100 per cent of cost in 1942 and about 66 per cent of cost in 1943.[47] According to press reports the action was taken only "after attempts to negotiate prices, which have been under way for over a year, proved fruitless. . . . The Lord Company has consistently refused to make any reduction in prices." [48] The company had also refused to accept voluntarily renegotiation proposals made by the government covering 1942 profits.[49] A repricing order was issued applying to all sales for government end use on both prime contracts and subcontracts. Because of an alleged failure of the company to comply with the order the government took over the plant and operated it during the remainder of the war.[50] Prior to issuing the order elaborate cost studies were necessary to

46. *Ibid.*, pp. 382–383.

47. These figures on profits and sales are taken from the letter of Robert P. Patterson, Under Secretary of War to the Chairman of the House Ways and Means Committee, April 21, 1945. See United States House of Representatives, Hearings before Committee on Ways and Means, 79th Cong., 1st Sess., pp. 30–32. See also *The New York Times*, Sept. 28, 1944, p. 27, and Press Release of Navy Department, Sept. 25, 1944.

48. *The New York Times*, Sept. 28, 1944, p. 27. For details of the attempts of the services to arrive at satisfactory prices voluntarily see letter from Patterson to the Chairman of the House Ways and Means Committee (note 47, above).

49. *Loc. cit.*

50. Executive Order 9493 (9 F.R. 12860). *The New York Times*, Oct. 26, 1944, p. 10.

establish over 600 different unit prices. Moreover, since sales to many subcontractors were involved, it was necessary to notify all such subcontractors and to see that the government benefited from the reductions received by them. The experience with this order confirmed the services in their view that mandatory pricing action, while necessary as a reserve power, was a pricing procedure which presented many problems of administration.

Under Title III of the Second War Powers Act various procedures were available to the services to require production by use of the priorities and allocations powers, such as issuance of preference ratings, set-aside orders freezing supplies or capacity for use of designated procurement agencies, and production directives requiring particular industries to allocate a certain percentage of their capacity to production of items deemed necessary for the war program. These orders generally affected an industry on an over-all basis and were administered by the War Food Administration in the case of subsistence items and by the War Production Board in the case of most other items. The question of price was in general not involved in such orders. As of the fall of 1944 over one hundred such directives had been issued by WPB and WFA. Most of these involved clothing, textiles, and food. Many of these had been issued at the request of the services in order to insure production of particular items which they had found it difficult to procure otherwise, often because other lines of production or sales to other customers were more profitable. The Committee on Mandatory Action of the Procurement Policy Board, reporting on its survey of the use of compulsory powers in the fall of 1944, found that "compliance has been satisfactory." Moreover, it concluded that "where a producer is unwilling to accept government business at all, the use of priorities powers as a means of compulsion may be far simpler administratively than the use of mandatory orders." [51]

Title XIII of the Second War Powers Act authorized the

51. Procurement Policy Board, *Report to Procurement Policy Board by Committee on Mandatory Action*, p. 6.

services to inspect the plant and to audit and inspect the records of war contractors. This power was essential to the conduct of effective negotiation and renegotiation and was also necessary to pricing under other compulsory powers. The services were, however, generally able to obtain the necessary access to plant and records voluntarily without formally invoking their statutory authority.

It is difficult to gauge the success of the services in their use of these mandatory powers. They did not invoke them frequently. They believed that a wide-spread or indiscriminate use of them was not the way to elicit the cooperation of industry which was necessary to insure maximum production. It is clear too that the services and WPB were particularly loath to invoke these powers where price was the primary obstacle. But the usefulness of mandatory powers as reserve weapons cannot be questioned. Many "voluntary" arrangements were doubtlessly effected which might have been difficult in their absence. The services have generally stated that they were prepared to use these powers if satisfactory voluntary arrangements were not possible. Nevertheless, they have been criticized for being reluctant to use their powers, for asking OPA for price adjustments which might have been avoided if they had used their mandatory powers more effectively, and for negotiating prices which did not measure up to their own standards of "fair and reasonable."

In many instances, however, the experience of the services with mandatory orders was not encouraging. This was especially true of the action of the War Department in invoking its power under Section 9 of the Selective Training and Service Act. Even with internal controls designed to insure prudence in the use of the powers, the record of the Quartermaster Corps was not outstanding. The wisdom of several orders on food and clothing items appears in retrospect to have been questionable. Yet these are items where standards of reasonable prices might be expected to be relatively clear because of the similarity of items procured to items previously purchased and because of the existence of numerous producers. How much more difficult the task would have been for many other items! The Title VIII action against the Lord Manufacturing Company indicated the great administrative difficulties involved when entering these areas quite apart from the technical problem of estimating costs.

It is undoubtedly true that some firms could have done a better job of pricing voluntarily and that more judicious rattling of the "big stick" might have helped. But judicious use of such threats depended upon more skillful negotiation, more explicit pricing standards, and more effective price and cost analysis. If these had been available, the need to invoke mandatory powers would doubtlessly have been less.

Conclusion

The evolution of policies for placing and pricing military contracts reflects clearly an attempt to adapt policies so far as possible to the over-all objectives of industrial mobilization outlined in Chapter I. At the outbreak of the emergency in 1939 the services depended principally on the competitive procedure to select sources and to determine prices. The price mechanism therefore was serving its normal function so far as military procurement was concerned. During the period from 1939 to Pearl Harbor there was a gradual movement away from price as the criteria for the selection of sources. Price still served, however, as an important device to induce particular individuals to convert to defense purposes. This was particularly important because of the reluctance to use direct controls and mandatory orders. Price and moral suasion were at the time the instruments for inducing conversion. Supplementary devices such as accelerated depreciation and various other financing devices discussed in Chapter VIII also aided. Price also served as the principal incentive to efficient production although during this period, which was characterized by a substantial though decreasing amount of unemployed resources, this objective did not receive much emphasis. Clearly the price system still served as the dominant method for determining individuals' disposable incomes although the excess profits tax of 1940 was enacted for the particular purpose of limiting one type of income.

The period from Pearl Harbor to the fall of 1942 was the period of the least emphasis upon price as a mobilizing device. The emphasis in this period was upon the completion of the process of conversion. The need to place contracts quickly in order to facilitate production planning by industry as well as the lack of properly qualified and trained personnel made it certain that price would play a subsidiary part. It was considered important only that price should not be a deterrent to the conversion of resources and to the allocation of these resources in accordance with the criteria established by WPB Directive No. 2.

From 1943 to 1945 was a period in which the various controls of production and materials flows were perfected. But despite these controls there was still room for price to play a part in the allocation of resources. WPB by its limitation orders, allocation controls, etc., shook resources loose from the civilian economy for the production of military goods. Priorities determined what end products should come first. But the prices negotiated by the services on prime contracts were still useful in determining what and how much a contractor should produce. Moreover, during this period there was increasing emphasis upon price as a device for inducing efficiency in the use of labor and materials. Finally, although wages and salaries were controlled and profits subjected to renegotiation and excess profits taxation, the price system still served to determine people's disposable income.

In line with the democratic objectives of insuring respect for the individual and the maximum possible decentralization of decision-making every effort was made to effect procurement by voluntary action and with a minimum use of mandatory orders directed at individuals. To be sure, the policies were by no means ideal and their adoption was often unduly delayed. Moreover, operations under these policies were necessarily imperfect. It is clear, however, that throughout the defense and war periods we were consciously attempting to continue to use price as an organizing mechanism and to devise systems of procurement which were consistent with our democratic institutions and aspirations whenever this could be done without jeopardizing the overriding objective of maximum and expeditious production of military goods.

VIII

RISKS: THE NON-CONTRACTUAL APPROACH

THE war program called for the construction of new manufacturing facilities at a cost of $25 billion.[1] It required the as-
sumption by industry of prime supply contracts of over $193
billion from June, 1940 to March, 1945 [2] and an unknown
volume of subcontract commitments. These contracts necessitated the adaptation of operations by many contractors to
the production of items with which they had had no previous
experience. It also called for an increase in the working force
of manufacturing industry from 10.4 millions in June, 1940
to 17.2 millions in November, 1943.[3] The magnitude of the
problem of training this increased force for its wartime purposes was increased by the need to train many new and inex-
perienced persons to replace experienced people who were
drawn off into the armed services.

It was clear from the very early stages of the defense program that business faced many risks in expanding and converting its plant for this productive effort. Would there be a war
or would the defense program fizzle out? If war came, how
long would it last? What would happen to wage rates and
material costs? What volume of production might a firm expect? What about the availability of labor and materials?
Would new wartime plants be useful in the postwar world?
These and many other problems were faced by any contractor
contemplating defense production. The government had
either to find ways to reduce these risks and uncertainties, to
relieve industry by assuming the risks itself, or to compensate

1. WPB, *Wartime Production Achievements and the Reconversion Outlook*,
p. 7; Army Industrial College, *Financial Aids to Contractors* (1945), "Study of
Experience in Industrial Mobilization in World War II," pp. 19–20.
2. WPB, Program and Statistics Bureau, *War Supply and Facility Contracts
by State, Industrial Area and County*, June 4, 1945, p. 4.
3. United States Department of Commerce, *Survey of Current Business*, July,
1945, p. 24.

industry for assuming these risks through contract prices or other devices.

Many of the risks were not within the contractors' control. This was true of wage increases granted by the WLB, increases in material prices authorized by OPA, and the termination of contracts brought about by the changes of military strategy or by the end of hostilities. Other risks were to a large extent within their control. This was generally true of the internal management of their plants, although even here forces outside of their control might interfere with their obtaining trained labor or with the smooth flow of materials. It was recognized from the beginning that if contractors were to exercise the maximum initiative in production and in reducing wastes of labor and materials those risks which were within their control should be left upon them and that they should be compensated for assuming them through contract prices. On the other hand, it was agreed that wherever possible those risks over which contractors had no control should be assumed by the government. It was believed, quite rightly, that the total cost to the government would be less by assuming these risks directly than by assuming them indirectly through higher contract prices. Moreover, it was recognized that this method of assuming risks would reduce materially the inflationary tendencies of the mobilization program.[4]

The services' approach to the problem of risks was threefold: (1) minimizing certain risks through direct controls over materials, manpower, wages, and prices; (2) allocating appropriately some risks through provisions in supply contracts, *e.g.*, escalation clauses; and (3) allocating other risks through non-contractual arrangements or arrangements out-

4. This philosophy dominated the thinking of the NDAC and its successors. It was clearly embodied in the Statement of Purchase Policies adopted by the Tryon Conference. "Under war-conditions, the Government can better obtain close prices and estimates and reduce the need for heavy allowances for contingencies by assuming certain unpredictable risks affecting performance, such as allocations, material shortages, and other factors resulting from Government action." Army Industrial College, *Contract Pricing: Principal Developments*, p. 139. See also Glen A. Lloyd, "Pricing in War Contracts," *Law and Contemporary Problems*, X (Autumn, 1943), 248.

side of the supply contracts such as special provisions to finance new investments, tax arrangements, and provisions for the guarantee of loans. The present chapter will discuss this latter approach, while Chapter IX will be devoted to the approach through provisions in supply contracts.

Accelerated Amortization

From the earliest period of the defense program it was clear that methods of financing the expansion of facilities and equipment would be critical to the success of the mobilization program in general and to the pricing program in particular. Industry was clearly reluctant to undertake the expansion of facilities which was necessary to implement the defense programs authorized in the summer of 1940 without adequate insurance against the risks involved. Some of the facilities required were clearly of a type which would have no appreciable value to industry at the conclusion of the emergency. Other facilities were adaptable to peacetime use, but with the experiences of the 1930's vividly in mind industry was fearful that these facilities might remain idle at the end of hostilities despite their technical usefulness.

The government under the guidance of the NDAC and successor agencies approached the problem from two directions: (1) stimulating private expansion through special tax incentives for new facilities and (2) providing expansion by use of public funds. It has been estimated that the cumulative value of new war manufacturing facilities put in place during World War II totaled $25 billion.[5] Of these about $16 billion were financed by government funds and $9 billion by private funds. About 95 per cent of the $16 billion financed by public funds was publicly owned. Of the government-financed facilities, 19 per cent was for aircraft facilities and 29 per cent for ordnance.[6]

The principal method used to encourage expansion with

5. See above, p. 111, note 1.
6. Army Industrial College, *Financial Aids to Contractors*, p. 18.

private funds was the accelerated amortization provisions of
the Second Revenue Act of 1940.[7] The accelerated amortization program was designed to give special tax treatment to
firms which undertook expansion of facilities necessary to
the war effort at their own expense. It gave assurance in advance that such firms could charge off facilities for tax purposes at a more rapid rate than was provided by Treasury
rulings for normal peacetime facilities in return for assuming
the risk of being loaded with excess facilities at the end of the
war. During World War I there had been provision for accelerated amortization, but under that program the determination of the rate of amortization was postponed until the end of
the war and tailored to the circumstances of each contractor.[8]
The rate of acceleration depended on the actual estimated
value of the facilities to the taxpayer in terms of its actual
use or employment in his going business or in terms of its
sale or scrap value. The *ex post* method of determining amortization had certain logical merits, but it had proved very difficult to administer and had led to innumerable delays and end-
less litigation. Moreover, it did not meet with favor from
industry, which wanted greater certainty through some *ex
ante* system which would make it possible to determine amortization in advance. Although there was some feeling that the
Treasury already had the power to provide relief under existing legislation through appropriate change in the Internal
Revenue Code, this view was not shared by the Treasury.

Under the provisions of the Second Revenue Act of 1940
a contractor who acquired or constructed with his own funds

7. Pub. Law No. 801, 76th Cong., 3d Sess. (Oct. 8, 1940), secs. 301 and 302.
Also Internal Revenue Code, secs. 23 and 124. For extensive discussion of the
legislative background of the accelerated amortization provisions and of the
problems incident to its administration, see David Ginsburg, *The Amortization
Deduction*, address before Practicing Law Institute, New York City, March 24,
1941 (issued as press release by the Office of Emergency Management, P.M. 252);
Ethan P. Allen, *Policies Governing Private Financing of Emergency Facilities,
May 1940 to June 1942*, "Historical Reports on War Administration: War
Production Board," Special Study No. 12; R. P. Patterson, *A Report to the Sec-
retary of War on the Administration of Section 124 of the Internal Revenue Law
Relating to the Issue of Necessity Certificates* (Feb. 15, 1945).

8. Ginsburg, *op. cit.*, pp. 18–22.

facilities which were necessary to national defense could, upon securing a certificate of necessity, amortize the cost over a five-year period at the rate of 1⅔ per cent per month in lieu of the ordinary deduction for depreciation based on useful life. If before the facilities had been fully amortized the emergency period ended or the Secretary of War or Navy certified that the facility was no longer necessary to national defense, the contractor might reopen his tax returns and recompute his amortization on the basis of the shorter period as thus established.

The act in its original form provided that accelerated amortization would not be permitted if directly or indirectly "the tax payer has been or will be reimbursed by the United States for all or part of the cost of any emergency facility pursuant to any contract with the United States . . ." unless the appropriate agencies issued a certificate indicating that the government's interest in the facilities had been protected.[9] This meant that, except where a certificate of government protection had been issued, supply contracts were to be priced on the basis of normal depreciation rates rather than on the accelerated rates. This pricing policy had been incorporated in the approved policy at the insistence of NDAC. This limitation, however, proved especially difficult to administer and was repealed on February 6, 1942.[10] The effect of repeal was to place upon contracting officers the burden of insuring that the contractor was not reimbursed for plant at a rate in excess of normal depreciation or that provision was made to protect the interest of the government in the facilities. Procurement policies continued to call for the consideration only of normal depreciation in negotiation of price,[11] although in renegotiation the accelerated amortization was an allowable cost.[12]

Necessity certificates totaling more than $6 billion were issued between September, 1940 and August, 1945.[13]

9. Pub. Law No. 801, 76th Cong., 3d Sess., sec. 302(i).
10. Pub. Law No. 436, 77th Cong., 2d Sess. (Feb. 6, 1942).
11. APR, par. 238.1.
12. RR, par. 383.2.
13. WPB, *War Production Board Facilities Actions* (Sept. 15, 1945).

The net effect of the accelerated amortization provision was to give the contractor the privilege of charging off for tax purposes facilities necessary for the war at a high rate during the war when presumably profits and tax rates were high, and at a lower rate in the postwar years when profits and taxes might be lower.

Public Financing of War Facilities

The use of government funds to aid the expansion of manufacturing facilities was another approach to the problem of reducing contractors' investment risks. This was done in various ways, in part by making funds available for the construction of privately owned plants and in part through the construction of government-owned plants which were turned over to private industry under various arrangements for operation. Of the new war manufacturing facilities totaling $25 billion, over $16 billion were owned by the federal government. Of the new privately owned facilities of about $9 billion, about $815 million were financed through one type of government financing or another.[14]

The emergency plant facility contract was developed early in the defense period as a means for encouraging expansion of privately owned facilities.[15] This was known as the "bankable" contract plan, since under it the contractor was able to assign the contract in order to borrow the necessary funds. The method of financing was optional with the contractor and was often done by loan from the Reconstruction Finance Corporation (RFC). Title to the facilities was vested in the contractor who was reimbursed by the government in sixty equal payments. If the supply contracts for which the facilities were acquired were terminated or ran out before the sixty month period was completed within which the contractor was to be reimbursed, the monthly payments by the government were accelerated accordingly. Prices on supply contracts

14. See H. B. Yoshpe, *Production Control in the Quartermaster Corps, 1939–1944,* chap. iv, for discussion of the Quartermaster's facilities activities.

15. Allen, *op. cit.,* pp. 28–41; 5 F.R. 4147.

for the output of the facilities were to include no charge for the facilities in question. At the end of five years, or earlier if payments were accelerated, the contractor was completely reimbursed for the use of the facilities by the government. At this time the contractor had the option of letting title to the plant pass to the government or of repurchasing the plant from the government. The repurchase price was either at an option price based on cost less depreciation at predetermined rates or at some lower price that the government and contractor might negotiate. This gave the contractor a method of financing expansion without risk to himself and left him completely free for five years or until the end of his contracts to determine whether he wished to acquire the facilities permanently. This arrangement was used particularly in the early period but was soon replaced by the more flexible arrangements offered by the Defense Plant Corporation when it started operating.

The creation of the Defense Plant Corporation (DPC) as a subsidiary of the RFC in August, 1940 opened a new opportunity for expanding capacity with a minimum of risk to industry.[16] At the request of the services DPC built industrial plants necessary for the war and leased these to contractors under a five-year lease. At the time of original negotiations an option price was determined at which the contractor might purchase the facilities at the end of the five-year period. The lease called for rentals of one of two types: (1) where the contractor would sell his entire output to the services, a rental of $1 per year, or (2) where sales would also be made to private customers, a rental large enough to amortize the entire cost of the plant during its useful life. The DPC financed plants to a total value of $8 billion, most of which had some prospective civilian use in the postwar period.[17]

The second method by which new publicly owned indus-

16. DPC was established at the request of the NDAC on August 22, 1940, under authority of amendment to the original RFC Act on June 25, 1940. Pub. Law No. 664, 76th Cong., 3d Sess.

17. Army Industrial College, *Financial Aids to Contractors*, p. 22.

trial facilities were financed was through construction by the services themselves from their appropriations. Such facilities were then leased to industry for operation. This method was used frequently in the early defense period and later where the facilities had no prospective civilian peacetime use. The War Department financed in this manner industrial facilities valued at over $5 billion.[18] The Navy financed another $3 billion in the same way.[19]

Financing Working Capital

Steps taken to provide contractors with working capital provided another facet to the program for facilitating production with minimum risk to the contractor and minimum cost to the government. This was accomplished in several ways, including advance and progress payments, direct loans to industry, government advances to industry of materials and equipment, steps to strengthen the credit standing of industry, and even the payment of excessive prices. The financing of contractors by intentional payment of excessive prices was contrary to established policies of the services. But to the extent that excessive profits were earned and held for any period, however unintentionally, the contractor was being financed by free government funds until the time of payment of his renegotiation refund.

The services had long had authority to make progress payments on prime contracts to an amount not in excess of the value of the work done, such payments to be protected by a lien upon the articles produced.[20] In the summer of 1940 both the services were authorized to make advance payments on war contracts in an amount not to exceed 30 per cent of the contract price. In December, 1941 the discretion of the services was widened by Title II of the First War Powers Act which, together with Executive Order 9001, authorized the

18. *Op. cit.,* p. 20; Army Industrial College, *Construction of New Facilities,* pp. 116–120.

19. Secretary of the Navy, *Annual Report,* 1945, p. A-132.

20. 37 Stat. 32, August 22, 1911 (Navy); 41 Stat. 975 (Army).

services "to make advance, progress, and other payments" on their contracts without limit whenever in their judgment this would facilitate the prosecution of the war.[21] Although early advances were made without interest charge, after the late spring of 1942 interest was charged at the rate of 2½ per cent on the outstanding balance of such advances.[22]

Advance payments and progress payments were an important source of working capital during all phases of the emergency. The cumulative total of advance payments to contractors made by the War Department alone from 1940 to September, 1945 exceeded $7 billion.[23] The Navy Department made advances of approximately $2 billion.[24] The Navy Department and Maritime Commission used progress payments very largely to finance their ship construction programs.

Advance and progress payments did not solve the whole problem of the working capital needs of contractors. The services could make such payments directly only to prime contractors. Subcontractors had to depend upon the prime contractor to relay to them their share of any advance. This procedure did not always work well. Moreover, even in the case of prime contractors the procedure often involved difficult problems of administration and accounting particularly where a contractor held several contracts involving several bureaus or technical services. To solve these problems the Board of Governors of the Federal Reserve System issued, in the spring of 1942, Regulation V, which created the so-called "V-Loan." By this arrangement the War and Navy Departments and Maritime Commission were each authorized to guarantee a loan from a commercial bank to a prime contractor or subcontractor whose work was "necessary, appropriate or convenient for the prosecution of the war" [25] up to 90 per

21. Pub. Law No. 354, 77th Cong., 1st Sess.; 6 F.R. 6787.
22. The Navy instituted such charges on April 11, 1942 (NPD, par. 12, 231) and the War Department followed on June 8 (APR, par. 321.12).
23. Army Industrial College, *Financial Aids to Contractors*, p. 40.
24. *Analysis of Navy Department Procurement in World War II* (mimeographed, no date), p. 35.
25. Executive Order 9112, 7 F.R. 2367 (March 26, 1942).

cent of the principal. The interest charge on such loans was
not to exceed 5 per cent. From this charge a guarantee fee,
which depended on the percentage of the loan guaranteed, was
paid to the government. Guaranteed loans under Regulation
V reached a cumulative total of over $10 billion by the end of
1945.[26] This program did much to aid small contractors. Over
58 per cent of the total number of guaranteed loans authorized
were for loans of $250,000 or less.[27] The total credit available
at any one time under V-loans reached its peak of over $6 bil-
lion in October, 1944.[28] Authorizations were always considerably in excess of the actual loans outstanding. The latter
reached their peak of about $2.0 billion in July, 1944.[29]

Other steps taken to facilitate the financing of working
capital requirements of contractors include the Assignment of
Claims Act of 1940, which permitted contractors to assign
their government contracts as collateral for loans; [30] a limited
number of loans made by the services directly to contractors; [31] and the practice of the services in certain cases of agree-
ing as part of a supply contract to buy and furnish to the contractor certain specified materials or components.[32]

Conclusion

By these various devices much was done to facilitate the
conversion of American industry to wartime production. By
reducing the risks the contractors faced these devices aided in
the negotiation of reasonable prices on supply contracts and
went a long way toward limiting the inflationary tendencies
arising from military procurement particularly in the early
part of the emergency.

26. *Federal Reserve Bulletin*, March, 1946, p. 245.
27. *Loc. cit.*
28. *Loc. cit.*
29. *Loc. cit.*
30. Pub. Law No. 811, 76th Cong., 3d Sess. (Oct. 9, 1940).
31. Army Industrial College, *Financial Aids to Contractors*, p. 45.
32. *Loc. cit.*

IX

CONTRACTUAL INSTRUMENTS AND THEIR USE

THE negotiated contract provided an opportunity for adapting the services' purchasing arrangements to the peculiar conditions of each contractor giving due consideration to his facilities, know-how, financial status, efficiency, and risks. During World War II the services developed many types of contractual arrangements; in particular, they developed many variations of the fixed-price contract. But the objective of all of these arrangements was the same: to facilitate maximum and expeditious production of war materials by appropriate allocation of risks and the provision of effective incentives. Some of these arrangements such as the simple fixed-price contract and the CPFF contract were well-established methods of contracting long before the war. Others were completely new to government procurement although in some cases they had been widely and effectively used in private purchasing.

The flexibility permitted by the negotiated contract represented a challenge to procurement officers and industry to work out arrangements which would further the over-all objectives of mobilization. The appropriateness of any type of arrangement depends upon the circumstances of the particular procurement, *i.e.*, upon the type of item purchased, the conditions of the contractor, the particular phase in the mobilization cycle, and the general context of controls over materials, manpower, wages, and prices within which it is used. Moreover, the effectiveness of each type of contractual arrangement must be analyzed in terms of the effects upon incentives of the excess profits tax and renegotiation.

It will not serve our purposes to classify contractual arrangements as good or bad. The usefulness of any particular contractual arrangement to the government and its acceptability to industry can be determined only in terms of the particular circumstances in which it is used. The purpose of the negotiated contract is to permit flexibility. It serves no good purpose, consequently, to surround the discretion of contracting officers with rigid rules. The problem of efficient procurement by the negotiated contract can be solved not by rigid rules on the use of particular contractual devices but rather by the selection of personnel experienced and trained in the methods and techniques of efficient purchasing.

This chapter will outline the major contractual arrangements used by the services during World War II. Brief reference will be made to the various "boiler plate" provisions required by statute or administrative order. It must be recognized that although the War and Navy Departments operated on the same general principles, in some cases they evolved different types of contractual arrangements to deal with the same problems. In the beginning of the emergency contract forms were controlled by the Treasury. As the emergency developed the services found it necessary to have greater freedom in developing variations in their contract forms.[1] As a result the system of uniform contract forms which had been built up between the wars broke down. The NDAC and its successor agencies exercised some unifying control, but this was confined for the most part to general principles. After the delegation of the clearance of contracts to the services in the spring of 1942 this control was increasingly loose.[2] The records of the Procurement Policy Board indicate that although there was much discussion by the two services of their evolving contractual instruments, many differences were allowed to go unresolved. In reviewing the contractual policies of the services it is also important to remember that there is inevitably a wide difference between professed policy and practice.

1. Production and Purchases Division, ASF, *Purchasing Policies and Practices*, pp. 34–35.
2. See above, pp. 55–56.

Letter of Intent and Letter Contract

The letter of intent or unpriced letter contract is essentially an interim device by which the contractor can be authorized to proceed with production before detailed contract terms are agreed upon.[3] It was used during the war where speed in production became so important that it was necessary to induce a contractor to acquire facilities or materials, make provision for a labor supply, or even begin production before the contractual terms were agreed upon or perhaps even before the specifications were stabilized. It is expected that a letter of intent will be followed by a formal contract. In fact the letter of intent usually specifies the time within which negotiations for such a contract are to be completed. The letter of intent insures the contractor of reimbursement of costs incurred in case of termination. In some cases a maximum limit to the expenses to be incurred is written into the letter. Often the approval of the cognizant contracting officer is required in advance for certain types of expenditures made by the contractor under the letter, such as machinery and equipment, or for each expenditure in excess of some specified amount. In the case of letters issued early in the war the Navy did not allow any profit on terminated letters. However, in the case of terminated letters entered into after November 1, 1944 by either of the services, a reasonable profit might be included in the negotiated settlement.

The letter of intent is primarily an emergency device. Although it was authorized and used throughout the war, its greatest use was during the period right after Pearl Harbor. During the first four months of 1942 the Navy made commitments including letters of intent and firm contracts of $8.4 billion of which $5.3 billion were in the form of letters of in-

3. The Navy Department used only the letter of intent. The War Department had both a letter of intent and also a letter contract. The latter was used where the items, quantities, and delivery schedules were known and specified but where there was insufficient time to negotiate the other contractual provisions. Production and Purchases Division, ASF, *op. cit.*, pp. 35–36. For the standard letter order forms used by the War Department see APR, pars. 1307–1311.

tent and $0.5 billion were contracts superseding previous letters.[4] Similarly after Pearl Harbor, the War Department issued instructions for more intensive use of the letter of contract "in the interest of expediting procurement." [5]

Although the letter of intent is an excellent device for expediting production, it is the least effective device for allocating risks and providing incentives to efficiency. The principal risk which the contractor takes under a letter is the risk of termination. For this reason it is important that all letters should be converted into firm contracts as soon as possible. Various administrative devices were used during the war to encourage procurement officers to convert them.[6]

Costs-plus-fixed-fee Contract

None of the other contract forms used during World War II has been the subject of as much debate as the cost-plus-fixed-fee (CPFF) contract. It, along with the cost-plus-percentage-of-cost (CPPC) contract, had been prominent in World War I.[7] But the CPPC contract was held responsible for much of the inefficiency and profiteering of that war and was consequently forbidden as early as May, 1918.[8] During World War II the CPPC contract was illegal from the beginning.[9] Early in the emergency, however, Congress gave the services power to negotiate CPFF contracts first for construction of overseas bases by the Bureau of Yards and Docks, then for continental construction by the Quartermaster Corps, and later for other procurements. By the time of Pearl Harbor the CPFF contract was well established as an instrument of policy. Although the First War Powers Act specifically prohibited the use of the CPPC contract, it did authorize the CPFF contract with a maximum fee of seven per cent of the estimated cost.[10]

4. H. S. Hensel, Affidavit in *U.S. v. Alexander Wool Combing Co.*, p. 8.
5. War Department, P. & C. General Directive No. 88, Dec. 17, 1941.
6. NPD, pars. 11,171–11,174; APR, par. 303A.
7. J. Franklin Crowell, *Government War Contracts*, p. 36.
8. *Ibid.*, p. 32.
9. See above, p. 87.
10. Pub. Law No. 354, 77th Cong., 1st Sess.

The typical CPFF contract provides that the contractor will be reimbursed to the extent of total allowable costs incurred in the performance of the contract plus a specified fee.[11] The content of "allowable costs" is specified in the contract in detail or by reference to some general statement of cost principles such as the statement of allowable costs promulgated by the Treasury under the Vinson-Trammell Act (generally referred to as T.D. 5000 or "the green book").[12] The fixed fee is specified in dollar terms and during the war generally could not exceed seven per cent of the estimated cost of performance of the contract exclusive of the fee. In some cases an incentive fee system is used, *e.g.*, where the fee increases if costs are cut below the estimate or if delivery schedules are exceeded. The contractor is required to keep detailed records of his costs on the contract and is generally required to have the prior approval of the cognizant contracting officer for certain specified expenditures, such as all expenditures for equipment and expenditures on subcontracts or for purchase of material over a certain amount. The allowable costs are subject to review first by the contracting officer and later by the Comptroller General. The extent to which the services reviewed operations and expenditures during World War II varied as between different bureaus and technical services. In some cases the review was confined to the question of whether an expenditure was "allowable." In other cases the services made elaborate studies of production and purchasing policies and brought considerable direct pressure to bear to improve these policies and reduce costs. The AAF had developed a particularly elaborate system of review. The decisions on "allowable costs" by the Comptroller General and the General Account-

11. For general discussion of the CPFF contract see Rear Adm. B. Moreell, *Notes on the Uses of the Cost-Plus-a-Fixed-Fee Form in Government Contracts* and Production and Purchases Division, ASF, *op. cit.*, pp. 228–286.

12. See Treasury Decision Internal Revenue 5000. The Navy adapted T.D. 5000 for most CPFF contracts. The AAF adopted it for early contracts, but later contracts of the AAF included additional language. Army procedures were later consolidated into TM 14–1000, "Administrative Audit Procedure for CPFF Supply Contracts" (April 1, 1944). See Office of the Fiscal Director, *History of Fiscal Services 1940–1945* (War Department Historical Files), chap. xliv.

ing Office have given rise to much controversy to which both the services and industry have been parties. The danger that expenditures will be disallowed by the Comptroller General even after approval by the services constitutes one of the principal risks of this contract form.

The CPFF contract is useful in a variety of circumstances. It has been widely used in construction contracts and for large production contracts, especially in the case of ships, aircraft, and ordnance. It has also been used on many research and development contracts. In the case of the latter, a special "no-fee" or "cost" contract has been developed for use with non-profit seeking organizations such as universities. This variation on the CPFF contract provides for reimbursement of "costs" only. In some such cases a nominal fee is provided to cover certain costs which are "disallowable" under the usual rules but which the services feel the universities should not be forced to bear. The Navy has been using a special type of CPFF contract on its research and development contracts in which certain costs, *e.g.*, labor and materials, are reimbursed on the basis of actual costs incurred, while burden and overhead rates are negotiated periodically on the basis of past experience. This reduces the cost problem materially and is especially useful in the case of small contracts with firms whose cost-accounting systems are not adequate to the segregation of overhead and burden on individual contracts.

Despite continuous criticism by Congress the CPFF contract was an integral and useful part of the procurement program during World War II and is likely to be continued over into peace. Table I indicates the importance of CPFF contracts of $10 million and over in relation to all contracts of $10 million and over for the period June, 1940 to December, 1944. During this period CPFF contracts represented 30 per cent of the total number of contracts of $10 million and over and 45 per cent of the total value of such contracts. These figures, however, overstate the importance of the CPFF contract in the total procurement program since it was more frequently used for large procurements than for small. It has

TABLE I

COST-PLUS-FIXED-FEE WAR SUPPLY CONTRACTS
OF $10 MILLION AND OVER *

Number and Value by Agency and Period of Award
June 1940–December 1944

Agency and Award Period	Number		Value (Millions of Dollars)	
	All Contracts	CPFF As Per cent of All Contracts	All Contracts	CPFF As Per cent of All Contracts
All Agencies—Total	*2,646*	*30.7*	*$110,497.1*	*45.3*
1940–1941	524	34.7	17,642.5	45.7
January–June 1942	529	35.0	25,353.0	51.8
July–December 1942	383	31.3	18,149.0	42.8
January–June 1943	441	27.2	18,397.7	41.1
July–December 1943	322	27.6	11,705.4	47.9
January–June 1944	316	25.9	15,218.2	41.5
July–December 1944	131	26.0	4,031.2	39.8
Army—Total	*1,490*	*31.6*	*70,526.6*	*46.6*
1940–1941	270	41.9	10,038.7	54.4
January–June 1942	287	34.5	15,854.5	50.7
July–December 1942	244	29.5	12,168.6	42.4
January–June 1943	257	26.8	11,773.8	42.1
July–December 1943	185	28.1	7,572.3	46.9
January–June 1944	186	24.7	11,026.2	43.5
July–December 1944	61	32.8	2,092.3	43.8
Navy—Total	*884*	*30.4*	*31,211.6*	*41.5*
1940–1941	181	30.4	6,377.0	35.0
January–June 1942	184	35.3	6,932.2	53.1
July–December 1942	110	33.6	4,996.9	40.5
January–June 1943	124	25.8	4,081.8	27.9
July–December 1943	118	31.4	3,786.9	54.4
January–June 1944	105	30.5	3,383.0	38.0
July–December 1944	62	17.7	1,653.8	32.4
Maritime Commission —Total	*257*	*28.0*	*8,473.9*	*49.5*
1940–1941	72	19.4	1,213.3	29.9
January–June 1942	57	36.8	2,556.3	55.0
July–December 1942	28	39.3	967.4	60.9
January–June 1943	58	32.8	2,453.3	59.5
July–December 1943	17	—	313.1	—
January–June 1944	20	20.0	729.5	31.6
July–December 1944	5	60.0	241.1	62.2
*Treasury **—Total*	*15*	—	*285.1*	—

* Excludes awards for foodstuffs, construction, and production facilities.
** All Treasury contracts have been reported as fixed-price.

Source: WPB, Bureau of Program and Statistics, *Cost-Plus Supply Contracts in the War Program* (March 8, 1945), Table I.

been estimated that "in terms of the value of all contracts, the proportion of cost-plus-fixed-fee contracts would be about 30 rather than 45 per cent; in terms of numbers the proportion is negligible." [13]

The period of greatest use in both absolute and relative terms was in the first six months of 1942, right after Pearl Harbor. Thereafter, the use of the CPFF contract declined continuously except for the period July to December, 1943. During this period the percentage of CPFF contracts increased because fixed-price contracts declined at a greater rate than CPFF contracts especially in the AAF and the Bureau of Aeronautics. The bulk of the CPFF contracts were awarded in the War Department by the AAF and Ordnance and in the Navy by the Bureaus of Aeronautics, Ships, and Ordnance.

The reasons for using CPFF contracts are several. Often they are used because of the need for speed in placing contracts despite uncertainty concerning specifications. This was true in the early part of the emergency of many of the construction contracts for overseas installations and for training facilities in this country. Uncertainty of specifications is also a common characteristic of many research and development contracts. Even in the case of production contracts where the specifications are relatively stabilized, it is often true that there is great uncertainty concerning costs in the early stages of production especially when a contractor takes a large contract to produce items he has not produced before. This may arise from instability in wage and material costs or from uncertainty concerning the probable trend of productive efficiency. Although the services developed other techniques for dealing with these uncertainties as the war progressed, such as escalation and redetermination clauses, these considerations seem to have accounted for many of the earlier contracts, especially for aircraft. Another consideration which was important in the case of aircraft was the risk to the contractor resulting from the large size of his contracts in relation to his

13. WPB, Bureau of Program and Statistics, *Cost-Plus Supply Contracts in the War Program, June 1940–December 1944* (March 8, 1945), p. 1.

capital. In some cases active contracts were as much as one hundred times as large as the contractor's capital investment. Under these circumstances a small error in negotiating a fixed price might wipe out the contractor's entire investment. Again other contractual arrangements developed by the services in the later stages of the war might have protected the contractor against some such risks. Finally, the CPFF contract proved very useful in the case of government-owned-contractor-operated (GOCO) plants, where the contractor was remunerated for his services by the payment of costs plus a fixed fee for operations. Despite much criticism of the CPFF contract in general and many attempts to eliminate it, the use of this arrangement in the case of GOCO plants was never seriously questioned.

While Congress specifically authorized the use of the CPFF contract, Congress and the public has always looked upon it with grave misgivings.[14] Many of the shortcomings of the procurement program have been attributed to it. The services have been called to account repeatedly for using it and on several occasions proposals were made to prohibit its further use.[15] For this reason among others those responsible for top policy within the services have attempted to limit its use while at the same time insisting before Congress that its use should not be prevented altogether.[16]

The usual criticism of the CPFF contract was that it failed to provide incentives to productive efficiency. This, of course, could be remedied. In fact the Bureau of Ships used an incentive scheme from an early date and the War Department Procurement Regulations eventually provided for similar schemes.[17] But the legal upper limit on the fee of seven per cent of estimated costs circumscribed narrowly the limits within which incentive fees might be used. Moreover, it still

14. 88 Cong. Rec. 3586–3595; 89 Cong. Rec. 7834.
15. 87 Cong. Rec. 4908–4910; 89 Cong. Rec. 7697 (S. Res. 80, 78th Cong., 1st Sess.; H.R. 3523 and H.R. 3558, 78th Cong., 1st Sess.).
16. Letter from Brig. Gen. B. Somervell and Robert P. Patterson, 87 Cong. Rec. 4908–4909.
17. APR, par. 378.

remained true that the CPFF contract provided an incentive to keep up costs on one contract in order to establish higher estimated costs and therefore high fees on subsequent contracts. Furthermore, knowledge that the contractor was operating on a CPFF contract was often destructive of morale within the plant, especially the morale of the foremen and superintendents. The services themselves had other reasons for discouraging the use of the CPFF contract. One, of course, was the fact that it led to constant public and Congressional criticism. Another reason was the administrative burden which it imposed on the services to approve expenditures under the contract and to audit the accounts.[18] The services were faced with a serious shortage of competent accountants. Finally, since such contracts raised many more questions of interpretation than the various alternatives, the administration of such contracts was more likely to be questioned by the General Accounting Office and the settlement reopened. This meant uncertainty for the contractor and delay in settling accounts, both of which were conducive to confusion and ill will.

For these reasons there was intermittent pressure from top policy makers in the services to convert existing contracts to some type of fixed-price contract and to reduce the number of new ones negotiated. In these attempts they were only partially successful.[19] The greatest difficulty seems to have arisen in connection with contracts awarded by the AAF. The problems of conversion arose in part from the fact that some contractors themselves seemed happy with their relatively riskless contracts. Moreover, for a long time the General Accounting Office appeared to require a shut-down to take physical inventory and to set up such other conditions on conversions that the contractor could not be sure that conversion would relieve him of further audit by the General Accounting Office. These difficulties were not ironed out

18. NPD, par. 10,551.
19. For detailed discussion of such attempts in the War Department see Production and Purchases Division, ASF, *op. cit.*, pp. 228–286.

until the spring of 1945, when the Under Secretary of War ordered the conversion of all CPFF contracts except those for research and development, initial production contracts for items not previously produced, GOCO contracts, and contracts for services.[20] Before this program had proceeded very far V-J Day had arrived and wholesale terminations were in order.

The fees actually allowed on CPFF contracts varied widely. As has been pointed out, fees were based on estimated costs exclusive of the fee. The Bureau of Yards and Docks, which had been authorized to pay fees up to 10 per cent of the estimated costs for its advanced bases, actually awarded its three initial contracts for bases in the Pacific Islands, Alaska, and San Juan at 6 per cent, 5.83 per cent and 5.607 per cent of estimated costs respectively.[21] The total estimated cost including fees of all CPFF contracts awarded by the Bureau of Yards and Docks from August 5, 1939 to September 30, 1943 was $3,987 million. These were awarded at fees which averaged 2.84 per cent of the estimated costs.[22] In the early stages of the war the fees on the contracts of the AAF generally reached the statutory limit of 7 per cent of estimated costs, but they were subsequently reduced to 4 per cent as the volume of awards increased.[23] The fees for Army Ordnance contracts varied depending on the circumstances, the efficiency, risk, financing, etc. They ranged from 6.2 per cent of actual cost for GOCO smokeless powder plants, to 1.3 per cent of estimated costs for large GOCO shell-loading plants.[24] A frequent arrangement in the early ship contracts was a fee of 3 per cent of estimated cost with a bonus for lowering costs or anticipating the scheduled delivery date, which might go up as high as an additional 4 per cent of estimated costs. In later

20. Memorandum from Under Secretary of War to Commanding General, ASF, and Commanding General, AAF, March 8, 1945 reproduced in *ibid.*, pp. 254–255.
21. Moreell, *op. cit.*, p. 52.
22. *Ibid.*, p. 78.
23. Production and Purchases Division, ASF, *op. cit.*, p. 260.
24. *Ibid.*, p. 263.

ship contracts the maximum bonus was cut to 2 per cent.[25] Since costs were extremely difficult to estimate in the circumstances in which the CPFF contract was typically used, it is not surprising to find that estimated costs and actual costs usually differed considerably. In consequence, profits as a percentage of actual costs were often far above 7 per cent. However, CPFF contracts like other contracts were subject to renegotiation.[26]

The merits of the argument that CPFF contracts are conducive to inefficiency are by no means established. In logic they seem persuasive. But there are many who have defended the contrary thesis with considerable vigor. The available evidence on the matter is not conclusive.[27] The problem of efficiency is a relative matter, and, as will appear later, even in logic the merits of fixed-price contracts as actually administered during the recent war are much less convincing than the uninitiated might imagine. Such efficiency as the CPFF contract attains, except in the case of contracts with incentive fees, must result from the direct pressures of those administering the contract for the services and from the basic drive of American industry to excel in productive efficiency. Apparently the AAF devised the most elaborate procedures for administering CPFF contracts, for reviewing prices on purchased materials and parts, and for bringing direct pressures upon contractors to improve their efficiency. An extensive and unbiased survey of the different techniques used by various bureaus and technical services to encourage efficiency under these contracts would be desirable. This might suggest ways to improve the administration of CPFF contracts in the future. Moreover, it might shed light on the controversy as to the relative merits of CPFF and other contractual forms, a con-

25. Army Industrial College, *Contract Pricing: Principal Developments*, p. 125.

26. RR, par. 332.4.

27. For examples in the production of aircraft engines and propellers of lower costs by CPFF contractors than by fixed-price contractors producing identical items see Army Air Forces, *Purchasing Policies, Controls and Procedures Affecting AAF Material* (War Department Historical Files), p. 28.

troversy which has been waged to date largely in the realm of pure speculation.

Fixed-price Contract

The mobilization plan promulgated in the 1930's had called for two basic types of contracts: the fixed-price contract for standard civilian items and the adjusted compensation contract for all military items.[28] The latter was a cost contract in which the fee was to be some predetermined percentage of the value of capital investment devoted to the contract. This contractual form raised all the problems of accounting and auditing associated with the CPFF contract together with the question of determining the value of the contractor's capital and the proportion thereof applicable to the contract. These plans were abandoned early and much of the energy of the services was devoted to trying to adapt the fixed-price contract to all items, specialized military goods as well as civilian products.

Industry and the services alike were agreed that the CPFF contract was not feasible for the mass of contracts because of the accounting burden which it placed on both parties and the problem of review by the General Accounting Office. Beyond this the objectives of industry and the services diverged. Many contractors sought a contract which approached as closely as possible the CPFF contract in its risklessness but carried the higher profit associated with risk-taking. While the services were willing to assume many of those risks over which the contractor had no control, they sought a fixed-price contract which had sufficient pricing risk to provide incentive to efficiency and at the same time would not yield profits which were too excessive when viewed at the completion of the contract. The result of this conflict of interest was a wide variety of contractual forms in which risks, rewards, and incentives were mixed in various ways. It is not an exaggeration to say that as a result we came closer than is generally realized to financing this war on a disguised CPPC basis.

28. See above, pp. 41–42.

The basic problem in the negotiation of the fixed-price contract arises from uncertainty concerning costs. In part this is due to the lack of adequate cost systems for determining costs on past production. The services found and OPA has since confirmed [29] that many firms, in fact most firms in terms of number, do not have accounting systems which permit the accurate estimate of unit costs on a product or item basis. If firms cannot tell what it has cost to produce their customary items in the past, how much more difficult it is to estimate future costs! In the early stages of the war these difficulties were accentuated by the multiplicity of new products and changing specifications and by the fact that many firms called into production had not had previous experience in producing even the conventional military items. Moreover, most firms were experiencing an unprecedented increase in volume which was certain to affect their costs, although there was by no means agreement as to the direction and extent. In addition, there was uncertainty concerning the probable trend of wage rates and raw material costs, the extent to which a prime contractor would subcontract, and the terms of such subcontracts. Even in the later stages of the procurement program many of these problems remained: new products were being produced, the future volume and its composition as between high-profit and low-profit items was uncertain, and many firms still did not have adequate records of past costs.

Simple Fixed-price Contract. In view of the uncertainties concerning costs, the simple fixed-price contract could not be used much except for the purchase of stock items or for items to be produced in a short period of time. It was used, however, for many emergency purchases and small purchases of clothing and provisions as well as small purchases of many standard commercial items produced for stock. Although the total number of such contracts and purchase orders were undoubtedly large, their value was unquestionably relatively small.

29. OPA, Accounting Department, *Cost Accounting Records in Industry* (June 30, 1946), pp. iii–iv.

Escalation for Material and Labor Costs. From an early period in the emergency the policy was adopted of including an escalation clause in many fixed-price contracts which was designed to protect the contractor in part against increases in wage rates and in material costs which were not within his control. This was particularly important prior to the imposition of price and wage controls in 1942.[30] Many of the early contracts included a provision whereby the price was increased automatically by a specified factor which was dependent upon the change in some index of material prices and wage rates.[31] Some of the early clauses, especially those used for ships, proved to be defective in that they provided for an application of the wage index to the contractor's actual wage bill, which itself already included the effect of increased wage rates, rather than to his deflated wage bill.[32]

The theory of escalation in this early period was that certain risks of cost increases were not within the control of the contractor and that the government would find it less expensive to assume these risks directly through a special escalation clause than to provide a contingency factor in the price of the contracts. The escalation clause provided reimbursement only if the risks actually materialized, and then only to the extent of the actual increase as calculated by the formula. But in order to encourage the contractor to use his labor and materials efficiently and discourage him from bidding up prices and wages unnecessarily, these clauses sought to tie escalation to some general index which was pertinent to the risks at hand but not too much influenced by the policies of the contractor in question.

As direct controls of wages and material prices were extended during 1942 the justification for such general escalation

30. For discussion of some of the early escalation clauses and industry's experience therewith see National Industrial Conference Board, *Escalation Protection in Contracts* (March 19, 1941).

31. For discussion of these clauses see OPA, *Escalator Clauses in War Contracts,* "Price Policy Series," No. 3 (Jan., 1942). See also War Department, P. and C. General Directive No. 48 (Sept. 17, 1941) and No. 86 (Dec. 17, 1941); War Department, Proc. Reg. 10-T (April 30, 1942).

32. NPD, par. 17,301.

disappeared. In the statement of principles adopted by the Tryon Conference in November, 1942 it was stated that "escalator clauses based on indices should no longer be used." [33] With the development of OPA controls, however, there was a tendency to ask for clauses which would provide for automatic increases in contract prices with increases in OPA ceilings. The use of such automatic escalation was resisted. The Tryon Conference concluded that "provisions for *automatic price increases* based on costs of specific items or on OPA ceiling should not be allowed unless the Government controls the actual price of items and not merely the maximum price." [34] Moreover, the Procurement Policy Board agreed unanimously in June, 1943 to eliminate escalator clauses which were tied to OPA ceilings [35] and reaffirmed this policy the following year.[36] This policy was based on the theory that in many cases the services were able to buy below OPA ceilings. An exception to the general policy was made in the case of several items, notably lumber, steel, coal, and petroleum, where automatic escalation was permitted by the amount of the increase in the OPA ceiling prices.[37] Likewise, in the case of products involving rubber as an important material automatic escalation was permitted as changes were made in the sales price of rubber by the Rubber Reserve Corporation.[38]

As an alternative to automatic escalation where price or wage ceilings were increased by action of a government agency such as OPA or WLB, the services provided for "negotiated escalation." Under this scheme if ceiling prices were increased by OPA action or wage costs through the action of WLB, either the contractor or the contracting officer might initiate a reopening of the contract price. Thereupon, the two parties would negotiate an equitable adjustment which might call for a greater or lesser change in the contract price

33. Army Industrial College, *op. cit.*, p. 140.
34. *Loc. cit.*
35. Procurement Policy Board, *Minutes,* June 2, 1943. See also APR, par. 1232.
36. Procurement Policy Board, *Minutes,* March 29, 1944.
37. NPD, pars. 17,341–17,354, 17,371–17,375; APR, par. 351.
38. APR, par. 1232.2.

than the change in the contractor's costs.[39] This made it possible for the services to force the contractor to absorb some or all of the increased costs when it appeared that his over-all position made this possible. It was the general policy of the services to permit escalation only in circumstances where the contracting officer was satisfied that the contractor had excluded from his price all or substantially all contingency allowances for the putative increases in costs.

Maximum-price Contracts. One important variation on the fixed-price contract used by both the War and Navy Departments is the maximum-price contract which provides for a single downward redetermination of price after a certain period of time or, more frequently, after production of a specified portion of the contract. This type of contract is used where circumstances are such that accurate cost estimates are not possible at the time of award but can be obtained after an initial test run. In some cases the redetermined price is applicable only to the undelivered portion of the contract, while in others it applies retroactively to the delivered portion as well. Typically the contract calls for negotiation of the redetermined price without limit as to allowable profit, although in some cases the dollar profit to be allowed is specified in the contract.[40] This later procedure was proposed in the early part of the war as a means of providing an incentive to cost reduction. Experience indicated in many cases that the redetermined prices were often substantially lower than the maximum price, so that a dollar profit which appeared appropriate for the latter price appeared excessive for the former. Consequently, this procedure was not used much. This procedure should be useful as a cost reducing device, however, where initial prices can be negotiated on a more reasonable basis. When a maximum price contract was used, however, an attempt was generally made to reward the contractor with

39. See, for example, the so-called Forrestal War Labor Board clause (NPR, pars. 17,361–17,365). This type of clause was used frequently on textile and clothing items as protection against increases in OPA ceilings on materials.

40. See NPD, par. 10,552 and pars. 10,568–10,569. Proc. Reg. 10-T (April 30, 1942).

a higher profit in proportion to his effectiveness in reducing costs.

The decision as to the point in the contract at which the redetermination should be made is particularly important. If made too early in the contract, costs are influenced unduly by high starting costs and the difficulty of estimating costs for future delivery is correspondingly great. If price is redetermined late in the contract, the price risk of the contractor is reduced and the incentives to efficiency are ineffective. The problem is complicated by the fact that the compilation of data and negotiation of the redetermined price take time. At the time of final redetermination the data is often already out of date. During the war policy varied, but in general an attempt was made to effect redetermination at some point between 25 per cent and 40 per cent of the completion of the contract. If price was not redetermined until after the completion of the contract, there was the danger that the General Accounting Office would interpret the contract as violating the statutory prohibition of cost-plus-percentage-of-cost contracts.

The difficulty of the maximum-price contract is the basic problem of how to negotiate reasonable prices with real incentives in the face of uncertainties concerning costs. It is difficult when redetermining prices to avoid pricing on a disguised cost-plus-percentage-of-cost basis. There is a natural tendency at the time of redetermination to be liberal in estimating future costs and to arrive at the redetermined price by applying to these liberally estimated costs an allowance for profits in line with renegotiation allowances. To the extent that the contractor expects the services to follow this procedure his incentives to cost reduction are weak. The services' great problem with the maximum-price contract is to convince the contractor that they will not set redetermined prices on an estimated cost plus conventional profit but that they will allow greater dollar profit for greater success in increasing efficiency. A further limitation of the maximum-price contract, in the case of contracts running for a long period, arises from the fact that at the time of redetermination future risks may still appear large and the corresponding cost estimates may include sizable contingencies. For these reasons, among others, the War Department was led during the war to devise a series of more elaborate price adjustment clauses.

War Department Price Adjustment Clauses. To carry out the principles established at the Tryon Conference for close pricing on fixed-price contracts the War Department developed an elaborate array of price adjustment clauses which provided for adjustment of prices upward was well as downward and provided for periodic adjustment as well as a single adjustment. These clauses went through some changes between the early part of 1943 and the close of the war.[41] The main features, however, are relatively simple. These clauses were used extensively by the War Department but were never adopted by the Navy. In fact the Navy as a matter of policy never approved any price-adjustment arrangement which called for upward adjustment of price without consideration except where it was necessary to insure supplies.[42]

The broad objective of these price-adjustment articles was to provide a kit of tools which could be adapted to various conditions and which would permit risks to be shifted from the contractor to the government wherever these risks arose from abnormal, war-caused uncertainties and hazards over which the contractor had no control.[43] It was hoped thereby

41. See 9 F.R. 1344–1362 (Feb., 1944) and 9 F.R. 4842–4857 (May, 1945).

42. The First War Powers Act (Pub. Law No. 354, 77th Cong., Dec. 18, 1941) and Executive Order 9001 (6 F.R. 6787, Dec., 1941) authorized the services to amend and modify contracts without reference to existing provisions of the law "whenever he deems such action would facilitate the prosecution of the war." The War Department took the position that this permitted upward adjustments of prices without consideration in accordance with their price articles which were designed to effect close prices which in turn "would facilitate the prosecution of the war." In the case of all upward adjustments without consideration the Navy Department took a more rigorous interpretation of the requirement that the contract amendment must "facilitate prosecution of the war." It required a showing that failure to make such upward adjustment would prevent the contractor from fulfilling his contract and thereby threaten delivery of necessary supplies.

43. For a discussion of the basic thinking behind these clauses see G. A. Lloyd, *Law and Contemporary Problems*, X, 235–261.

to facilitate the negotiation of close prices from which substantially all contingency allowances had been eliminated.

Table II gives a quick view of the various clauses as they had been developed and perfected by the spring of 1945. Forms I-A, I-B, and I-C provided for periodic repricing either upward or downward at fixed intervals. Prices set thereunder were to be based on cost projections for a single pricing period. Under Forms I-A and I-B the price revisions applied only to future deliveries and the price set in the contract for the first period was not subject to revision. These articles could be applied only in cases where there was sufficient cost experience to enable reasonably accurate cost projections for the first period. Where this was not possible, Form I-C was in order. Forms II-A and II-B provided for optional price adjustments at the initiative of either the government or the contractor with specific limitation as to the frequency of revision. Under Form II-A price revisions were to be applied to prospective deliveries only, while under Form II-B the prices for the first period might be changed retroactively.

These general forms were designed to make it possible to review prices and costs frequently and to adjust prices, especially prospective prices, in the light of changing circumstances. Their effectiveness depended upon the skill of the procurement officer in analyzing the causes of changes in costs and using this analysis in negotiation. If these forms were to be used to encourage efficiency, the contracting officer had to distinguish between changes which were within the control of the contractor and those which were not and administer appropriate rewards for efficiency resulting from control of the former. Failure to accomplish this meant that these clauses would result in a disguised form of cost-plus-percentage-of-cost contracting. Their effectiveness depended, then, upon highly competent cost analysis and negotiation.

The other forms included in Table II need little comment. Form III represented the War Department's approach to retroactive wage increases by the WLB. Prospective wage increases could be handled adequately under Forms I-A, I-B,

TABLE II

WAR DEPARTMENT PRICE REVISION ARTICLES

(Adapted from Table in APR, par. 370.5)

Effect of Article	Conditions for Use	
Form 1–A	*Applicable to Particular Article*	*Applicable to all Form I and Form II Articles*
Upward or downward price revision negotiated at fixed periods, with prospective effect only.	1. Contract is such that both parties should be bound by price for the first period. Pricing periods range from 3 to 4 months in length. 2. Price is based on projections not extending beyond end of first period. 3. Periods should conform with operation of contractor's cost accounting system and need not be of equal length. 4. Periods may be measured in time or production or delivery of items.	1. Contract is fixed price contract for supplies or services. 2. There is an absence of competition as that term is defined in paragraph 371.1(2). 3. Price is negotiated on understanding that particular article is to be included in contract and is a close price containing substantially no contingency charges. 4. Contractor employs proper estimating methods. 5. Contractor's cost accounting system is sufficiently reliable and accurate for proper operation of article. 6. One article is not to be substituted for another without express authority. 7. Alternative provisions for disagreements are provided. See paragraphs 372.2, 372.8, 373.2 and 373.7.
Form 1–B Upward or downward price revision negotiated at fixed periods, with prospective effect only and with first period price based on experience under prior contract for same or similar item.	1. Production under prior contract will continue to beginning of production under new contract. 2. Where new contract is of short duration, it may constitute one period. 3. Price is based on projections which do not extend beyond end of first period. 4. Periods should conform with operation of contractor's cost accounting system and need not be of equal length. 5. Periods may be measured in time or production or delivery of items.	

Effect of Article	Conditions for Use
Form I–C Upward or downward price revision negotiated at fixed intervals, with retroactive revision at end of first period and prospective revision thereafter.	1. Contract is such that neither party should be bound by price for first period. First period not to extend beyond 40% of production under contract. 2. Price is based on projections not extending beyond end of first period. 3. Periods should conform with operation of contractor's cost accounting system and need not be of equal length. 4. Periods may be measured in time or production or delivery of items. 5. Article may provide for one repricing, both retroactive and prospective, in appropriate cases.
Form II–A Upward or downward price revision negotiated upon demand of either party, with prospective effect only, and subject to specified limitations on frequency of demands.	1. Contract is such that both parties should be bound by initial price. 2. Price is based on projections extending over life of entire contract, taking into account reasonably expected cost decreases. 3. Date before which first demand cannot be made is specified. Ninety-day limitation effective thereafter may be varied by chief of technical service.
Form II–B Upward or downward negotiated price revision, with first period fixed and subject to retroactive revision, and	1. Contract is such that neither party should be bound by initial price. 2. Price is based on projections not extend-

Effect of Article	Conditions for Use
with prospective revision thereafter upon demand of either party, subject to specified limitations on frequency of demands.	ing beyond completion of initial portion of contract. 3. Ninety-day limitation on frequency of demands may be varied by chiefs of technical service. 4. Percentage figure in paragraph (b) (1) of article to be kept as low as possible and never is to exceed 40%.
Form III Negotiated price revision in event of retroactive changes in wages, salaries or employment conditions ordered or authorized by War Labor Board or any other authorized Government Agency.	1. Contract must contain one of the Form I or Form II price revision articles. 2. Price must contain substantially no charge for changes in wages, salaries or employment conditions.
Form IV Downward price revision negotiated upon contracting officer's demand after completion or termination of contract.	1. Contract amount is $100,000 or less. 2. Initial price bears reasonable relationship to expected final price under contract. 3. Items are strictly developmental or experimental in character. 4. Contractor's cost accounting system is sufficient to show costs under contract.
Form V Downward or limited upward price revision negotiated after completion or termination of contract.	1. Maximum price does not exceed $1,000,000. 2. Contract calls for experimental or developmental items or services for tests in laboratories or field operations or similar experiments. 3. Form I–C or II–B cannot be used in contract. 4. Price is as close as circumstances permit. Maximum price bears reasonable relationship to initial price. 5. Contractor has or will establish adequate cost accounting system. 6. Prior written approval of Director, Purchases Division is required before article is used in any contract.
Form VI Upward or downward price revision negotiated upon happening of spec-	1. Contingency or basic assumption must be clearly stated in article. 2. Contingency must come within one of specified categories.

ified contingent event and limited to that event and its direct effect.

3. Certain events are excluded as possible contingencies.

4. Price contains no charge or allowance on account of specified contingency.

5. Article may be used even though one of Form I or Form II articles is used in same contract.

I-C, II-A, or II-B. Forms IV and V, which called for retroactive price revision, were applicable to developmental and experimental contracts only. Form VI provided revision in case some specified contingency materialized, such as inability to get a subassembly from a specified supplier or a change in freight costs as a result of government allocation or priority orders.

Incentive Contract. The services have sought continuously a fixed-price contract with an incentive reward tied directly to the specific accomplishments of the contractor in reducing his costs. As indicated above some of the CPFF contracts, especially those used by the Bureau of Ships, had such incentive provisions. The limitation of such schemes arose from the difficulty in estimating costs on which the initial schedule of fees was based, the problems of administering and auditing cost contracts, and the complications of post-audit by the General Accounting Office. Moreover, the upper limit to fees established by statute at seven per cent of estimated costs restricted the size of incentives which might be offered.

In an effort to circumvent these difficulties the Navy Department developed a fixed-price incentive contract which it used with some frequency after 1943 on large contracts for ships, air frames, and some ordnance items.[44] The War Department did not adopt this form of contract until late in the war and by June 30, 1945 had only one such contract in effect.[45]

The price under an incentive contract consists of the actual costs of production plus a profit which varies with actual costs in accordance with a formula specified in advance. There is,

44. For details of the Navy contract see NPD, pars. 10,565–10,566.
45. Production and Purchases Division, ASF, *op. cit.*, p. 156. See APR, par. 378 for the War Department incentive contract.

however, a ceiling price. If actual costs of production rise above this ceiling, the contractor absorbs all such costs, thus operating at a loss. If actual costs are below the ceiling, savings are shared between the government and the contractor on some prearranged basis. The final price is determined after completion of the contract and is based on the actual costs plus the profit indicated by the specified formula. Final costs are determined by negotiation on the basis of a statement of costs submitted by the contractor rather than by audit. The Navy has typically reserved the right to audit costs, however, if it has reason to question the cost data submitted on completion of the contract.

The profit schedule is worked out so that at a base cost, which the Navy considers a reasonable estimated cost, the contractor receives a moderate profit about equal to the fixed fee which would be allowed on a CPFF contract with the same estimated cost. This profit is less than a contractor might anticipate on a simple fixed-price contract because of the protection of the ceiling price. At costs above the base cost the contractor's dollar profit declines and at costs below the base his dollar profit increases. The formula for sharing savings in cost may be simple, say twenty five per cent to the contractor. Or it may provide for a large percentage of the savings in costs going to the contractor in the neighborhood of the ceiling price and a lower percentage as costs decline.

The Navy apparently believes that it has had considerable success with this type of contract. The prerequisites for success are three: (1) that the Navy should have a fairly accurate estimate of what reasonable costs should be; (2) that the contractor should have an adequate system of segregating costs on each incentive contract from other costs; and (3) that the two parties should have confidence in one another's willingness to negotiate final costs in an equitable manner. Perhaps the greatest danger in the use of this contract arises from failure to estimate base costs accurately. If base costs are estimated too high, the reward to the contractor becomes a reward for over-estimating costs rather than for controlling costs. Since many incentive contracts have covered production for a long period of time, some have included an escalation provision with respect to wages and material. This makes it possible to eliminate any contingency for wage or price increases in estimating the base cost. In this way one factor which might give rise to overestimating base costs is eliminated.

The fixed-price incentive contract developed by the Navy appears to be well adapted to large contracts, where the contractor's accounting system allows segregation of costs, and where there has been sufficient prior experience to make it possible for the two parties to agree in advance on a reasonable base cost. It provides a real incentive to the contractor to lower his costs and at the same time provides that the government will have a substantial share of the resulting savings. It has an advantage over the CPFF contract in that the final price depends upon negotiated actual costs and thereby eliminates continuous auditing by the services and post-audit by the General Accounting Office. This saves valuable manpower and other administrative costs to the government.

Other Contractual Provisions

The previous discussion has been confined primarily to the pricing provisions in contracts with the services. These contracts had, of course, many other clauses, some of which were more or less directly related to the pricing provisions of the contract while others were only incidental to our present problem. Many of these clauses were standard so-called "boiler plate" clauses required by either legislative or administrative order.[46]

Most contracts included a change clause specifying the procedures for effecting changes in specifications and corresponding changes in the contract prices. They also included a tax clause specifying what excise taxes were payable on goods used by the armed services and the procedures to be followed in case such excise taxes were changed. Contracts also included

46. For details concerning these various clauses see *Army Procurement Regulations* and *Navy Procurement Directives*.

standard clauses stating that they were subject to repricing under Title VIII of the Revenue Act of 1943 and specifying the conditions under which the contract should be subject to renegotiation. Other clauses specified the procedures for termination and the basis of remuneration in such event. Still other clauses specified the conditions of employment to be followed by the contractor in fulfilling his contract. These included a specific prohibition of discrimination against employees or applicants for employment because of race, creed, color, or national origin and a provision that the contractor was to abide by the Walsh-Healy Act in the payment of wages. Other clauses specified the conditions for inspection of goods supplied, for payments under the contracts, for the treatment of classified contracts, and for reports of evidences of espionage, sabotage, or subversive activities. Finally, most contracts had a disputes clause specifying the procedure to be followed in case of any dispute as to matter of facts in the administration of the contract.

The patent problems of the services gave rise to another series of contract clauses. Although this is not the place to review extensively the patent policies of the services during the recent war, brief reference will be made to three principal aspects of their patent policy. In the case of research and development contracts it was common practice for the services to leave to the contractor patent rights on inventions resulting from performance of the contract and to reserve to the government only a non-exclusive, royalty-free license. Sometimes there was in addition an option for the government to purchase a non-exclusive license under designated "background" patents necessary for military, naval, and defense purposes or a provision granting the government a free license under such "background" patents. In relatively few cases provisions were made for the assignment of patent titles to the government rather than to the contractor, but the record indicates that relatively little use was made of this provision. These patent clauses had the effect of providing industry with most commercial rights to patents resulting from research and development financed by the government. This policy has been criticized recently in a report by the Attorney General.[47]

It was also customary for the services to incorporate clauses specifying the liabilities which the services would assume in case of infringement suits brought against contractors for alleged infringement of patents in the performance of war contracts.[48] Finally, it should be mentioned that provision was made in accordance with Congressional statute for the review and adjustment of patent royalties paid by contractors on patents used in the performance of government contracts.[49] In view of the substantial increase in volume of many items subject to patents it was provided that the services might adjust royalty payments downwards. Upon notice of any adjustment of royalty payments the contractor was forbidden to pay royalties in excess of the stipulated amount for patent privileges used in the performance of war contracts.

Conclusion

The preceding discussion has indicated briefly the types of contractual instruments which were most frequently used by the services in World War II. It should be emphasized that these were simply the typical forms on which there were many variations. Each arrangement represented a different approach to the problem of allocating risk, providing incentives, and avoiding excessive profits under conditions of uncertainty concerning future costs. The success of each of the methods in attaining its objectives depended eventually upon the services and the contractor arriving at a reasonably accurate estimate of costs and in using this estimate to negotiate an equitable contract. There was no easy solution, no magic formula which circumvented the need for accurate and imaginative price and cost analysis and skillful negotiation.

47. For discussion of the services' policies see United States Department of Justice, *Investigation of Government Patent Practices and Policies*, 3 vols. (1947). For clauses used see APR, pars. 335.1–335.2 and NPD, par. 13,823.

48. APR, pars. 335.4–335.8 and NPD, pars. 13,821–13,823.

49. Pub. Law No. 768, 77th Cong., 2d Sess. (Oct. 31, 1942); APR, par. 1,112 and NPD, pars. 13,851–13,869.

X

PROBLEMS OF NEGOTIATION

THE development of a comprehensive policy and suitable contracting forms is not enough to insure the successful negotiation of contracts. There are four other prerequisites for success: (1) the selection and training of experienced personnel; (2) the development of methods of price and cost analysis; (3) the development of adequate sources of information; and (4) the development of cooperation with industry.

The prewar experience of the services had not provided them with experience in the use of negotiated contracts nor with the type of personnel necessary. Purchase by the formal competitive bid system did not require much business judgment or elaborate systems for obtaining and analyzing price and cost data. After the outbreak of the emergency leadership in the adoption of approved purchasing practices came from outside the services. It came in large part from the group of industrial purchasing specialists who were brought into the NDAC by Donald Nelson and later transferred to the services. These were joined by experts in production and finance, economists, accountants, and lawyers. These various groups were eventually molded into effective purchasing teams which pioneered in the adaptation of successful business practice to the needs of the services in war. Despite many difficulties and mistakes the accomplishments of these teams were substantial. The development of policy and its successful execution were dependent upon the abilities and perseverance of these men who contributed their several talents to the joint undertaking.

Personnel

The success of a well-conceived procurement program in time of war depends above all else upon the experience and training of the personnel who implement it. Good policies and procedures are not enough. Successful negotiation depends upon the development of a team of able men with varied talents who have been trained in the objectives and techniques of military procurement. The team will generally include negotiators, lawyers, accountants, and price analysts, as well as the technical men who design the product and production men who understand the contractor's production problems.

The key to successful purchasing lies in the good judgment of the negotiator and his sense of responsibility to all parties concerned. There is no magic formula for choosing such people. A successful negotiator must have imagination and aggressiveness as well as a conviction of the importance of his job. He must be able to lead a team of experts and to make the maximum use of specialized knowledge and experience of the members of his team. His principal purpose is to insure maximum and expeditious production. He must bring the particular deal to a successful conclusion upon terms which will encourage the contractor to be efficient in the use of labor and materials, realizing that this will generally involve the assumption by the contractor of some pricing risk.

With this in mind, there is something to be said for choosing people who have had experience in competitive industries in which the risks are great and in which success depends in large part upon aggressive buying. This suggests recruiting personnel with broad experience from mail order houses, department stores, and chain stores as well as from manufacturing concerns in fields such as the automotive, electrical, and radio industries. These sources, of course, are not the only ones from which capable personnel can be recruited. But it should be recognized that the negotiator has to resist many forces, within and outside of the services, which make for "conservative" or riskless pricing in which the incentives to efficiency may be absent. If the negotiator is to succeed in the task of incentive pricing, he must have a sympathy for the basic idea. It is clear that there are some lines of industry and finance which are more conducive to developing the appropriate attitudes than others.

It is important that the various members of the team receive careful instruction in the objectives of the program. The negotiator's job is not simply to conclude the deal, but rather in the light of all available data and the advice of his teammates to conclude a deal which will provide incentives to efficient and expeditious production. Likewise, the lawyer's function is not simply the narrow one of protecting the government by drafting a water-tight document, but rather to devise contractual arrangements tailored to the particular circumstances which, while protecting the government, will further the general plan of the negotiator. Finally, the tasks of the accountant and price analyst are not simply to record data on past transactions, but rather to collect and analyze all available data with as much imagination as possible and make it available in intelligible form to the negotiator.

It was unfortunate that during the last war time and facilities were not available early in the war to train members of the purchasing groups who were recruited from civilian life. While the policies and procedures adopted by the services during the war were patterned upon those developed by industry, it was necessary to use many who had not had wide industrial experience in these fields. Moreover, the objectives and procedures of government purchasing had certain characteristics which differed from those of private industry. It is possible, however, to devise training programs for negotiators, price analysts, and lawyers which would introduce them to the objectives and procedures of wartime purchasing in a very short period of time. Some steps in this direction were taken by the War Department when the Army Industrial College was reactivated in 1944 and more elaborate experience in this type of training was gained by both the War and Navy Departments in training personnel for the terminations and surplus property disposal programs.

The training program in the objectives and techniques of negotiation should not be confined solely to the purchase teams. Purchasing is not an independent function operating in isolation. It depends for its success upon the understanding and cooperation of the technical and production groups which draft specifications and often originate procurements. As has been argued above,[1] efficient purchasing cannot be effected if the function of drafting specifications is divorced from the function of purchasing. The technical requirements of the services can often be satisfied by products of several specifications. One of the considerations in choosing the product to be purchased is the relative costs of the alternatives. Successful purchasing policy depends upon the cooperation of the technical and production groups with the purchasing groups. It also depends upon the proper understanding of the objectives of the purchase groups by higher echelons. Consequently it is important that the technical and production groups as well as the higher echelons in the material services and bureaus should be well trained in the objectives and the techniques of the purchasing program.

Price and Cost Analysis

With the transition from competitive bidding to the negotiated contract the services found themselves without many of the traditional bench marks of good purchasing established by market forces. It was necessary to devise new methods and techniques of price analysis which would enable them to arrive at reasonable prices. The problem faced by the services was somewhat similar to that faced by public utility commissions in the regulation of public utility rates, but fortunately the legal framework in which the services worked was more favorable to aggressive pricing and experimentation.[2] The tools and techniques at hand were several.[3] They included all

1. See above, p. 33.
2. For discussion of problems of inducing efficient operation and cost control by utilities see John M. Clark, *Social Control of Business* (2nd ed., 1939), p. 346–349; Irston R. Barnes, *The Economics of Public Utility Regulation* (1942), chap. xviii. It would be profitable for our public utility regulatory authorities to review their present techniques in the light of the experiences of the services in pricing military procurements during the war.
3. For a discussion of these techniques see *Pricing in War Contracts*, Army Service Forces Manual M601 (Aug., 1943); G. A. Lloyd, *Law and Contemporary Problems*, X, 239–246.

those which are normally available to industrial purchasers. Moreover, the services' position was strengthened by their mandatory powers to acquire information and to determine prices. To be sure, the services were limited somewhat in their ability to press their advantage in negotiation with industry by the fact that they were agents of the government, subject to pressures of public and Congressional opinion. But the tools were available which, in the hands of experienced personnel, should have enabled the services to do a purchasing job which would compare favorably with that done by many of the most alert business organizations.

The first technique of price analysis is the development of active competition of an informal sort. Negotiation does not necessarily preclude competition. It precludes only the special formalized procedure required by Section 3709, a procedure which often reduces rather than fosters competitive forces. The extent to which rival bids can be developed under a system of negotiated purchases will depend upon the state of the market and the extent to which criteria for the selection of sources other than price narrow the market. But the selection of a source and negotiation of a contract should be done only after all possible sources have been considered and, wherever practicable, definite negotiations undertaken with several of them. This technique will not be as successful in war as in times of peace, but it should prove useful in some cases even in time of war. Part of the usefulness of this procedure arises from the incidental information which is gained from negotiations with several firms. Various companies will generally have different cost estimating systems, will pad their costs in different ways, or will view the inherent risks differently. The incidental intelligence arising from several preliminary negotiations will often do much to narrow the bargaining range. It remains true, however, that the development of informal competition may not be possible in many cases. This is especially true in time of war when all sources must be used. It is also true of most research and developmental work at all times. It will also be of limited use for production contracts following de-

velopmental contracts and in some repeat production contracts where new producers face large initial costs.

Another tool which may be used, even where active competition is not available, is the analysis of comparative prices.
Comparison of prices for different firms requires considerable
care to make allowance for all variables. The lowest price does
not necessarily represent the best contractual arrangement.
Allowance must be made for differences in volume, specifications, delivery schedules, government-furnished equipment,
the extent of government financing or government facilities,
and provisions for escalation or other price adjustment. Moreover, under the peculiar conditions of war production, it is
often not feasible for one firm to meet the prices of another
for legitimate reasons, such as differences in know-how, plant
layout, production process, type of equipment, the extent of
subcontracting, the labor supply, etc. Yet a high-cost firm
may be necessary to satisfy military requirements. Wartime
price policies clearly visualized differential pricing geared to
the peculiarities of each contractor. In certain areas, however,
particularly in the case of food, clothing, and many standard
commercial articles, comparative prices are of considerable
value even under wartime conditions. Moreover, differences
in quoted prices often suggest the need for closer examination
of costs. Comparisons of prices typically lead to further comparisons of costs and cost breakdowns, which in turn may suggest the need for careful study of the contractor's production
methods, his purchasing policies, or pricing methods.

In some areas, comparisons of price changes or of the trends
of prices are even more revealing than the comparison of the
level of prices. Where several firms convert to the production
of the same product, initial prices may vary substantially, due
either to differences in conditions of production or to differences in skill in negotiation. As contractors move into mass
production, they can anticipate a decline in costs with corresponding changes in prices. A failure of one contractor's
prices to follow the trend of others will often raise questions
which should lead to further investigations. The technique of

comparing price trends is also applicable to non-identical products where the production processes and other factors influencing cost are similar. Such comparisons will often raise more questions than they answer, but to the extent that they lead to more careful analysis of production methods, purchasing policies, or pricing methods, they serve their purpose. Even under wartime conditions, differences in price trends for products where costs are subject to similar influences call for an explanation.

To a very large extent successful pricing in wartime depends on good cost estimating. As developed above, differences in prices and price trends suggest the need for cost comparisons. But even in those many areas in which circumstances are such as to make cost comparisons meaningless, cost analysis is the key to incentive pricing.

The type of cost information which is available and the use to which it should be put will vary with different procurements. In some areas during the last war, *e.g.*, some ordnance items and ships, the services had good cost data based on operations in government-operated plants. In other cases the services can break a product down into its components and make reasonably accurate estimates of many of the components of cost. This, of course, requires persons skilled in production and purchasing. In still other cases the services can get a useful record of the contractor's costs for past operations either through the certification by the contractor as to his past costs or through government inspection and audit of the contractor's books. The availability and reliability of this previous cost data depend in large part upon the contractor's accounting system.

For the purpose of pricing future deliveries the important question is not past costs but future costs. Far too much emphasis has often been placed on the data on past operations and far too little attention given to estimating future costs. Actual costs on past operations are only the beginning point for estimating future costs. Moreover, for new products or even for old products produced by new companies there may be no past costs with much relevance to the problem. For these reasons much reliance must be placed upon cost estimates.

During World War II it was the practice of the services on all important procurements to require the contractor to submit a cost estimate on each contract together with a breakdown of the cost estimate into its components, for example, material, direct labor, manufacturing overhead, engineering expense, selling expense, administrative expense, and other cost factors. This cost breakdown was interpreted in the light of other price and cost data mentioned above and of past operating statements broken down, if possible, between renegotiable and non-renegotiable business. Often a budget of future overall operations was the focal point of all price analysis and price negotiation.

The reliability of a contractor's cost estimates depends on the nature of his cost-accounting system, the degree of uncertainty concerning the factors influencing future conditions, and the contractor's disposition to price closely. One of the important problems is to make certain that a contractor's cost-estimating system takes into account the effect of increased volume upon burden and overhead rates. Cost estimates based on normal rates will often overstate costs substantially under conditions of increased volume. Another problem is to insure that research and development costs and other non-recurring costs are broken down so that estimates of production costs will not be unduly inflated.

It is the function of those responsible for procurement to verify the reasonableness of these estimates through price and cost analysis and the art of negotiation. The methods for doing this are various. Where there are several firms producing an item, a comparison of estimates of material costs is significant. Where conditions of production do not vary greatly, a comparison of other elements of the cost estimate may be useful. Even where items are similar but not identical many elements other than material costs may be usefully compared.

Where there are no other producers of the same or similar items, cost comparisons between firms are not possible. There are, however, various other ways of analyzing a contractor's cost estimates. In some cases the service may find it feasible to set up a cost estimating unit of its own which will make separate estimates of the material and labor components. Since estimates of other components are often based on these two items, correct estimates of these are particularly important. If the contractor has produced the item in the past, it may be feasible to work from his previous costs. If these can be ascertained, they may be projected forward with appropriate allowances for changes in the prices of major materials and in wage rates. Where production is such that costs tend to decrease with additional output, it is sometimes possible to project past costs into the future by use of learning curves developed from past experience with cost trends on related items. Thus, cost analysts for ships and air frames have frequently found that the costs of most contractors on quite different models tend to follow a standard pattern as they move from the developmental stage into large-scale mass production.

A comparison of cost estimates with past operating statements will often prove enlightening. This is particularly fruitful where the bulk of a contractor's output is for one item or a series of items produced by similar processes and under similar conditions. The relation between components in the cost breakdown may be compared with the relation between similar components in the operating statement. If, for example, selling and administrative expense in the cost breakdown should appear as 15 per cent of the total cost, while in the past operating statement it appears as only 10 per cent, an explanation is in order. Likewise if the contractor anticipates greater volume in the future than in the past, failure of the selling and administrative expense to be estimated as a smaller percentage of total cost for the future will also call for an explanation.

An example taken from Navy experience will indicate the way in which a comparison of prices, cost breakdowns, and past operating statements may be used to illuminate a cost estimate.[4] In 1943 some four companies were producing four

4. Adopted from a Navy Department document, prepared by the Price Analysis Division, OP&M (no date).

different models of an important component of four different types of bombers. The prices varied all the way from $3,500 to $8,500. But these differences in price were in part due to differences in design. By 1944, however, it was noted that the prices of company X, the high-cost company, had declined only 9 per cent while prices of two other companies had declined 47 per cent and 30 per cent respectively. Since investigation revealed that 88 per cent of the business of company X was in the production of this one item, it was clear that a comparison of its cost estimates on the particular item with its past operating statement would be relevant. Company X's past cost estimates on contracts in production in 1943 had included an estimated profit of 6 per cent, but its operating statement for the year 1943 showed that it actually made profits of 19 per cent on sales. A comparison of its estimated cost breakdowns submitted on contracts in production during 1943 with its actual operating statement for the year indicated that estimates of manufacturing overhead and labor expense had been overly generous. Yet the new cost breakdown submitted for 1944 production showed a pattern very similar to its previous estimates. This analysis suggested the need for a detailed audit of actual costs and resulted in a lowering of X's prices on 1945 operations from $8,500 to $6,150 per unit.

The methods of cost and price analysis are various. The best techniques and their merits will vary from one contract to another and from one time to another. In the early stages of procurement they will be least effective. New products, new firms, and new techniques involve too many uncertainties for accurate cost estimating. Experience in World War II indicated, however, that as the procurement program progressed costs became more stable, additional information became available, and staff became more skilled. Consequently, it was possible as time went on to do an increasingly better job of cost and price analysis. Planning in advance for price and cost analysis should make it possible to do effective work earlier in a future emergency.

Sources of Price and Cost Data

A successful program of price and cost analysis depends upon careful planning of methods and techniques for collecting the requisite information. Price data on past procurements can be collected and analyzed by the services from the record of past contracts. Both the War and Navy Departments developed such programs during the last war. Some of the summary results of these studies are presented below in Chapter XIII. The most important price data for procurement, however, are not the summary indexes presented below but the basic price series from which these indexes were derived. But the indexes and subindexes themselves are of some value in so far as they indicate trends in prices on related items with which the price trends of particular firms may be compared.

Data on each contractor's over-all operations were developed during the war in connection with renegotiation and the company pricing programs.[5] This included much general information concerning the products and operations of the contractor as well as detailed balance sheets and profit and loss statements. The annual data collected by the renegotiation boards, although often out of date by the time it was available to procurement officers, had the advantage of segregating costs and revenues between renegotiable and non-renegotiable business. The company pricing program made a particular effort to get interim financial data on a quarterly basis wherever possible. For many companies quarterly financial data were also filed with OPA under the financial reporting program sponsored by that agency.[6]

The cost inspection groups, particularly those assigned to firms with CPFF contracts, had a good deal of information about the cost systems and cost estimating methods of the

5. For discussion of the company pricing program see below, Chapter XII.
6. See Office of Temporary Controls, Office of Price Administration, Office of Research, *Corporate Profits 1936–1946, Part I, Profits Growth to Wartime Peak* (1947), "War Profits Study," No. 16; also Federal Trade Commission, *Reports on War Time Costs and Profits for Manufacturing Corporations, 1941–1945* (Oct. 6, 1947).

larger firms with which they worked. These groups were also available for special cost studies whenever these seemed desirable in a particular negotiation.

Equally fruitful as a source of data were the negotiations themselves. As has been pointed out, it was customary to require the filing of an estimated cost breakdown in each major procurement. While a single unsupported cost breakdown in itself may be of little value, a series of such breakdowns in connection with other data may prove very illuminating. Moreover, skillful negotiation can do much to smoke out missing information and to reduce the bargaining area. Thus, an initial CPFF contract calling for conversion to a fixed-price contract or a maximum-price contract calling for redetermination are devices which make it possible to postpone fixing a price until more information is available. Consequently, the choice of contractual arrangement which is proposed to the contractor as a basis of negotiation may be dictated by the information which it is desired to obtain as well as by the immediate objective of correct pricing.

Perhaps the greatest problem of the services lies in providing procedures by which all the information available to them and relevant to a particular negotiation can be brought to bear on the negotiation. This is particularly difficult because of the functional and geographical decentralization of purchasing operations. Unification of the armed services may reduce these problems somewhat through elimination of duplicating procurement groups, but functional and geographical decentralization of purchasing operations is sure to persist. Moreover, the problem of integrating the activities of renegotiation and company pricing groups with one another and with original procurement will remain. Considerable progress was made in developing procedures for rapid interchange of information between the relevant groups during the recent war. In planning for another war, particular attention should be given to improving the methods by which all pertinent information can be brought to bear upon each negotiation, particularly in the early period of mobilization.

Cooperation with Industry

The cooperation of the services and industry in the purchasing program is an equally important prerequisite to success. The development of a common purpose and mutual respect can do much to simplify operations and facilitate the whole mobilization program. The calibre and attitude of the purchasing personnel selected by the services will do much to determine the extent of cooperation. It is clear that much of the success in the last war was due to the respect in which many of the procurement personnel were held by contractors. Another means for developing a common purpose is to provide for consultation with industry in the formulation of major policies. This can be done in advance of an emergency but it must also be continued throughout the period of crisis or war. It is inevitable that policies and procedures will change. If industry is to be expected to adapt itself readily to changing policies, it is important that broadly representative groups from industry be given an opportunity to express their opinions on major changes of policies and procedures. Finally, once policies and procedures have been settled, it is important that the policies and procedures as well as the major objectives should be explained carefully to contractors and their interested employees. This can be done through the press and trade journals, through trade associations and other industrial groups, and through the organization of procurement clinics and industrial training programs. Relatively little of this was done in connection with procurement during the recent war. The services did, however, develop such programs of cooperation with industry in connection with the programs of terminations and disposal of surplus property. The highly satisfactory experience with reference to these programs indicates the advantages which may flow from systematic attempts to develop cooperation with industry through prior consultation and systematic exposition of policies, procedures, and objectives. The Industrial College of the Armed Forces is currently working along similar lines in peacetime.

XI

PROCUREMENT AND THE LEVEL OF PROFITS

In view of the discussions between the wars concerning war "profiteers," it is not surprising that considerable attention was given to the profits of war contractors during World War II. One approach to the problem was the attempt to negotiate contract prices which would not yield "unconscionable profits." But the problem of profits was also attacked by the imposition of excess profits taxes and the introduction of renegotiation.

There are substantial differences between the problems of developing a profit policy on military contracts in peace and in war. In peacetime the services must depend upon profit incentives to induce contractors to produce military goods. Consequently peacetime profit policy will generally be determined by conditions in civilian markets which are in large part outside the services' control. Only in the case of certain industries in which the services' purchases represent a large share of total output, such as aircraft and shipbuilding, do they have much latitude to determine profit policy. In such markets they are responsible consciously or unconsciously for the general level of profits. They have a degree of freedom to formulate a positive policy for profits in such industries, limited only by the inducements necessary to maintain the scale of investment required to satisfy their needs.

In wartime the problem is substantially different. The unlimited demand of the services for goods and the development of scarcities on a broad scale leads to a condition in which profits may increase almost without limit. On the other hand, it is no longer so necessary to use profit incentives alone as an inducement to the allocation of resources to military needs because of the direct controls over the use of materials, productive capacity, and labor which serve to shake resources loose from the civilian economy for the production of military goods. Unrestricted profits in a major war will serve no purpose either in allocating resources or in inducing efficiency in the use of labor and materials. Moreover, unrestricted profits will be destructive of both civilian and military morale.

The problem of controlling profits in wartime is made difficult by the fact that war profits may develop for any of several reasons. First, many profits develop because of the great increase in the volume of production incidental to the war. This greater volume makes it possible to distribute overhead and general administrative expenses over more units of production so that with prewar prices the rate of profits on sales or on net worth is increased substantially. A second source of wartime profits is the inability of the government and contractors to negotiate reasonable prices because of other uncertainties affecting costs such as wages, material prices, or availability of labor or because of lack of personnel to estimate costs and negotiate such prices. A third source of profits arises from the willfulness of a small fringe of contractors who take advantage of war conditions to raise their prices. In some cases this may be the result of collusive or monopolistic action, but under wartime conditions market forces can lead to substantial price increases even without such action. Finally, some profits are the result of the efficiency of the contractors' operations. Whether because of their facilities, careful management, the superior morale of their labor force, or control of patented devices or secret processes, some contractors are able to produce at substantially less cost than others.

Vinson-Trammell Act

The interwar years saw a great deal of concern with the profits of munitions makers. Although Congress debated the problem at length, the sole attempt at the direct control of profits on military procurement during the interwar years was that embodied in the so-called Vinson-Trammell legislation.[1] This was peacetime legislation applicable only to the shipbuilding and aircraft industries and aimed at profits rather than prices. Upon the approach of war it proved inadequate and was suspended.

The immediate occasion for the legislation was the proposal in early 1934 to authorize the construction of certain vessels which would bring the composition of the Navy up to the limits established by treaties signed at the Washington Conference in 1922. An amendment limiting profits was incorporated in the act at the insistence of Representative C. W. Tobey [2] despite the objections of the Navy Department that the proposal was unworkable and would be expensive to administer.[3] This amendment provided that on all contracts or subcontracts for construction of complete naval vessels, naval aircraft, or any portion thereof where the award exceeded $10,000, the allowable profit was to be limited to 10 per cent of the total contract price.[4] The contractor or subcontractor was required to file with the Navy Department upon the completion of each separate contract or subcontract a report showing his profit thereon and to pay direct to the Treasury any excess over the allowable profit. Persons subject to the act were required to maintain records adequate to segregate costs on particular contracts. Accounting principles to be applied in estimating costs and methods of ascertaining excess profits were to be determined by the Secretary of the Treasury in agreement with the Secretary of the Navy.

This in effect provided a maximum profit of 10 per cent of the contract price. Up to the point where the contractor made such profit he had an incentive to reduce costs, but any

1. For brief history of the act and statement of procedures thereunder see *Statement of Treasury Department Regarding Profit-Limiting Provisions of the Vinson-Trammell Act and Procedure Thereunder*, reprinted in United States Senate, Hearings before the Subcommittee of the Committee on Finance, 77th Cong., 2d Sess., *Renegotiation of Contracts* (1942), pp. 96–115. See also H. S. Hensel and R. G. McClung, *Law and Contemporary Problems*, X, 202–205, 213.

2. 78 Cong. Rec. 1629.

3. United States Senate, Hearings before Committee on Naval Affairs, on H.R. 6604, 73d Cong., 2d Sess., *Construction of Certain Naval Vessels* (1934), *passim*.

4. 48 Stat. 505, sec. 3 (March 27, 1934).

cost reductions below a level equal to 90 per cent of the contract price reverted to the Treasury. Thus the Vinson-Trammell Act placed upon the contractor more risk and more incentive to efficiency than a straight CPFF contract, while at the same time it left the contractor with less incentive to efficiency than a fixed-price contract without profit limitation. It should be noted that this arrangement differed from the CPPC contract in that the maximum profit was based on the contract price fixed in advance and not upon his costs.[5] An excessively high initial contract price, however, had the effect of increasing the allowable profit.

In 1936 the act was amended so as to simplify its administration and to allow the offset of losses against profits.[6] This amendment permitted the prime contractor or subcontractor to combine all such contracts or subcontracts completed in any tax-year when estimating profits on contracts subject to profit limitation. In consequence the contractor might offset excess profits on one contract against losses or deficiencies of profits on other contracts. It was pointed out that this process of averaging profits was the method used in determining profits under the income tax law and would place contractors subject to the Vinson-Trammell Act on a basis of equality with other contractors. Otherwise a contractor subject to the Vinson-Trammell Act might net less than another contractor not subject to the act who had the same volume of contracts and same distribution of profits thereon.[7] This amendment also simplified the accounting problems for many contractors and the problem of auditing by the Treasury. The 1936 amendments provided further that a contractor or subcontractor who incurred a net loss in one year on contracts subject to profit limitation might take the loss as a credit in determining excess profits, if any, in the next succeeding year.

5. For the contrary view see Hensel and McClung, *op. cit.*, p. 213.
6. 49 Stat. 1926 (June 25, 1936).
7. For examples of the way in which contractors subject to the Vinson-Trammell Act might be discriminated against due to inability to average profits see United States Senate, Hearings before Committee on Naval Affairs on H.R. 5730, 74th Cong., 2d Sess., *To Amend the Act Establishing the Composition of the U.S. Navy* (1936), pp. 30–32.

In 1939 the provisions of the Vinson-Trammell Act were extended to Army aircraft in order to place the War and Navy Departments on an equal footing.[8] At the same time the allowable profit on aircraft for both the War and Navy Departments was raised from 10 per cent to 12 per cent while the allowable profit on naval vessels remained at 10 per cent. The carry-over provisions were liberalized with respect to aircraft only to allow a contractor or subcontractor to carry forward any net loss as a credit against excess profits, if any, during any of the next four income-taxable years. Moreover, if his profit in any year on contracts subject to the act was less than 12 per cent, he might carry forward such deficiency as a credit in determining excess profits during the next succeeding four income-tax years. These liberalized carry-over provisions were not applicable to naval vessels.

Prior to the acceleration of the defense program in the summer of 1940 no serious difficulty seems to have arisen from these profit limitations. In 1936 the Secretary of the Navy reported that the act had "been administered with little difficulty and with little criticism on the part of contractors."[9] In 1940 the Secretary of War reporting on the experience of the War Department during the first year in which its aircraft procurements had been subject to the act stated that "no major difficulties in aircraft procurement occurred as a result of the profit-limitation provisions."[10] But in June, 1940 when a rapid expansion of the services was contemplated, the maximum allowable profit on naval vessels and on Army and Navy aircraft was reduced to 8 per cent of the total contract price.[11] In order to remove the incentive for negotiating contracts with excessively high prices, thereby increasing the allowable profit, it was further provided that any profit in excess of 8.7 per cent of the cost of performing a contract (except in the case of prime contracts on a CPFF basis) should be considered to be a profit in excess of 8 per cent of the total

8. 53 Stat. 560, sec. 14 (April 3, 1939).
9. Secretary of the Navy, *Annual Report*, 1936, p. 24.
10. Secretary of War, *Annual Report*, 1940, p. 2.
11. 54 Stat. 677, sec. 2 (June 28, 1940).

contract price.[12] This in effect established the allowable profit at 8 per cent of the contract price or 8.7 per cent of the cost, whichever was lower. This reduction in allowable profit from 10 per cent on naval vessels or 12 per cent on aircraft to 8 per cent on both was made upon the initiative of the Senate in view of the expanded defense program and "the resulting opportunity for greater efficiency in operation and for spreading general and overhead expenses." [13] At the same time in order to encourage competition of small contractors and subcontractors and simplify the administration of the act it was provided that, for the duration of the national emergency, the profit-limiting provisions should be applicable only to contracts or subcontracts exceeding $25,000.[14]

These amendments of June, 1940 never became effective. The War and Navy Departments soon faced serious difficulties in placing new contracts.[15] This was particularly true of aircraft procurements. As a result of French and British orders for aircraft the prime contractors had a large backlog of orders.[16] While they had been making only about 4 per

12. Since the act provided for awarding of contracts on the basis of negotiation rather than competitive bidding, it was feared that the services might use their discretionary powers to negotiate high contract prices for the purpose of inflating dollar profits. See United States Senate, Hearings before Committee on Naval Affairs on H.R. 9822, 76th Cong., 3d Sess., *To Expedite Naval Shipbuilding* (1940), p. 91 *et seq.*

13. Senate Report No. 1863, 76th Cong., 3d Sess. (1940), p. 8.

14. 54 Stat. 677, sec. 3 (June 28, 1940).

15. See testimony of Secretary of War, Joint Hearings before House Committee on Ways and Means and Senate Committee on Finance, 76th Cong., 3d Sess., *Excess Profits Taxation, 1940* (1940), p. 24 and testimony by Assistant Secretary of the Navy, *ibid.*, p. 29; also United States Senate, Hearings before Subcommittee of Committee on Appropriations, 76th Cong., 3d Sess., *Second Supplemental National Defense Appropriation Bill for 1941*, pp. 68–69, 74, 190. Secretary of War, *Annual Report*, 1940, p. 3; Secretary of the Navy, *Annual Report*, 1940, p. 28.

16. For a summary of the importance of foreign purchases of aircraft in 1939 and 1940 see Industrial College of the Armed Forces, *Foreign Purchasing Competition before the Lend-Lease Act* (1946), "Study of Experience in Industrial Mobilization in World War II." Until the summer of 1940 aircraft and aircraft parts and accessories constituted between 70 per cent and 90 per cent of the value of military goods for which export licenses were granted (*ibid.*, pp. 57–58). By January of 1940 the leading aircraft manufacturers had a current backlog of orders of $533,000,000, equal to about 80 per cent of their rated annual capacity (*ibid.*, p. 58). During the first four months of 1940 additional licenses for export

cent on contracts previously [17] and consequently the profit limitations had not come into effect, they were now loaded down with lucrative foreign contracts. Moreover, the subcontractors on whom they depended increasingly for castings, parts, and subassemblies were resisting orders subject to profit limitations in favor of civilian orders or orders for other munitions free from such limitations.[18] It was clear that a profit limitation system, applying to only part of the munitions field, would interfere seriously with production of essential equipment under conditions approximating full utilization of specialized resources so long as industry was left a significant degree of freedom to accept or reject orders. Accordingly on September 9, 1940 at the request of the services and of the Council of National Defense, contracts and subcontracts for Army and Navy aircraft were exempted from the profit limitations.[19] Finally, when Congress enacted general excess profits legislation on October 8, 1940, all profit limitations under the Vinson-Trammell Act were suspended on contracts entered into after December 31, 1939 or uncompleted by October 8 by contractors or subcontractors who were subject to the excess profits tax.[20] This placed all industry, civilian or military, on an equal basis.

The Vinson-Trammell Act was clearly impossible as a wartime technique for controlling profits because of its limited applicability. If it had been generalized to apply to all military procurement, it might have been workable after effective priorities had been imposed. But even then it had the disadvantage of inflexibility in the level of allowable profit since it made no distinction between contractors as to the amount of

---

of aircraft and aircraft parts and accessories were issued to the extent of $89,431,974 (*ibid.*, p. 64). "The rate of increase was rapidly rising so that approximately 100 per cent more planes were licensed for export in the first four months of 1940 than in the last six months of 1939" (*ibid.*, p. 58).

17. United States Senate, Hearings before Subcommittee of Committee on Appropriations, 76th Cong., 3d Sess., *Second Supplemental National Defense Bill for 1941*, p. 80.

18. See testimony of General Arnold on Aug. 5, 1940, *ibid.*, p. 74 *et seq.*; also Admiral Furlong, *ibid.*, p. 190.

19. 54 Stat. 883 (Sept. 9, 1940).

20. 54 Stat. 1003, sec. 401 (Oct. 8, 1940).

their investment, the extent of subcontracting, the character and amount of risk involved, and many other factors which influence normal profit differences. The argument that it imposed substantial accounting burdens on industry and the government was of some validity, but the experience with renegotiation indicates in retrospect that this problem was not insuperable.

As a peacetime procedure for controlling the excesses of profits, it is not at all clear that the act was a failure. The Treasury reported that up to August 31, 1942 the total recovery had been $7,452,635.61 on Navy vessels and Navy aircraft and $70,068.02 on Army aircraft.[21] The small recovery on Army contracts is accounted for by the fact that the legislation only applied to contracts completed between April 3, 1939 and October 8, 1940 and also to the fact that this industry had evidently been a low profit industry until the placement of foreign contracts in 1939. There is no evidence, however, that prior to 1940 the act had caused the services any difficulties. In fact both the services testified to the contrary.[22] But the period from 1934 to 1939 was one of a substantial amount of unutilized resources. It is probable that under other peacetime conditions with quite a high level of employment of resources, such profit limitations would have seriously interfered with procurement. The Vinson-Trammell Act, which became inoperative upon passage of the Excess Profits Act in 1940, became operative again with the repeal of the excess profits tax in November, 1945.[23] The services, however, have requested that the act be repealed. This seems to have been a wise move. During peacetime there is a danger that the profitability of alternative employments will make contractors unwilling to take military contracts subject to such profit limitations. Moreover, it seems probable

21. United States Senate, Hearings before Subcommittee of the Committee on Finances, 77th Cong., 2d Sess., *Renegotiation of Contracts* (1942), pp. 97-98.
22. See above, p. 166, notes 9 and 10.
23. By the Revenue Act of 1945 contracts for naval vessels and aircraft entered into during a taxable year beginning after December 31, 1945 are subject to the Vinson-Trammell limitations. 59 Stat. 557 (Nov. 8, 1945).

that such limitations on profits will not be conducive to efficiency.

Renegotiation Statutes

The suspension of the Vinson-Trammell Act in October, 1940 represented a recognition of the paramount importance of profit incentives to industry in the expansion of aircraft and vessel capacity. In the absence of more effective direct controls over industrial production, of a type which we were not prepared to invoke in 1940, direct controls over the profits on military contracts were not feasible. The excess profits tax, applicable to all business, was relied upon to reduce the extraordinary profits accruing from the war for all producers, whether concerned with civilian or military production.[24] So long as the defense program was being imposed voluntarily on the civilian economy, a general excess profits tax seemed the only feasible method. This did not imply, however, that Congress or the public were indifferent to profits on military contracts.

As a matter of fact from the time the Vinson-Trammell Act was suspended in the fall of 1940 until the institution of statutory renegotiation in April, 1942 there was continuous public concern with the problem. In the first half of 1941 both the House Naval Affairs Committee [25] and the Truman Committee [26] began investigating profits of manufacturers and shipbuilders. In its report on January 15, 1942 the Truman Committee recommended that "some form of substantial review" be instituted so "that defense contractors will be prevented from taking advantage of the Government." [27] The report of the House Naval Affairs Committee on January

24. 54 Stat. 975 (Oct. 8, 1940).
25. United States House of Representatives, Committee on Naval Affairs, House Report No. 1634, *Investigation of the National Defense Program* (1942), 77th Cong., 2d Sess.
26. United States Senate, Hearings before Special Committee Investigating the National Defense Program, 77th Cong., 1st Sess., *Investigation of the National Defense Program* (1941), Part 5.
27. Senate Report No. 480, Part 5, 77th Cong., 2d Sess. (1942), p. 43.

20 summarized extensive studies of contractors' profits. While it found that "neither industry as a whole nor the major part of industry should be criticized," it recommended that "some method of profit limitation should be adopted to eliminate profiteering on defense contracts." [28] It pointed out that it had been cooperating with the Navy Department in voluntary renegotiation of some contractors whose excessive profits were large. Much publicity was subsequently given to committee hearings on the profits of Jack and Heintz Inc.[29] and other contractors.

Meanwhile the services, spurred on by the increasing evidence of excessive profits, began to initiate voluntary programs of renegotiation by which they recovered excessive profits already earned and negotiated price reductions on future deliveries.[30] The Navy had been particularly concerned with ship repair and alteration contracts on which there had been considerable evidence of excessive profits.

From late January the services redoubled their efforts to find some solution to the problem. The issue was finally brought to a head on March 28, 1942 when the House of Representatives adopted the Case Amendment providing for renegotiation of contract prices to eliminate all profits above 6 per cent.[31] The services were vigorously opposed to this proposal because it failed to provide sufficient flexibility and was likely to reduce incentives to efficiency.[32] Subsequently the services worked out with Senator McKellar and the subcommittee of the Senate Committee on Appropriations an alternative proposal. This contained the basic outline of the

28. House Report No. 1634, 77th Cong., 2d Sess., p. 26.
29. United States House of Representatives, Hearings before Committee on Naval Affairs, 77th Cong., 2d Sess., *Investigation of the Naval Defense Program,* vol. 1, March 23 and 25 and April 13, 1942, *passim.*
30. Affidavit of H. S. Hensel, *U.S. v. Alexander Wool Combing Co.,* U.S. District Court for District of Massachusetts, Civil No. 4121, pp. 39–49. Affidavit of Robert P. Patterson, *U.S. v. Alexander Wool Combing Company,* U.S. District Court for District of Massachusetts, Civil No. 4121, pp. 24–28.
31. 88 Cong. Rec. 3139–3140.
32. United States House of Representatives, Hearings before Committee on Naval Affairs, 77th Cong., 2d Sess., *Investigation of the Naval Defense Program* (1942), pp. 2473–2475, 2493–2517, 2577–2578.

renegotiation statute as finally adopted except for inclusion
of section (f) which provided a graduated scale of maximum
profit percentages ranging from 10 per cent on the first
$100,000 of the contract price to 2 per cent on everything
over $50,000,000. The services indicated that they were agree-
able to the McKellar proposal except for this section. A
substitute minus the controversial section (f) was finally
adopted.[33] The renegotiation statute gave formal recognition
to practices of informal renegotiation which the services had
been working out gradually in the preceding months. This
statute with minor clarifying amendments served as a basis
for renegotiation of war contractors for the years 1942 and
1943.[34]

The Renegotiation Act as amended in the fall of 1942 provided that the services, the Maritime Commission and the
Treasury might renegotiate the contracts of all prime contractors or subcontractors whose total renegotiable contracts exceeded $100,000 for the fiscal year.[35] All business for the end

33. Pub. Law No. 528, 77th Cong., 2d Sess., sec. 403, April 28, 1942 (56 Stat.
245).

34. The statute was amended on October 21, 1942 (Pub. Law No. 753, 77th
Cong., 2d Sess.) in line with recommendations of the contracting agencies. The
more important amendments at this time were as follows: (1) provided for renegotiation of contracts by the Treasury Department; (2) defined "excessive
profits" and "subcontracts"; (3) clarified procedures for recapturing excess
profits from subcontractors; (4) authorized renegotiation on an over-all basis;
(5) legalized the practice of the Treasury in allowing a contractor held liable
for repayment of excessive profits an offset of income and excess-profits taxes
already paid; (6) spelled out the exemptions from renegotiation. On July 1, 1943
the act was further amended to cover business under contracts with the Defense
Plant Corporation, Metals Reserve Company, Defense Supplies Corporation and
Rubber Reserve Company (Pub. Law No. 108, 78th Cong., 1st Sess.). On July 14,
1943 the act was amended to provide for renegotiation of fees or commissions
paid for procuring government contracts or subcontracts (Pub. Law No. 149,
78th Cong., 1st Sess.).

35. For more detailed discussion of the renegotiation statute see the symposium
published by *Law and Contemporary Problems*, X (Autumn, 1943), especially
W. John Kenney, "Coverage and Exemptions"; William Marbury and Robert
R. Bowie, "Renegotiation and Procurement"; Carman G. Blaugh, "Renegotiation
Standards and Practices"; Paul B. Boyd, "Administrative Machinery and Procedures." For an excellent discussion of the substantive effects of the renegotiation policies by the WPB representative on all three of the early renegotiation
boards see T. H. Saunders, "Renegotiation of Contract Prices," *Harvard Business
Review*, XXI (Winter, 1943), 164–182. See also N. C. Parkin, "Renegotiation of

use of the government was subject to renegotiation with some limited exceptions, especially "for the product of a mine, oil or gas well, or other mineral or natural deposit, or timber, which has not been processed, refined, or treated beyond the first form or state suitable for industrial use." [36] Moreover, the Secretary of each Department was authorized at his discretion to exempt contracts or subcontracts where "the profits can be determined with reasonable certainty when the contract price is established" and a portion of a contract or subcontract if the "provisions of the contract are otherwise adequate to prevent excessive profits." [37]

In February, 1944 the statute was amended and extended until December 31, 1944 with the proviso that if the President found, no later than December 1, 1944, "that competitive conditions [had] not been restored" he might extend renegotiation for a further period not to exceed six months.[38] Renegotiation was subsequently extended by the President until June 30, 1945 [39] and by Congress until December 31, 1945.[40] Although the amendments on February, 1944 affected rene-

War Contract Prices," *The Journal of Business*, XVII (April, 1944), 91–103; R. F. Watt, "Renegotiation: A Conscience for Procurement," *University of Chicago Law Review*, XI (April, 1944), 230–257; W. G. Katz, "Renegotiable Sales and Profits," *University of Chicago Law Review*, XI (April, 1944), 258–270; G. F. James, "Renegotiation: An Answer to a Problem," *University of Chicago Law Review*, XI (April, 1944), 204–221; G. M. Ferrand, "Renegotiation Legislation," *Columbia Law Review*, XLIV (March, 1944), 216–239; Richard C. Osborn, "Statutory Renegotiation, A Critique," *The Accounting Review*, XXII (April, 1947), 175–186. For a discussion of the way in which the renegotiation statute has fared in the courts, see John F. Sonnett and Robert Roy Dann, "Renegotiation in the Courts," *The Federal Bar Journal* (July, 1946). See also the *Report on Renegotiation of War Contracts* by the House Committee on Naval Affairs (House Report No. 733, 78th Cong., 1st Sess., 1943) and by the Truman Committee (Senate Report No. 10, Part 5, 78th Cong., 1st Sess., 1933) for discussion of the first year of experience with the act. For official history of the Navy's activities see Robert J. H. Powell, *History of Navy Department Renegotiation* (1947), 3 vols.

36. 56 Stat. 985.

37. *Loc. cit.*

38. Title VII of Revenue Act of 1943, Pub. Law No. 235, 78th Cong., 2d Sess. (58 Stat. 88).

39. Proclamation 2631, Nov. 14, 1944.

40. Pub. Law No. 104, 79th Cong., 1st Sess. (June 20, 1945). See United States House of Representatives, Hearings before Committee on Ways and Means, 79th Cong., 1st Sess., *Extension of Termination Date of Renegotiation Act* (1945).

gotiation very little in a substantive way, the changes in procedures were considerable. Under these amendments renegotiation was made the responsibility of a War Contracts Board consisting of six members representing each of the interested agencies. The War Contracts Board, however, delegated its administrative responsibility for renegotiation to the various contracting agencies reserving to itself determination of policy and general supervision. The statutory limit on exemption of renegotiable sales was raised from $100,000 to $500,000. Appeal was provided from decisions of the War Contracts Board to the Tax Court of the United States. The amended statute also provided some general standards to be considered in making a determination of excessive profits. Finally, the mandatory exemptions from renegotiation were extended and defined in more detail and the War Contracts Board was given discretionary power to grant exemptions where competitive conditions were such as to result "in effective competition with respect to . . . price" or in the case of standard commercial articles where "competitive conditions . . . will reasonably protect the Government against excessive prices."

The services insisted from the first that the renegotiation statute was basically a pricing statute designed as an integral part of the procurement process.[41] Its purpose was primarily to effect reasonable prices and not as a device to recapture past profits. It was on this basis that they distinguished renegotiation of *excessive* profits from taxation of *excess* profits. But the procedures which were actually worked out by the renegotiation boards under the original statute and which were continued in much the same way under the subsequent revisions placed the principal emphasis on recapture. Renegotiation came to be increasingly divorced from procurement in both philosophy and administration.

41. See Marbury and Bowie, *op. cit.*, pp. 218–231; W. John Kenney, "Renegotiation of War Contracts," lecture before Practicing Law Institute of New York, October 7, 1943, pp. 34–37, 92.

The repricing of future deliveries was left to officials responsible for the original procurement and was undertaken for the most part independent of the renegotiation process. This is to be explained on various grounds. During the early stages of renegotiation it appeared to be impossible to work out a procedure of repricing which could effect an expeditious handling of the thousands of cases awaiting renegotiation. The difficulties inherent in this problem led to the increasing separation of procurement and renegotiation groups. The latter, subject to continuous criticism from industry and investigation by Congress, were concerned with expeditious handling of the problem in a manner which would clear government and industry alike of charges of excessive profits and would at the same time induce general cooperation by industry. Many contractors had a genuine desire to be cleared of charges of excessive profits in an expeditious manner and at the same time to avoid undue risk. Repricing of future deliveries involved risk because it necessitated considerable crystal gazing, while recapture of excessive profits already earned offered a comparatively riskless method of inflicting necessary pain. The compromise was clear.

The procedures marked out by the renegotiation boards were designed to expedite and simplify the process. They provided that each contractor should be assigned to one department for the renegotiation of all his contracts subject to the act. After preliminary attempts to renegotiate each contract separately, it was decided that renegotiation should be on an over-all basis, covering all renegotiable business for a fiscal year. This made it possible to proceed on the basis of a general balance sheet and operating statement, appropriately adjusted to eliminate non-renegotiable business, and to avoid special cost and profit studies of each contract. The Joint Statement on Principles adopted by the interested services and departments provided that, in determining the existence and amount of excessive profits, the price adjustment boards would be guided by the following broad principles:

(a) That the stimulation of quantity production is of primary importance.

(b) That reasonable profits in every case should be determined with reference to the particular performance factors present without limitation or restriction by any fixed formula with respect to rate of profit, or otherwise.

(c) That the profits of the contractor ordinarily will be determined on his war business as a whole for a fiscal period, rather than on specific contracts separately, with the possible exception of certain construction contracts. Fixed price contracts are negotiated separately from fees on cost-plus-fixed-fee contracts.

(d) That as volume increases the margin of profit should decrease. That is particularly true in those cases where the amount of business done is abnormally large in relation to the amount of the contractor's own capital and company-owned plant, and where such production is made possible only by capital and plant furnished by the Government.

(e) That in determining what margin of profit is fair, consideration should be given to the corresponding profits in pre-war base years of the particular contractor and for the industry, especially in cases where the war products are substantially like pre-war products. It should not be assumed, however, that under war conditions a contractor is entitled to as great a margin of profit as that obtained under competitive conditions in normal times.

(f) That the reasonableness of profits should be determined before provision for Federal income and excess profits taxes.

(g) That a contractor's right to a reasonable profit and his need for working capital should be distinguished. A contractor should not be allowed to earn excessive profits on war contracts merely because he lacks adequate working capital in relation to a greatly increased volume of business.[42]

Under Secretary Patterson and Under Secretary Forrestal had previously announced the "broad rule" that "the margin of profit which a company makes on its expanded war sales

42. *Joint Statement by the War, Navy and Treasury Departments and the Maritime Commission: Purposes, Principles, Policies, and Interpretations under Section 403 of the Sixth Supplemental National Defense Appropriation Act, 1942* (March 31, 1943), pp. 7–8.

may be limited to one-half or one-third of the margin of profit on peacetime sales." [43]

The amendments of 1944 established the following standards to be considered in determining excessive profits:

(i) efficiency of contractor, with particular regard to attainment of quantity and quality production, reduction of costs and economy in the use of materials, facilities, and manpower;

(ii) reasonableness of costs and profits, with particular regard to volume of production, normal pre-war earnings, and comparison of war and peacetime products;

(iii) amount and source of public and private capital employed and net worth;

(iv) extent of risk assumed, including the risk incident to reasonable pricing policies;

(v) nature and extent of contribution to the war effort, including inventive and developmental contribution and cooperation with the Government and other contractors in supplying technical assistance;

(vi) character of business, including complexity of manufacturing technique, character and extent of subcontracting, and rate of turnover;

(vii) such other factors the consideration of which the public interest and fair and equitable dealing may require, which factors shall be published in the regulations of the Board from time to time as adopted.[44]

These standards left the services considerable flexibility in their determination of allowable profits.

Although the procedures for determining the existence of excessive profits were flexible, they followed a general pattern. Contractors subject to the act were required to file substantial certified data concerning renegotiable sales, costs, profits, and other aspects of their operations. These data were subjected to analysis by the services and supplemented by

---

43. *The New York Times,* Feb. 10, 1943, p. 20. This position has been sustained by the Tax Court of the United States. See *Aircraft Screw Products Co. v. War Contracts Price Adjustment Board,* 8T.C.1037 and *Crucible Steel Casting Co. v. Secretary of the Navy,* 9T.C.523.

44. Pub. Law No. 235, 78th Cong., 2d Sess., sec. 701 (4) (A).

other data available to the services on costs and profits as well as data on performance. If preliminary investigations indicated the existence of excessive profits, a meeting was held at which the data were reviewed and the contractor was given a chance to state his case. At this point the Price Adjustment Board made a determination of the amount of excessive profits, if any, and requested a corresponding refund.

If the contractor and the Price Adjustment Board agreed on the refund, a voluntary agreement of refund was signed which relieved the contractor of further claims. If not, the Price Adjustment Board could impose an order unilaterally. If the contractor failed to comply with a unilateral order, the government could withhold any funds due him or, in the case of a subcontractor, could direct his customers who were prime contractors to withhold payments due him.

The statute has been administered with a minimum of difficulty. By February 7, 1947 over 48,000 cases had been handled by the various boards exclusive of construction contracts renegotiated on a completed contract basis and also of brokers, agents, and sales engineers. Over 56,000 cases were canceled after preliminary investigation indicated that the contractor was not subject to the act or did not show excesssive profits. The total value of contracts renegotiated exceeded $190 billion and the gross dollar amount recovered in refunds was over $10 billion.[45] Disputes concerning the findings of the War Contracts Board which could not be resolved voluntarily occurred in only 1.2 per cent of the cases.[46] As of June 10, 1946 only 496 cases, involving sales of about $364,000,000 had been appealed to the Tax Court.[47] Clearly that statute has been administered expeditiously and with a minimum of friction with industry. It is unquestionably true that renegotiation has done much to clear industry of a record of "unconscionable profits." The public record is the record of profits after

45. United States Senate, Special Committee Investigating the National Defense Program, Senate Report No. 440, Part 2, *Renegotiation*, 80th Cong., 2d Sess. (1948), p. 14.
46. Sonnett and Dann, *op. cit.*, p. 1, note 1.
47. *Ibid.*, p. 2.

renegotiation refunds. These profits have the stamp of approval of the War Contracts Board and compare well with profits made by many concerns during the war on civilian business.

The Effects of Renegotiation

The net effect of renegotiation upon procurement is perhaps more hotly debated than any other aspect of the procurement policies pursued during World War II. Its effects are to be sought not in the dollars recouped but rather in its effect upon procurement and upon national morale. As was indicated above, excess profits may result consciously or unconsciously from the increase in volume due to the war and from uncertainties concerning other factors affecting costs. Moreover, they may result from the conscious efforts of a small group of individuals to take advantage of the war effort for their own profit. There is no question but that renegotiation was an effective device for recouping excessive profits arising from these sources. Cooperative contractors who found that they had made more than reasonable profits due to errors in estimating costs were provided an orderly procedure for rectifying these errors. The government was provided with a weapon to proceed against the minority of recalcitrant contractors who sought willfully to profit from wartime conditions. National morale and unity of purpose were unquestionably strengthened thereby. It does not appear that there are as many wartime fortunes or as large fortunes made from World War II as from World War I. Finally, renegotiation made a minor contribution to minimizing directly the budgetary cost of war although the excess profits taxes would have recouped the greater part of the excessive profits recouped by renegotiation and the indirect effects of renegotiation in discouraging efficiency probably more than offset this.

Renegotiation was also of considerable value both to procurement officials and to industry in setting a pattern of profits which might be considered reasonable under wartime conditions. It reset the sights of procurement officers and industry alike concerning the appropriate price and profit policies to be followed in pricing war contracts. Peacetime standards were clearly inapplicable. But what standards were to take their place? Through a case-by-case method, the renegotiation boards, staffed by men from industry and finance, developed a pattern of reasonable profits, a pattern into which each contractor was fitted with some allowance for his risks, his contribution, his efficiency, etc. Within limits the pattern might have been higher, or it might have been lower. The relative position of individual contractors might have been different. The important thing is that by a pragmatic and orderly process *a pattern* was established. Differences were not due solely to chance or differences in bargaining skill. The area for differences of opinion as to appropriate profits on new procurements was narrowed.

What was the effect of renegotiation upon procurement? Perhaps the principal contribution which renegotiation made to procurement was the wealth of information which renegotiation made available. Renegotiation was the occasion for summarizing the over-all contribution of each contractor to the war effort. The reports prepared for the Price Adjustment Boards indicated the total war business of each contractor, his technical contributions, his products, to whom he sold, his performance with respect to quality and delivery, his prices compared with those of competitors, and his over-all costs and their breakdown in terms of labor, materials, and overhead. This information was invaluable in the negotiation of particular contracts. Moreover, renegotiation gave the procurement officer some indication of the type of buying job he had done in previous purchases. In the case of multiple product firms, it might be impossible for a particular procurement officer to assess his previous procurement because over-all cost and profit figures were the result of sales of all products and not of a particular product. But, even in such cases a record of substantial excessive profits called for some explanation which an alert procurement officer was bound to seek. Renegotiation was in a real sense "the conscience of procurement."

Renegotiation also tended in many cases to make prime contractors somewhat more receptive to lower prices. If the contractor foresaw excessive profits from existing prices, he might be more inclined to make price reductions since they were practically costless to him. This was particularly true if he could be convinced that reasonable pricing policies would lead to more favorable treatment in renegotiation. On the other hand, it was frequently alleged that procurement officials, knowing that renegotiation would recoup excessive profits, were less prone to push vigorously for close prices than they would otherwise have been. This was doubtlessly true in some cases, especially in the early period. But as the pricing philosophy of the services became more articulate and procurement officers were trained in the techniques and arts of price analysis and negotiation, this tendency was lessened. Without the extensive knowledge of contractors' over-all operations and without some standard of reasonable profits, negotiators would have been in a poor position to seek close prices under the peculiar conditions of wartime procurement.

But this is not the whole story. The controversy revolves primarily around the effect of renegotiation upon the productive efficiency of contractors. The theory of renegotiation was that allowable profits should be determined in such a way as to reward the contractor who in the light of all circumstances controlled his costs well and sought to use labor and materials efficiently. For greater efficiency the contractor was to receive greater reward in dollar terms. It has been widely alleged, however, that renegotiation far from rewarding efficiency placed a premium on the incurring of high costs. It has been pointed out that renegotiators were often not in a position to distinguish effectively between an efficient and an inefficient firm because of the absence of adequate tests of relative efficiency. Moreover, it is quite widely believed that the range of allowable profits in terms of which the boards operated was too narrow to allow for significant variations in rewards. There is a general belief that once the pattern of allowable profits had been established, a contractor could expect about the same rate of profit on costs in subsequent years that he had been allowed in his initial renegotiation. Consequently it was argued that far from being rewarded for efforts at cost reduction the contractor had a positive incentive not to reduce his costs any more than necessary. This meant that renegotiation did not provide the contractor with incentive to improve his internal production set-up or to seek lower prices on his purchases of materials and subcontract items.

These charges, if true, are a serious indictment of renegotiation. Although there doubtlessly were cases where efficiency was not rewarded, particularly in the formative stages, it appears that a conscientious effort was made to reward efficiency. The difficulty arose in getting adequate measures of efficiency. Comparative costs and changes in costs, while often significant indicators of efficiency, were by no means conclusive. The problem of efficiency was a relative one, not an absolute one. The relevant question was whether the firm was conserving labor and materials as well as might be expected considering its available plant, its location, its labor market, etc. The mere fact that one firm's costs were as low as another's was not conclusive. A firm with an old converted plant might have much higher costs than another with a new plant geared for mass production. Yet in a relative sense the first firm might be more efficient than the other. In some cases a breakdown of unit costs might be illuminating, but often it would not be conclusive. And in the case of many multiproduct firms, meaningful unit cost data were not to be had. Analysis of cost trends could also be deceptive. If one firm's costs declined faster than another's, was this because its costs were inflated by a greater amount to begin with, because of more advantageous technical conditions, or because of a greater increase in efficiency? And what indicators should be used when there was no other firm producing the item or where cost data were not available? In general the renegotiation boards were not equipped to handle this problem. Although the cost analysis work of the procurement groups was designed to aid in these matters, this work was too little and too late to be of much significance in renegotiation. The evidence available to the Price Adjustment Boards was fragmentary and their judgments were inevitably highly intuitive. It is not surprising therefore that the spread between the profits allowed to efficient and inefficient firms was narrow. Nor is it surprising that the opinion became prevalent that cost reduction did not bring its rewards in renegotiation.

In the matter of rewarding those contractors who took the risks incident to close pricing equally difficult problems arose. The theory was that the renegotiation boards would allow substantially greater profits to those contractors who had made a conscientious effort to price their contracts in advance at a level which on the basis of reasonable anticipations would not yield excessive profits. This promise of better consideration in renegotiation was the incentive which the negotiator could hold forth to induce close pricing of initial contracts. While it appears that the renegotiation boards made some effort to follow through on this policy, many procurement officers were of the opinion that the difference in treatment was not sufficient to warrant the assumption of the risk. But here again the renegotiation boards faced serious problems in determining the extent of the pricing risk that the contractor assumed. The problem was to visualize the risks as seen in advance. If a contractor ended the year with large excessive profits, this might be due to a conscious attempt to inflate his cost estimates. But was it? Might it not have been due to a failure to assess the various elements of uncertainty correctly? If at the time of negotiation the procurement officers accepted the cost estimate as reasonable, could they question a contractor's claim that he thought that he was taking a pricing risk? Might not these excessive profits have been due to unexpected success in controlling costs? If so, should the renegotiation boards penalize him for his efficiency? Only where a strong case could be made that the firm had followed a policy of padding its costs knowingly was it feasible to penalize a contractor severely for failure to take a pricing risk.

The difficulties of administering rewards for efficiency and risk-taking arose from the basic problem which inevitably harasses wartime procurement, *i.e.*, the problem of devising standards of reasonable unit costs. Even with adequate cost techniques, close pricing in initial procurement would be difficult. The prerequisite to close pricing on initial procurement as well as to the administration of incentives through renegotiation is the development of more adequate techniques for analyzing costs and production efficiency. If administrated incentives are to be effective, industry must be convinced that the administrators have the way as well as the will to determine the degree of efficiency and risk-taking. If industry is not convinced, there will be strong incentives to cushion costs and to pad profits.

It should also be pointed out that the excess profits tax limited seriously all attempts to administer financial rewards for efficient production or for the assumption of pricing risk. These taxes bore heavily on the increment of profit, particularly in the case of contractors who had experienced a substantial increase in the volume of sales over the base period of 1936–1939. An additional increment of profit before taxes did not appear to be very important to a contractor after excess profits taxes of 70 or 80 per cent had been paid. This was particularly true if the risks or the effort involved in efficient production and close pricing appeared large. Of course the contractor had a long-run interest in maintaining an efficient plant in anticipation of the return of peace and his need to compete in civilian markets. This consideration plus patriotic motives doubtlessly induced many contractors to maintain their plants at as high a level of efficiency as was feasible under wartime pressures.

It is probable that in wartime positive financial incentives to efficient production must necessarily play a minor role, but it is extremely important that there should not be negative incentives to efficiency. Renegotiation will do much harm if there develops a belief that allowable profits depend upon costs and that a contractor will be penalized for increased efficiency. Such a disguised form of CPPC pricing would be destructive of industrial morale.

Discretionary Exemptions from Renegotiation

In view of the difficulties of maintaining incentive prices so long as contracts were subject to renegotiation it is not surprising that an attempt was made to grant discretionary exemptions from renegotiation in appropriate circumstances. The Tryon Conference had recommended that greater use be made of the power to exempt contracts from renegotiation where it was feasible to negotiate close initial prices.[48] It was contemplated that this would be done both by exemptions of specific contracts and by the over-all exemption of specific contractors for limited periods of time. The amendments to the renegotiation act in February, 1944 were designed to encourage this.

While the Navy never looked with much favor on exemption from renegotiation except in the case of incentive contracts,[49] the War Department officially encouraged exemption in specified circumstances. Army Procurement Regulations provided that exemptions should be granted only if certain rigorous conditions were satisfied which were designed to insure that the contract prices were reasonable.[50] But many of the contractors who could and would satisfy these conditions wished the clean bill of health which renegotiation offered, while many who wanted to escape renegotiation were not able or willing to satisfy the rigorous conditions. Moreover, in order to qualify for exemption of certain contracts, the contractor had to have an accounting system which en-

48. Army Industrial College, *Contract Pricing: Principal Developments*, p. 140.
49. Records of the Navy indicate that only about thirteen contracts were exempted from renegotiation by the Navy, most of which were incentive-type contracts.
50. APR, par. 1205.

abled him to segregate costs of the exempted contracts from costs of other contracts subject to renegotiation. Despite the encouragement of exemption by high policy echelons, the technical services of the War Department do not seem to have granted many exemptions. The official history of the Purchases Division, ASF, concludes that "it is possible that exemptions from statutory renegotiation have not contributed materially to the effectuation of pricing policies." [51]

It is unfortunate that greater use was not made of these discretionary powers to grant exemptions from renegotiation, particularly after the early years of the war. It should have been possible in the case of contractors producing goods similar to their peacetime products to have negotiated close initial prices free from renegotiation for limited periods of time. Experience of many contractors in numerous other fields also indicates that close pricing could have been effected once the uncertainties of the early war years had been passed. The greatest difficulty seems to have risen from the need to segregate costs on exempted contracts from those which were not exempted. The appropriate solution to this problem, which is discussed in more detail in Chapter XII below, was to develop an over-all forward pricing policy covering all future sales for war use whether on prime contracts or subcontracts. This would have avoided the need for segregating costs on individual contracts. A wider use of the discretionary powers to exempt contractors from renegotiation would have required courage on the part of the services, but it would have put the procurement officers upon their mettle. Moreover, it would have provided a striking opportunity to recognize contractors who were doing a conscientious job of pricing and would have increased the incentives to cost control particularly among the many small contractors who are particularly sensitive to financial incentives and for whom it is not easy to devise other systems for inducing efficiency in the use of labor and materials.

51. Production and Purchases Division, ASF, *Purchasing Policies and Practices*, p. 182.

Conclusion

Renegotiation was unquestionably of considerable use in the early stages of the war. It should be credited with having set a pattern of allowable profits and with having limited the "unconscionable profits" resulting from errors of judgment or from the efforts of a willful minority. It contributed much to the development of public morale except on the part of those managements which became convinced that efficiency did not pay. But as the war progressed renegotiation became increasingly removed from procurement. Some contractors evidently concluded that renegotiation penalized those who succeeded in improving the efficiency of their operations. If it was to be used as an essential part of the pricing policy of the services, it should have been kept closer to the procurement function. Moreover, its success was dependent upon the development of more convincing tests of efficiency and risk-taking and upon a greater willingness to make significant differences in allowable profit between contractors who controlled their costs and those who did not. If such tests were developed, it should have been possible to make wider use of the discretionary powers to grant exemptions from renegotiation after the initial stages of the war. As it was, renegotiation was too far removed from procurements, too much emphasis was placed upon recouping excessive profits after they had been earned, and too little emphasis was placed upon the proper pricing of a contractor's future deliveries on an over-all basis.

XII

COMPANY PRICING PROGRAM

THE company pricing program inaugurated by the services in the spring of 1944 represented an innovation in pricing procedures which warrants careful consideration in any planning for the future.[1] The program was designed to provide some missing links in the services' pricing program: (1) to provide more effective procedures for pricing subcontracts and (2) to bridge the gap between pricing for future delivery, which was done on an individual contract basis, and renegotiation of past deliveries, which was on an over-all basis. This aspect of the services' pricing program has not received the attention which it deserves.

Although it is fair to say that the program was not outstandingly successful, the program as originally conceived had distinct merits. On another occasion, if inaugurated at an earlier period in the procurement cycle and appropriately integrated with original procurement and renegotiation, it might serve to make the pricing problem both simpler and more effective.

Background

The company pricing program was a natural outgrowth of the services' previous attempts to develop an effective pricing program. By the end of 1942 the services had developed a reasonably clear pricing program: (1) procurement officers

1. "Company pricing" was the designation used by the War Department. The parallel program of the Navy was "repricing" or "price revision." The present discussion is based largely on the author's personal experiences. For general discussion of the program see National Industrial Conference Board, *Repricing War Contracts under the Company Pricing Program* (1944), "Studies in Business Policy," No. 8; ASF Manual M 609, *Company Pricing* (May, 1945); Production and Purchases Division, ASF, *Purchasing Policies and Practices*, pp. 184–190, 383–386; *Business Week*, Dec. 16, 1944, pp. 15–16.

strove for close prices on each contract at the time of negotiation; (2) in cases where prices turned out in retrospect to have been excessive, they were corrected through a refund of excessive profits on an over-all basis. These two aspects of price policy were undertaken to a large extent by separate groups. Although these two groups were responsible ultimately in each service to the same authority, they operated with a high degree of independence and without adequate coordination. This separateness was further emphasized in February, 1944 when the renegotiation boards operating within the services were made responsible on matters of policy and procedure to the War Contracts Board, which was established by Congress to operate outside of the services.

This *modus operandi* which had been developed between initial procurement and renegotiation was far from satisfactory. While it was reasonably effective in recouping excessive profits after they were earned, it did not provide an effective means of negotiating incentive prices in prospect. This failure was due in part to the crystal-gazing nature of the problem of pricing for future delivery and to the conflict of profit control with incentive pricing.

But much of the difficulty arose from the fact that there were several missing links in the system for pricing military contracts. In the first place there was no adequate method for controlling prices on subcontract items. Since it has been estimated that fifty cents out of every dollar spent by the services on prime contracts went for the purchase of subcontract items and materials, the failure to control subcontract costs was a major problem. Due to a tendency to pyramid profits on costs, excessive prices on subcontract purchases tended to be reflected in even more excessive prices on end products. Except where the services were able and willing to put exceptional pressure on prime contract prices, there was often no real incentive for prime contractors to try to negotiate low prices on their subcontracts. Moreover, in many cases prime contractors did not have the evidence of excessive prices of their subcontractors which was available to the services, and the latter were loath to give them this data. In certain cases subcontractors were reluctant to depart from established prices, a reluctance which a prime contractor might find it very difficult to break down. This was true of many subcontract items sold by a single seller, by sellers with well-established list prices, or by industries with well-established price leadership. Consequently, many industrial purchasing departments tended to devote themselves to order-placing and expediting and to become quite insensitive to price considerations.

In some cases, but by no means all, these subcontract prices were subject to OPA controls. These controls, however, were far from adequate. The evidence indicates that in many cases the rate of profit attainable under these ceiling prices were far above those deemed reasonable on war contracts. But industry was often reluctant to make subcontract sales below the established ceilings, even for use on war contracts.[2]

The services had made some attempts to exercise indirect control over subcontract prices, but these had not proved very effective. In the case of major components, they sometimes reviewed the prices of subcontracts when negotiating prime contracts. It was not feasible to do this in many cases, however, because of the multitude of relatively small subcontracts involved and because at the time of the negotiation of a prime contract the contractor was often in no position to know who his subcontractors would be. Even in the case of CPFF contracts, where cost inspectors had to approve invoices for materials, the inspectors often confined their review of prices to determining whether there had been gross overpricing in terms of conventional standards of reasonable prices. Since the prime contractor was legally responsible for delivery and performance, the cost inspectors were loath to substitute their judgment on pricing matters for that of the contractor's purchasing agent. Various proposals to extend the review of the purchase prices on subcontracts to all major prime contractors raised many administrative problems. Moreover, to

2. See above, pp. 76–77.

have done so would have placed a serious burden on many subcontractors who were selling to several prime contractors under the jurisdiction of several contracting offices. Such subcontractors would have found their sales prices being reviewed by many procurement offices with all the burdens of filing of information and negotiation which this would have involved. And even if an attempt had been made to review prices on all major subcontract purchases, this individual subcontract approach was bound to fail, not only because of the administrative burden involved, but also because of the inherent weakness in the individual contract approach.

This leads to the second broad weakness in the prevailing system of pricing contracts. Pricing for future delivery was done on an individual contract basis, but incentive pricing for future delivery to be successful depends on accurate estimating of the future over-all operations of the firm. In the case of those few firms whose total operations were confined to one or a few contracts under the jurisdiction of a single procurement office, it was feasible in negotiating prices to consider the future operations of the firm on an over-all basis, including total volume, probability of contract increases or cancellations, changes in the composition of output as between high-profit and low-profit items, changes in delivery schedules, and the many other variables which might be relevant to future costs. The typical case was quite different. Many of the prime contractors, both large and small, had numerous contracts with several different technical services or bureaus. The various contracts were priced by different procurement offices and at different times. The procurement officer was often ill-advised concerning the total future operations of the firm since he did not have a composite over-all view of the firm's existing orders and delivery schedules and of the future intentions of other procurement offices. Yet in order to arrive at a reasonable estimate of future costs or to assess an estimate submitted by the firm, it was necessary to make some assumptions concerning future over-all operations. Here was a situation calling for real coordination of procurement effort between procurement offices often located far apart and purchasing quite unrelated products.

The situation was further complicated by the fact that some contractors took advantage of the situation to play various procurement officers off against one another in an effort to gain from all the most favorable conditions offered by any. To some extent this is inevitable under a system of decentralized purchase operations. Under such a system considerable discretion must be given to the individual procurement officer, no matter how rigid the regulations. But the process goes much further than necessary. Closer relations between operating procurement officers could do much to minimize the confusion resulting from this process and to develop a united front against constant nibbling at the standards of pricing established by the services.

The pricing philosophy of the services required for its success that each contract, or at least the aggregate of all contracts of each firm, should be priced sufficiently closely to provide an incentive to efficient production. Failure to price closely any important group of a firm's contracts gave the firm a cushion against loss on other contracts and thereby reduced the risk which it should assume. The good work of one contracting officer might come to naught if another contracting officer failed in his responsibility. A similar problem was presented by the case of firms which were producing on both prime contracts and subcontracts. Close pricing by all procurement officers on the former, if possible, might come to naught because the subcontracts were not reasonably priced.

These two problems, the absence of effective checks on the prices of subcontracts and the failure to provide an over-all approach to prices for future delivery, were the basic problems which the company pricing program was designed to solve.

As indicated above, the company pricing program was in reality a logical development in the evolution of the services' pricing policies. In the fall of 1943 the Assistant Director for Pricing, ASF, had pointed out the difficulties inherent in approaching pricing through the individual contract and had urged greater use of over-all review of contractors' pricing policies in connection with renegotiation.[3] Likewise, in the fall of 1943 procurement officials in the Navy Department had initiated studies of ways and means to follow up renegotiation by more effective steps to reduce prices on future deliveries. Renegotiation, which had originally been conceived as a device to effect repricing, had clearly failed in this respect. To be sure, the Price Adjustment Boards would incorporate a forward pricing clause in their agreement where the contractor was willing. Although these clauses varied from case to case, a clause used quite frequently provided:

The contractor agrees to re-estimate its costs from time to time during its current fiscal year, giving consideration to its cost experience for the latest fiscal year covered by this agreement, and from time to time during the current fiscal year to adjust its prices under contracts and subcontracts subject to renegotiation under the provisions of the Act, to eliminate the accumulation during such current fiscal year of profits thereunder regarded by the contractor as excessive. The provisions of this paragraph, however, shall be without prejudice to subsequent renegotiation pursuant to the Act, relating to any fiscal year subsequent to the fiscal year covered by this agreement.

Many contractors acted in good faith and brought their pricing policies into line with the services' objectives. But these pledges lacked teeth and their administration proved difficult where the contractor did not take them seriously. It is not surprising that these clauses came to be referred to as "boyscout" pledges.

The passage of the Revenue Act of 1943, signed by the President on February 25, 1944, provided an additional impetus to find a new solution to the problem of incentive pricing.[4] Title VII of the act extended renegotiation through December 31, 1944 with the proviso that the President might extend it six months more if competitive conditions warranted.

3. G. A. Lloyd, *Law and Contemporary Problems*, X, 255–261.
4. Pub. Law No. 235, 78th Cong., 2d Sess. (Feb. 25, 1944).

Title VIII gave the Secretary of each of the procurement departments the power to establish prices for future delivery by order if he was unable to arrive at fair and reasonable prices voluntarily by negotiation. The debate preceding the extension of the renegotiation statute had indicated a feeling on the part of several influential Congressmen that by 1944 the procurement program should have been sufficiently stabilized and the services should have had sufficient cost information to negotiate initial prices so well as to make renegotiation unnecessary. The discussions incident to extension of renegotiation led the services to renew their efforts at close pricing with increased vigor, so that their contract prices would be on a satisfactory basis if renegotiation should lapse. Moreover, Title VIII was interpreted as an indication by Congress that such a policy was in order.

Procedure of Company Pricing

The solution chosen was one of supplementing existing procedures by a periodic over-all review of each firm's prices and price policies in order to revise them where necessary and to bring them in line with current conditions and future operations. To accomplish this was a major administrative task. Primary administrative responsibility for the review was assigned to the procurement personnel of the same service which was responsible for renegotiation.[5] In the case of the War Department, company pricing was the responsibility of the established procurement offices of the technical services and of the AAF. In the Navy Department it was the responsibility of the Price Revision Division established in the Office of Procurement and Material. In the case of certain shipbuilders, air frame contractors, and some other contractors where a single bureau was responsible for the bulk of the procurement it was the practice in the Navy to leave repricing activities in the hands of the bureau of principal cognizance.

5. In some cases firms were assigned to a service other than that responsible for renegotiation. This was true particularly where the service responsible for renegotiation did not have a dominant interest in the company pricing review.

Although a single group had administrative responsibility for repricing, it was necessary that all parties interested in the contractor should be represented in negotiations. In many cases this meant that all procurement offices having contracts with the firm would participate in company pricing discussions and meetings. In other cases, particularly where their interests were minor, the parties concerned would indicate a willingness to accept any arrangement effected by the group responsible for the review, provided the arrangement did not affect existing contractual arrangements in any manner except by reducing prices. In any event, so far as prime contracts were involved no arrangement could be concluded which was not acceptable to the contracting officer who had legal cognizance of the contract.

Company pricing reviews were generally undertaken by a team of negotiators, price analysts, and lawyers. The board responsible for renegotiating the company was also frequently represented. A company pricing meeting was supposed to be preceded by a detailed examination of the contractor's existing orders, his past financial operations, current and past prices, prospective cost trends, and his budget of future operations. It was necessary, therefore, to pool all available information from the various procurement offices and from the cognizant Price Adjustment Board and to supplement this data with the most recent interim financial data available and with an estimated budget of future operations. The period for which a company pricing arrangement was effective varied anywhere from three months to a year. The importance of the period arose from the fact that the longer the period, the greater the risk, while the shorter the period the less effective were the incentives to efficiency. Three months was the most frequent period for which arrangements were effective.

The specific ends to be reached as a result of a company price review varied.[6] The purpose was to examine the prices and pricing policies of the firm and, where there was evidence

6. For examples of typical arrangements see ASF Manual M 609, *Company Pricing.*

of excessive prices over-all or maladjustment in the structure of prices, to determine the cause and the most effective remedy. In some cases the mere collection of data and its review by the assembled procurement officers gave the latter the means for negotiating satisfactory prices for their respective contracts. In other cases it developed that the cost-accounting system on which the firm had been relying was such as to overestimate costs systematically under conditions of large volume production. The company pricing meeting served in such cases as a stimulus to the contractor to revise his cost system or to revise his pricing policy based thereon. In such cases the burden for repricing could be placed on the contractor. In the case of other contractors, particularly firms producing a multiplicity of items without adequate individual product cost data, the solution was a uniform percentage reduction in prices on all items sold for the end use of war contracts or a uniform discount on all such sales. Where cost information was such as to distinguish costs and profits on broad classes of items, the reductions or discounts were often varied as between the different classes of products. Although there were instances where voluntary refunds of excessive profits from past sales were accepted as part of the company price review, this was generally recognized as the function of renegotiation.

A special rebate arrangement was devised for use in certain specified circumstances on subcontract sales. Under this arrangement the contractor agreed in advance to rebate directly to the government a specified percentage of all sales for the end use of war contracts made during the period.[7] Under this arrangement the sales price remained artificially high but the net realization of the firm was reduced. This differed from an agreement to refund profits in excess of a certain percentage in that the amount of refund on each dollar of sales was agreed upon in advance and the contractor presumably had an incentive to reduce his costs. In this respect it avoided the cost-

7. See *ibid.*, pp. 19–20 for a discussion of the pros and cons of the rebate arrangement.

plus-percentage-of-cost virus which infects most refund arrangements. The disadvantage of this technique arose from the fact that it failed to reduce prices to the immediate customer so that the costs of contractors purchasing from the subcontractor remained artificially high. Since customers presumably continued to calculate their prices on this artificially high basis, it resulted in artificially high prices on prime contracts.

The regulations established by the services provided that the rebate arrangement should be used only with respect to subcontract sales and then only under two circumstances: (1) where the seller could not distinguish at the time of sale between sales for end use of war contracts and civilian end use, and (2) where the contractor could not change his price structure without serious postwar damage. In the latter case a rebate arrangement was to be used only if the services were convinced "that the existing price structure has developed through a long previous competitive period; that present prices are comparable to those prevailing before the war; that the price structure was a firm one, and not simply a list from which competitive discounts were quoted; that the articles involved will be sold after the war in similar form to the form in which they were sold before the war; and that changed prices in wartime would clearly be likely to disrupt the postwar market." [8] These conditions were clearly designed to limit the use of the rebate article. Although the War Department made rather frequent use of the rebate article, the Navy used it in only three or four cases and then only because of the impossibility of distinguishing between war and civilian end uses.

Evaluation

The accomplishments of the company pricing program are difficult to assess. The program was initiated in the spring of 1944 but was not launched as a major program until early

8. *Ibid.*, p. 20.

fall. Just as the program was gaining momentum the prospect of victory in Europe began to loom over the horizon. Negotiations during the winter of 1944–1945 were complicated by the uncertainties arising from prospective cutbacks and by the need to perfect company pricing techniques and explain the program to industry.

Nonetheless, pricing policies of many concerns were revised in line with the services' objectives. Moreover, in the case of several of the major holders of prime contracts general discussion between top executives of the company and all interested procurement officers led to a revision of over-all company policy to bring it more closely in line with the services' policy. In the case of large decentralized concerns, this approach through top management afforded an excellent method for developing desirable pricing techniques with a minimum of administrative burden to the services and for developing better relations between the operating groups of industry and the services.

Perhaps the greatest accomplishment of the company pricing program was with respect to the pricing of subcontracts, a field which was relatively untouched when the program began. Here the services succeeded in negotiating price reductions, discounts, and rebate agreements in many situations which would otherwise have been untouched except by renegotiation. Figures of price reductions, rebates, or refunds, however, cannot measure the over-all accomplishment of the program. The significance of the program is to be measured not by the dollars saved but solely by the materials and hours of labor saved as a result of incentive pricing. On this there is no evidence.

The company pricing program, in contrast to renegotiation, was administered at all times as an essentially voluntary program. Moreover, it was administered by procurement personnel. The inducement to participate was the prospect of better treatment at the time of renegotiation. To be sure, mandatory action under Title VIII was available for use against recalcitrant contractors, but there was general reluctance to invoke these powers. The problem of inducing voluntary compliance was complicated by the fact that many contractors believed that renegotiation boards would not make any significant difference in allowable profits as between firms which had taken the risks of close pricing and those which had not. Consequently some firms which were unwilling to conclude arrangements acceptable to the services were allowed to continue their pricing policies unmolested.[9] Such failure to invoke mandatory powers, if continued, might have undermined the whole program. But by the time such cases had been winnowed out in the late spring of 1945 there was little enthusiasm for drastic action in view of the rapid tapering off of the procurement program.

As the newest technique for the pricing of military procurements, the company pricing program had to fight for recognition in an environment in which procurement and renegotiation groups were well established. It was seriously hampered by the fact that it was never recognized as a co-partner with renegotiation, and the policies and procedures of these two approaches to pricing in terms of the over-all business unit were never adequately integrated. It was claimed by many that the program was merely a profit-skimming scheme, which did in a slipshod manner what renegotiation could do with greater skill. There is an element of truth in this charge, especially with respect to the earlier arrangements. This was not, however, inherent in the program. The really significant charge against the program is that in their haste to show tangible results the responsible company pricing groups proceeded far too often on the basis of inadequate over-all operating statements and failed to make sufficiently intensive studies of the contractor's operations, his cost system, price methods, and future budget. This resulted from inadequately trained personnel, uncertain policies, and a preoccupation with paper results.

Whatever the faults of the program as actually administered in 1944–1945, the company approach to pricing for future

9. Production and Purchases Division, ASF, *op. cit.*, p. 386.

delivery has real merit. This approach to pricing is the logical result of the basic philosophy of incentive pricing developed by the services in 1942 and 1943. In the pricing of some procurements, particularly products with close civilian counterparts, comparative prices may afford a useful standard for pricing. But for the large volume of specialized military procurement this standard is not adequate.

Wartime contractors for specialized military equipment are to a large extent unique. The conditions of production differ so greatly between contractors that there are often no standards of pricing except those which look primarily to the conditions of the particular contractor. It has been customary in the past to develop a price policy for the firm on a piece-meal basis by attempting to negotiate reasonable prices on each contract at the time of its award. In many cases these original prices were redetermined one or more times after a review of cost experience on the particular contract. This required not only elaborate analysis of costs and negotiations upon the award of the contract, but further filing of information and negotiations in accordance with provisions for redetermination. Although this approach is justified in the case of large contracts, it is an inexcusably cumbersome and expensive method for dealing with the large mass of small-sized and medium-sized prime contracts, which constitute the bulk by number of the contracts which must be priced. This procedure leads to the maximum confusion and irritation of contractors since redetermination on several contracts with different procurement officers will call for the filing of duplicate information to be analyzed and used in as many different ways as there are contracts to be redetermined. Moreover, these negotiations will seem, and often are, futile since close pricing on one contract will serve little purpose if other contracts, whether prime contracts or subcontracts, are free of control. An approach to subcontract pricing through each individual prime contract would be even more burdensome and costly to all concerned. A pricing and repricing policy based on a consideration of the over-all company position recommends itself as a means for effecting the pricing objectives of the services with a minimum effort on the part of both industry and the services. It will produce a minimum of friction between the two parties.

Even if applied only to the one hundred companies holding the largest volume of prime contracts and a similar number of leading subcontractors the procedure would accomplish much. During the last war the one hundred largest prime contractors held about 67 per cent of the total prime contracts.[10] Several of these companies, *e.g.*, General Motors and General Electric were also important subcontractors. In anticipation of another war a start should be made even before the coming of the emergency at developing company pricing agreements with such companies. These might take the form of master pricing agreements which would specify the information to be supplied and the way in which prices would be determined on all sales to the services. The policies established with various contractors should be consistent with one another and with the general pricing policies of the services, while at the same time they should be tailored to the circumstances of the particular contractors. With a core of company pricing arrangements of this type, it would then be possible in the event of an emergency to spread the program to include smaller prime contractors and subcontractors.

This procedure holds an important key to preventing the disastrous effects of competition for industrial capacity and know-how between government buying offices under conditions of decentralized procurement operations. Periodically all interested purchasing offices would review jointly the overall position of each contractor and would negotiate revision of prices and price policies if this seemed necessary. The government would in effect approach each contractor as a single buyer rather than as a host of rival buyers with different and conflicting buying policies. Company pricing is an answer to the critics of decentralized purchasing operations.

10. Smaller War Plants Corporation, *Economic Concentration and World War II*, pp. 29-31.

XIII

PRICES AND PROFITS ON MILITARY GOODS IN
WORLD WAR II

It is difficult to judge the over-all effectiveness of the services' pricing policies and procedures during World War II. The major objectives of the services were to insure the fulfillment of their requirements and to promote harmony and unity through furthering the stabilization program. Price policy on military purchases was designed to contribute to these objectives through facilitating conversion to war production, promoting productive efficiency in industry, and minimizing excessive profits from military contracts.

To what extent did the price policies and contractual arrangements facilitate the allocation of resources to military production? To what extent did they provide the maximum incentives to efficiency in the use of labor and materials consistent with prompt delivery of necessary goods? To what extent did they promote economic stabilization by minimizing excessive profits? These questions would by their very nature be difficult to answer even if all possible data were available. The most that can be attempted here is a brief survey of the trends of production, prices, and profits on military goods.

Production

Perhaps the best and most conclusive evidence of the effectiveness of any component of the mobilization program are the indexes of production, including particularly the production of the weapons of war. Our production record in World War II is impressive. The Federal Reserve Board index of adjusted total industrial production showed an increase from 121 in June, 1940 to a peak of 247 in November, 1943. This represented an increase in the adjusted index of durable manufactures from 131 to 376 and in the adjusted index of non-durable manufactures from 114 to 180.[1] The trend in munitions production is indicated in Chart IV, which gives the volume of production of munitions in the United States measured in terms of standard unit costs.[2] We accomplished an outstanding feat of production. But this was the combined result of a large group of policies, public and private. Did the price policies of the services facilitate or hinder this accomplishment?

Prices

The services have compiled an extensive record of price changes on major military items from January, 1942 through August, 1945. These data have been conveniently summarized in index form.[3] The compilation of these data was undertaken in part to satisfy the agreement to provide OPA with information on prices and profits and in part as an aid to the services' program of cost and price analysis. No comparable record of prices of military purchases has ever before been compiled. The items included represent over 50 per cent by value of the total purchases of the War Department and 60 per cent by value of the purchases of the Navy Department. The items were carefully selected to represent various important types of products and contractual arrangements. In compiling the data and in developing statistical techniques for their summary the War and Navy Departments followed similar procedures and had extensive advice and assistance from the Bureau of Labor Statistics.

The peculiarities of military procurement necessitated sev-

1. *Federal Reserve Bulletin.*

2. Standard munitions dollars are derived by multiplying the number of units of each munitions item produced by its unit cost in August, 1945. They provide a measure of physical munitions output which is not distorted by price changes. Since fixed unit costs are used, standard munitions dollars do not represent actual expenditures.

3. For details see Production and Purchases Division, Headquarters, ASF, *Indexes of Contract Price Changes;* Price Analysis Division, OP&M, Navy Department, *Indexes of Navy Contract Prices.*

CHART IV

United States Munitions Production
Monthly
July 1940–December 1945
(In standard 1945 munitions dollars)

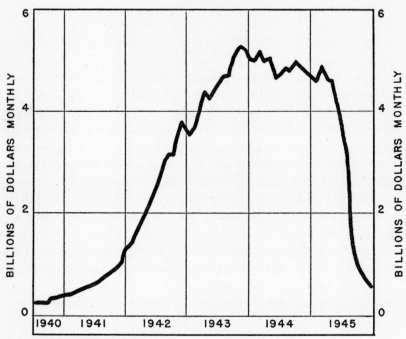

Source: Civilian Production Administration.

eral departures from usual practices for constructing price indexes. The basic data were compiled from the record of initial contracts and contract changes. The indexes record all changes in contract prices negotiated with individual companies for identical or closely similar products. They record, therefore, changes in contract prices negotiated with individual companies and not changes in average prices negotiated or changes in average prices paid. The indexes do not reflect voluntary refunds on past deliveries. If, however, voluntary refunds were accompanied by corresponding revision of existing contract prices for future delivery or by lower prices on new contracts, such reductions are reflected in the indexes. Finally, the indexes do not reflect refunds incident to renegotiation.

As a result of the use of the company method, the introduction or dropping of high-price or low-price firms does not affect the level of the index. This method was used because the services' prices were tailored to a large extent to the peculiarities of each individual contractor. Consequently, there were often substantial and persisting differentials between prices for the identical item negotiated with firms producing under different conditions.

The company method of index computation gives a smoother index than the conventional average price index. But it does not differ significantly from the conventional average price index except where new firms are brought into production or dropped out at prices substantially higher or substantially lower than those negotiated with other firms. This was often true during the period of conversion in 1941 and early 1942, when high-cost firms were often brought in, and again in the later period of the war, when high-cost firms were often dropped first. As a result of these influences the indexes probably tend on balance to understate the total decline in average contract prices from 1942 to 1945. There were also a few items, particularly in aeronautics and electronics, where conditions of the war necessitated a shift from low-cost to high-cost firms or vice versa and where, consequently, the

CHART V

Contract Price Changes
War Department
January 1942–August 1945
(October 1942 = 100)

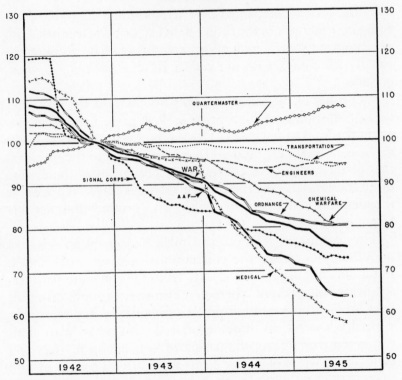

Source: War Department. See Appendix C for detailed data.

CHART VI

Contract Price Changes
Navy Department
January 1942–August 1945
(October 1942 = 100)

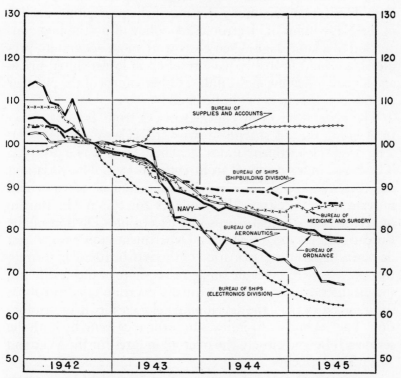

Source: Navy Department. See Appendix D for detailed data.

technique adopted gives results somewhat different from those which would result from the conventional index methods.

It should be recognized that the contractual method used may have a substantial effect on the trend of the indexes. Thus, under the pressure to convert letters of intent to contracts as soon as possible the Navy converted many letters for electronic items to maximum-price contracts with admittedly high initial prices before the items had moved completely from the developmental stage into the stage of mass production. This factor accounts for some of the precipitous decline in the Navy index of electronics. A policy of postponing conversion to a later stage when costs were more accurately predictable would probably have resulted in lower initial prices and a smaller decline in the index. Other effects of the peculiar contractual practices might be cited.

The general trend of contract prices from January, 1942 to August, 1945 is sharply downward (Charts V and VI). The War Department index declined from 108.6 to 75.4. The Navy index declined from 106.0 to 78.1. The variations between the trends of the various technical services and bureaus are interesting. The indexes for the AAF, Bureau of Aeronautics, Signal Corps, the Electronics Divison of the Bureau of Ships and the Medical Department show the greatest declines. In part the explanation of this is to be found in the fact that they were responsible for a greater share of the new items, the production costs of which usually decrease substantially as the items move from the developmental stage into mass production. The decline in the indexes for ordnance items by both the services followed closely the over-all indexes for the War and Navy Departments.

Perhaps most noticeable are the trends for the Quartermaster Corps and the Bureau of Supplies and Accounts, both of which tended to rise. These two groups were responsible for the purchase of many items produced in the same or similar form in times of peace such as food, clothing, and petroleum. Many of these items were subject to OPA controls from an early period so that initial prices were not inflated. Moreover,

since many of these items were the same as or similar to peacetime civilian goods they did not involve such serious problems
of cost estimating as did specialized military items. Furthermore, since these items or closely similar items had been produced in peacetime on a volume basis, they were not subject
to the same increasing economies of mass production. Finally,
in several classes of items, *e.g.*, textiles and foods, Congressional policy encouraged increases in raw material prices.

It is interesting to compare the price changes on the services' contracts with the corresponding changes for similar
goods in civilian markets. In Table III comparisons are made
for some six classes of commodities where the items purchased
by the services were the same as or similar to those sold in
civilian markets. It will be noted that between January, 1942
and June, 1945 the percentage increases in contract prices for
the Navy Department were less than the percentage increases
in civilian wholesale prices in the case of cotton textiles,
woolen textiles, and metal and metal products. For the same
period the War Department contract prices increased less
than civilian wholesale prices in the case of footwear and
woolen textiles. In the case of Navy purchases of petroleum
products and footwear and War Department purchases of
cotton textiles the services' increases were greater. The service's increases were also greater in the case of clothing, but in
this connection it is significant that the BLS index probably
understates the increase in prices of civilian clothing because
of failure to consider quality deterioration. These comparisons
must be used with care. The products included in the sample
vary for the different indexes and the bases of computation
of the indexes are different. Moreover, there is no way of
determining whether the prices on government contracts were
in line with prices in civilian markets in the base month,
January, 1942. Despite these limitations the comparisons do
suggest that in several lines the services' prices did not change
in an adverse manner compared to civilian prices and in several
lines price increases on the services' contracts were more
moderate.

TABLE III

COMPARISON OF PRICE CHANGES ON MILITARY CONTRACTS WITH WHOLESALE PRICE CHANGES, 1942–1945

	BLS Wholesale Price Index	Navy Department Index	War Department Index
Petroleum			
Index January 1942	59.5	97.4	
Index June 1945	64.2	106.9	*
% Change Jan. 1942 to June 1945	+7.9	+9.8	
Footwear			
Index January 1942	121.1	95.8	95.8
Index June 1945	126.3	110.6	98.4
% Change Jan. 1942 to June 1945	+4.3	+15.4	+2.7
Clothing			
Index January 1942	101.1	89.1	96.4
Index June 1945	107.4	103.6	104.4
% Change Jan. 1942 to June 1945	+6.2	+16.3	+8.3
Cotton Textiles			
Index January 1942	110.5	96.9	96.2
Index June 1945	119.7	102.4	114.3
% Change Jan. 1942 to June 1945	+8.3	+5.7	+18.8
Woolen Textiles			
Index January 1942	103.0	95.4	100.3 **
Index June 1945	112.7	88.1	101.1
% Change Jan. 1942 to June 1945	+9.4	+7.7	+0.7
Metals and Metal Products			
Index January 1942	103.5	116.1	
Index June 1945	104.7	100.3	*
% Change Jan. 1942 to June 1945	+1.2	+13.6	

* Not available.
** War Department index is for June, 1942.

Source: Navy Department, Price Analysis Division, OP&M, *Indexes of Contract Prices;* War Department, Production and Purchases Division, Headquarters, ASF, *Indexes of Contract Price Changes;* Bureau of Labor Statistics.

The bulk of procurement by dollar volume was made by the AAF, Army Ordnance, Signal Corps, Bureau of Aeronautics, Bureau of Ordnance, and the Bureau of Ships. These groups were responsible for the procurement of most of the distinctly military items, many of them new and without closely similar civilian counterparts. It was in the purchase of these items that the difficulties of cost estimating were greatest and in which adequate bench marks for judging prices were most difficult to devise. The indexes of contract prices for these technical services and bureaus all declined markedly. The meaning of these price trends is open to considerable question. The price declines reflect two basic factors, declines in costs and declines in profit margins. Cost declines were to be expected as contractors moved into mass production on new items or on items which were at least new to them. But some of the decline was clearly due to the fact that prices in January, 1942 were too high. Either they were based on cost estimates which appear in retrospect to have been exaggerated or they had contemplated excessive profits. Consequently, differences in the rate of decline of the various indexes are by no means indications of greater effectiveness in pricing. On the contrary, a precipitous decline in prices may indicate that initial prices were excessive while a more moderate decline may simply mean that initial prices were more realistic.

Were contract prices negotiated closer to costs as the war progressed? Was there an increasing pressure put on contractors to reduce costs? Or did prices simply follow costs downward at a leisurely pace? On these issues the price indexes tell us nothing. The data on profits to be discussed below indicate that the margin between realized profits and allowable profits narrowed as the war progressed, *i.e.*, the margin of safety declined. This might suggest that pressures to control costs increased. The evidence, however, is not conclusive. It might well be argued that the elements of uncertainty decreased as the war progressed, particularly uncertainty concerning wage rates, material prices, allowable profits, and productive efficiency so that narrower margins did not increase the pricing risk. It is significant, however, that the services did succeed in reducing prices more rapidly than costs so that the cushion was reduced. This was an important accomplishment. A constantly increasing margin of safety, particularly in view of the control of profits by renegotiation, might have reduced the incentives to efficiency materially.

Profits

The profit record of American industry during the war will also throw some light on the effectiveness of the pricing policies pursued by the services. As might be expected, total profits before taxes of manufacturing industry during the war period increased substantially over their prewar level. (See Table IV.) This was true of both war and non-war industries alike. A good deal of this increase was due to the increase in volume of business and might have been expected with any recovery to something approaching full employment. But there was also a substantial increase in the margin of profit before taxes as a percentage of sales. As indicated in Table IV, however, the increases in the profit margins before taxes in war industries were generally not as great as the increases in non-war manufacturing industries. It appears that while the non-war industries experienced a lesser percentage increase in total sales and profits, they experienced a greater increase in profit margins.[4]

An interesting aspect of wartime profit experience has been the relatively greater improvement in the profits of small concerns as compared with large concerns. This trend has been observed in three different studies, in each of which the size of firms has been measured in terms of assets.[5] The general trend is indicated in Table V which shows that before the war

4. The classification of war and non-war industries is admittedly arbitrary. Most industries and many firms produced for both war and non-war uses. However, other scraps of information confirm this conclusion. It is hoped that when complete data on renegotiation are published they will throw more light on the differences between changes in profit rates on war and non-war business.

5. United States Department of Commerce, *Survey of Current Business,* January 1946, pp. 10–16, compares profits before taxes to equity by size for 1941 and 1942 with previous years. Office of Temporary Controls, OPA, Office of Research, *Corporate Profits 1936–1946, Part I, Profits Growth to Wartime Peak* (1947), "War Profits Study," No. 16, pp. 41–50. This study, based on a sample of 2,500 corporations, compares profits before taxes as a percentage of sales for 1944 to average profits for the years 1936–1939 for corporations classified by asset size in 1939. *Federal Reserve Bulletin,* XXXI (1945), pp. 16–26. This study compares profits before taxes for the years 1940 and 1943 expressed as a percentage of sales and of net worth for some 1,260 manufacturing concerns classified by asset size as of the end of 1941.

TABLE IV

CORPORATE PROFIT MARGINS BEFORE TAXES

Manufacturing Industries 1936–1939 and 1942–1945—(Millions of Dollars)

Industry	Sales			Profits before Taxes				
	Annual Average		Per cent	Annual Average		Per cent	Per cent of Sales	
	1936–39	1942–45	Increase	1936–39	1942–45	Increase	1936–39	1942–45
Total Manufacturing	56,152	136,166	142.5	3,158	12,847	306.8	5.6	9.4
War Industries	22,146	74,064	234.4	1,690	7,580	348.5	7.6	10.2
1. Iron and Steel	5,559	19,101	243.6	289	1,811	526.6	5.2	9.5
2. Non-ferrous metals	1,945	3,955	103.3	148	379	156.1	7.6	9.6
3. Machinery (except elec.)	3,493	10,297	194.8	335	1,357	305.1	9.6	13.2
4. Electrical machinery	1,557	6,710	331.0	143	759	430.8	9.2	11.3
5. Transportation equip. (except auto)	715	18,409	2474.6	45	1,555	3,355.5	6.3	8.4
6. Auto and auto equip.	3,966	3,614	-8.9	289	286	-1.1	7.3	7.9
7. Chemicals and allied prod.	3,945	9,114	131.0	402	1,155	187.3	10.2	12.7
8. Rubber products	966	2,864	196.5	39	278	612.8	4.0	9.7
Non-War Industries	34,006	62,102	82.6	1,468	5,267	259.2	4.3	8.5
1. Food and kindred prod.	11,982	22,470	87.5	442	1,422	221.7	3.7	6.3
2. Tobacco manufactures	1,273	2,081	63.5	130	175	34.6	10.2	8.4
3. Textile mill products	3,998	7,729	93.3	112	818	630.4	2.8	10.6
4. Apparel	2,239	3,970	77.3	26	241	826.9	1.2	6.1
5. Lumber	860	1,634	90.0	40	178	345.0	4.7	10.9
6. Furniture	1,040	1,913	83.9	33	144	336.4	3.2	7.5
7. Paper and allied prod.	1,698	3,300	94.3	97	386	297.9	5.7	11.7
8. Printing and publishing	2,228	3,225	44.7	121	475	292.6	5.4	14.7
9. Petroleum and coal	4,929	8,902	80.6	221	731	230.8	4.5	8.2
10. Leather	1,239	2,083	68.1	28	147	425.0	2.3	7.1
11. Stone, Clay, Glass	1,385	2,346	69.4	130	269	106.9	9.4	11.5
12. Miscellaneous	1,135	2,449	115.8	88	281	219.3	7.8	11.5

Source: United States Department of Commerce, "National Income," Supplement to Survey of Current Business, July 1947, Tables 17 and 29.

average profit margins rose in an orderly progression with the size of firm, while in 1944 average profit margins show little difference between firms of different sizes.

The preceding data have referred to profits on war business and non-war business alike. More pertinent as a guide to the effectiveness of military procurement policies are the data developed by the various Price Adjustment Boards on profits on renegotiable business alone. Although complete data on renegotiation are not yet available, there is sufficient data available to indicate the general profit experiences on renegotiable sales.

TABLE V

PROFITS BEFORE TAXES AS PERCENTAGE OF
SALES BY 1939 ASSET SIZE

Manufacturing Companies, Average for 1936–1939 and 1944

1939 Asset Size (*millions*)	All Companies		Durables		Non-Durables	
	1936–39	*1944*	*1936–39*	*1944*	*1936–39*	*1944*
Total of all cos.	8.4	10.6	10.2	10.5	8.5	11.1
Small (under $1)	3.6	9.5	5.1	10.7	2.9	8.3
Medium ($1 to 9)	6.2	10.5	7.6	10.5	5.7	10.8
Large ($10 to 99)	7.4	10.1	9.8	10.1	7.9	10.6
Giant ($100 and over)	10.0	11.2	11.4	10.9	9.9	11.6

Source: Office of Temporary Controls, OPA, *Profits Growth to Wartime Peak*, pp. 55–56.

A comparison of profits before taxes and before renegotiation on renegotiable sales with profits before taxes but after renegotiation on adjusted renegotiable sales is most significant for our present purposes.[6] It should be recognized that this comparison does not tell the whole story. The data on profits before renegotiation reflect profits as recorded on the contractor's books at the end of the year. As the war progressed some firms followed the policy of making voluntary refunds of profits earned before the close of the fiscal year. These profits did not show in their accounts as profits subject to renegotiation at the year's end. Consequently, the amount of profit

6. Adjusted renegotiable sales are sales before renegotiation minus the refund made in renegotiation.

cushion which such a contractor had was understated by his year-end statement.

Table VI shows profits before and after renegotiation for the year 1943 for some 3,745 corporations who made refunds to various renegotiation boards for that year. It indicates that for the year 1943 corporations who made renegotiation refunds had profits before renegotiation and before taxes of 18.4 per cent on renegotiable sales. These profits were reduced by renegotiation to 10.7 per cent on adjusted sales. There was a tendency for profit rates before renegotiation to be somewhat higher for the smaller firms. This was probably due in part to the larger percentage of CPFF contracts held by the larger firms. It is clear that as a group these firms were operating with a comfortable profit cushion in 1943.

TABLE VI

PROFITS BEFORE TAXES AS PERCENTAGE OF RENEGOTIABLE SALES

3,745 Refund Cases, Fiscal Year Ending in 1943
(Corporations Only, Renegotiated by all Departments)

			1943 Total Sales (thousands of dollars)				
	All Cos.	*Under 500*	*500 to 999*	*1000 to 1999*	*2000 to 4999*	*5000 to 9999*	*Over 10,000*
No. of cases	3,745	150	645	880	1,052	484	534
Before renegotiation	18.4	24.3	22.9	20.7	19.9	20.9	17.8
After renegotiation	10.7	11.8	12.0	10.8	10.6	11.2	10.6

Source: 91 Cong. Rec. 6255.

Data covering fixed-price sales by all contractors making refunds to all renegotiation boards through February 7, 1947 are given in Table VII. For the war years 1942–1945 average profit margins before taxes and before renegotiation showed a continuous decline from 21.4 per cent to 16.1 per cent of renegotiable sales before adjustment. Profit margins before taxes but after renegotiation declined from 11.1 per cent to 10.4 per cent of adjusted sales. The cushion between profits before renegotiation and profits after renegotiation became smaller in each successive year.

The data available for firms renegotiated by the Navy give a more detailed picture of this group of contractors for the four year period 1942–1945.[7] This group of cases includes over 24,000 cases or about 20 per cent of all cases assigned to

TABLE VII

COMPARISON OF PROFITS BEFORE AND AFTER
RENEGOTIATION ON ALL RENEGOTIABLE
SALES INVOLVING REFUNDS *
THROUGH FEBRUARY 7, 1947

(thousands)

Fiscal years ending	Number of cases	Before adjustment			After adjustment		
		Fixed price net sales	Fixed price basic profit (before taxes)	Per cent of sales	Fixed price net sales	Fixed price basic profit (before taxes)	Per cent of sales
1942	5,294	$26,101,326	$5,573,759	21.4	$23,079,982	$2,565,701	11.1
1943	4,870	39,871,011	7,504,386	18.8	36,285,979	3,870,529	10.7
1944	3,805	33,709,029	5,529,057	16.4	31,664,858	3,397,458	10.7
1945	1,360	5,367,492	862,208	16.1	5,054,830	524,611	10.4
1946	52	120,920	17,384	14.4	115,758	11,753	10.2
Total	15,381	$105,169,778	$19,486,794	18.5	$96,201,407	$10,370,052	10.8

* Figures do not include CPFF contracts, or construction contracts renegotiated on a completed contract basis. Neither do they include any renegotiations of brokers, agents, or sales engineers.

Attention is directed to the fact that 11,458 clearance cases, involving renegotiable sales of $54,970,865,000 and basic profits of $4,021,975,000 (7.3 per cent) have been eliminated from this tabulation. Also 56,618 cancellations have been eliminated since it is not possible to obtain statistical data showing sales and profits on all canceled cases.

Source: Senate Report No. 440, Part 2, 80th Cong., 2d Sess.

all boards for renegotiation. Table VIII indicates the profits before and after renegotiation for various types of cases broken down between fixed-price and CPFF business. For all fixed-price business the actual profit before renegotiation was 13.6 per cent which was reduced by renegotiation to 8.8 per cent. The refund cases showed profits on fixed-price business of 18.3 per cent before renegotiation for refunds resulting

7. The data on Navy cases are taken from Robert J. H. Powell, *History of Navy Department Renegotiation* (1947), III. Much of this data has been reproduced by Norman C. Parkin, "Control of War Contract Profits," *Harvard Business Review*, XXVI (March, 1948), 230–250.

from bilateral agreements and 15.3 per cent for refunds established by the renegotiation boards by unilateral determination. These profits were reduced by renegotiation refunds to 10.6 per cent and 10.2 per cent of adjusted renegotiable sales respectively.

TABLE VIII

RENEGOTIATION RESULTS BY TYPES OF CONTRACTS, 1942–1945

Navy Cases Only

	Per cent Profit before Adjustment	Per cent Profit after Adjustment	Per cent Profit Refunded
Clearances			
Fixed Price	6.4	6.4	—
CPFF	4.2	4.2	—
Total	6.1	6.1	—
Bilateral Agreements			
Fixed Price	18.3	10.6	47.4
CPFF	5.5	5.1	8.4
Total	17.3	10.1	46.4
Unilateral Determinations			
Fixed Price	15.3	10.2	37.4
CPFF	5.5	4.3	23.4
Total	14.7	9.8	37.0
Combined			
Fixed Price	13.6	8.8	38.4
CPFF	4.8	4.6	4.9
Total	12.7	8.4	37.1

Source: Navy Department, *History of Navy Department Renegotiation*, III, 137.

But these are only averages. The wide dispersion of actual profits before renegotiation is indicated in Chart VII. Profits ranged from 0.9 per cent to 74.9 per cent of renegotiable sales. In over 40 per cent of the cases profits were in excess of 20 per cent. In 14 per cent of the cases profits exceeded 30 per cent. The median average profit was 17.3 per cent. The modal profit fell between 14.0 per cent and 14.9 per cent.

The dispersion of profits after renegotiation on fixed-price contracts was from 3.0 per cent to 21.9 per cent (Chart VIII). The modal profit after renegotiation fell between 11.0 per cent and 11.9 per cent. In about 33 per cent of the cases profits

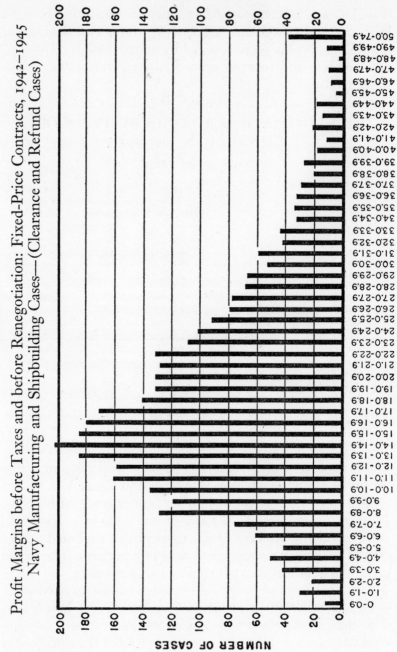

CHART VII

Profit Margins before Taxes and before Renegotiation: Fixed-Price Contracts, 1942–1945
Navy Manufacturing and Shipbuilding Cases—(Clearance and Refund Cases)

Source: Navy Department.

CHART VIII

Profit Margins before Taxes and after Renegotiation: Fixed-Price Contracts, 1942–1945
Navy Manufacturing and Shipbuilding Cases—(Refund Cases Only)

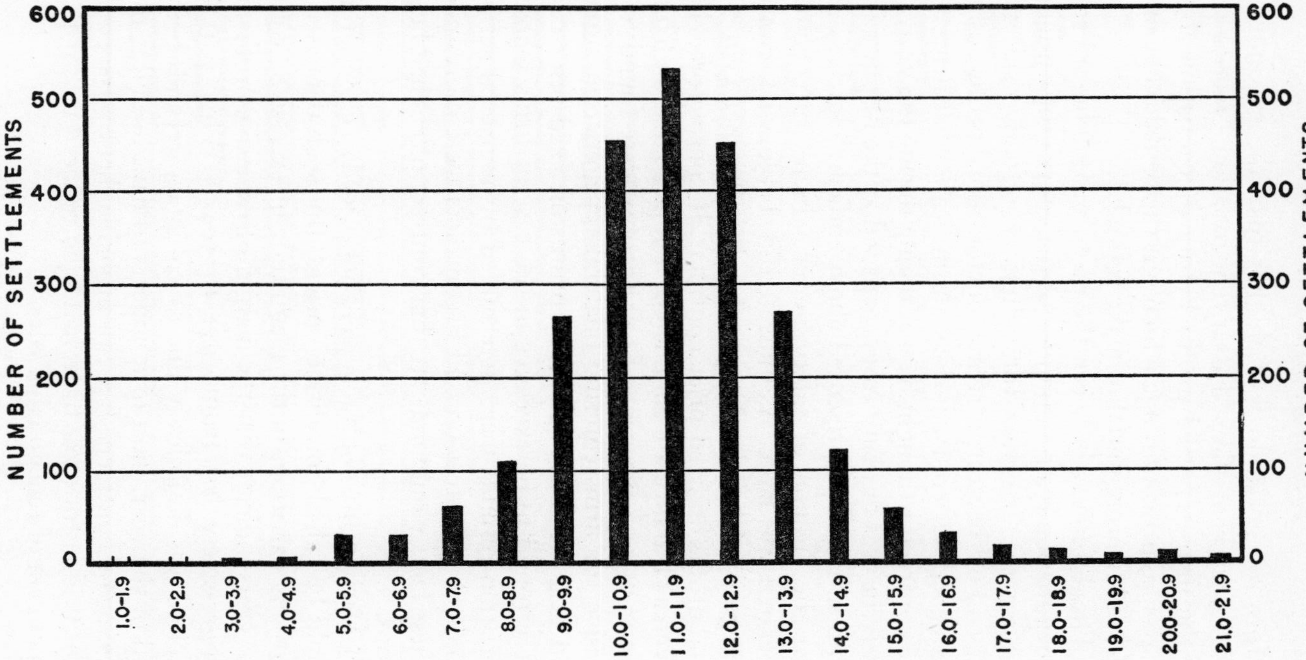

Source: Navy Department.

before renegotiation were higher than the maximum profit of 21.9 per cent allowed after renegotiation. Over 72 per cent of the firms reported profits before renegotiation above the 11.0–11.9 per cent range which was the modal range of profits allowed firms required to make refunds.

The difference between the profit margin before and after renegotiation is a rough index of the contractor's pricing risk. Subject to correction for voluntary refunds made prior to the end of the year, it represents the actual profit cushion experienced. Of course it does not indicate what degree of risk the contractor thought he was taking during the year. Doubtlessly he was in many cases surprised at the magnitude of his profits. The data presented above indicate clearly, however, that the cushion of safety under which many contractors operated was large. As indicated in Table VIII, contractors renegotiated by the Navy refunded 38.4 per cent of their total profits on fixed-price contracts. If contractors who were given a clearance are eliminated, it appears that on fixed-price contracts 47.4 per cent of total profits were found to be excessive for firms entering bilateral renegotiation agreements and 37.4 per cent of the total profits on fixed-price contracts were found to be excessive in the case of firms whose renegotiation refunds were determined by unilateral action. Refunds of fixed fees on CPFF contracts were more moderate. These facts would indicate that contract prices had been generous.

Clearly many contracts were not priced so closely that they could be called "incentive" prices. But such data as we have showing variations in the magnitude of excessive profits over the years indicate that the margin of excessive profits became progressively less from 1942 to 1945.[8] While part of this decline was doubtlessly due to voluntary refunds before the end of the year, most of it appears to have been due to closer pricing on contracts. It seems probable that by 1944 and 1945 the cushion for most firms had been reduced to 3 per cent or 4 per cent of renegotiable sales.

8. See Table VII above and also Parkin, *op. cit.*, p. 24.

Conclusion

The evidence of the over-all effectiveness of the services' pricing policies and procedures is not conclusive. As was indicated in Chapter IX, more elaborate study is needed of the costs and prices on specific contracts to determine the effects of various contractual arrangements on the incentives to cost reduction. But, judged by the final test of victory or by the increase in the volume of military goods and services produced, our record was impressive.

The data developed by renegotiation indicate, however, that the prices negotiated for many contracts were too high judged by the profits allowed in renegotiation. This was especially so prior to Pearl Harbor and during the early months thereafter. After January, 1942 the prices for most products showed a consistent downward trend except for some items purchased by the Quartermaster Corps and the Bureau of Supplies and Accounts. But even in these cases a comparison of the services' prices with wholesale prices for the same or similar goods sold in civilian markets does not reflect unfavorably upon the services. Moreover, the renegotiation data indicate that the margin of excessive profits became less each year after 1942. This suggests that closer pricing was being done through the efforts of industry and the procurement officers. Whether this reflects lesser uncertainties or a conscious effort to arrive at more reasonable prices it is difficult to determine. Whatever the cause, it is clear that once conversion to war production had been effected prices negotiated on military contracts became increasingly reasonable.

XIV

PEACETIME PROCUREMENT RECONSIDERED [1]

WITH the cessation of hostilities and the decontrol of our economy after World War II we are faced with important decisions concerning the purchasing policies and procedures to be followed by the armed services in the postwar world. It might be assumed that military purchasing would be undertaken again on the basis followed between the wars. As indicated in Chapter III, however, former peacetime policies and procedures were by no means adequate even for that period. Moreover, for the years ahead we must plan not only for peace as we have known it in the past but also for the possibility of peace with intermittent or continuing crisis. We seem likely to face for some time to come continuing international tension in a world of crisis. This has already led to large expenditures for the maintenance of our armed forces. These expenditures superimposed upon a full-employment economy have already created a situation which threatens serious inflation. Moreover, large military expenditures seem likely to continue. Expenditures for national defense which reached $10.6 billion for the fiscal year 1948 are estimated at $12.1 billion for the fiscal year 1949.[2] The President's Air Policy Committee recommended in January, 1948 a program for expansion of our air forces which it estimated may call for total military expenditures of $18 billion in the fiscal year 1952.[3] This compares with average annual expenditures of less than $1 billion per year for the period 1920–1939 and a maximum annual expenditure during that period of $1.7 billion in 1920.

1. This chapter is adapted in large part from my article "Military Procurement in Peacetime," *Harvard Business Review,* XXV (1947), 444-462.
2. *The New York Times,* Aug. 16, 1948, p. 6.
3. President's Air Policy Committee, *Survival in the Air Age,* p. 33.

In view of the prospect of large military expenditures for some years to come in an economy committed to a high level of employment and in view of the inadequacies of the pre-war peacetime system of military purchase it is not surprising that substantial changes have been made in military purchasing policies for peacetime. The Navy Department was authorized in August, 1946 to place its research contracts by negotiation without regard to traditional peacetime procedures.[4] A bill sponsored by the War and Navy Departments has been recently passed by Congress which, in addition to providing uniform legislation for Army, Navy, and Air Forces procurement and providing for use of negotiation upon declaration of a national emergency, broadens the authority of the services to place peacetime contracts by negotiation under specified circumstances rather than by formal competitive bidding.[5] This legislation is in line with recommendations previously made by the Procurement Policy Board after its review of the needs of the services and the limitations of pre-war powers [6] and was more recently approved by the President's Air Policy Committee.[7]

Objectives of Peacetime Procurement

Peacetime procurement methods adopted by the services should serve three major objectives: (1) to equip and maintain an effective military establishment which will implement our diplomatic strategy in time of peace and be capable of expansion to meet our needs in time of war; (2) to maintain an efficient industrial economy which can be readily expanded without undue delay in time of war to meet the needs of maximum strategic production; and (3) to preserve and strengthen our democratic institutions by insuring respect for the individual, wide-spread sharing of economic and

4. Pub. Law No. 588, 79th Cong., 2d Sess. (60 Stat. 780).
5. Pub. Law No. 413, 80th Cong., 2d Sess. (Feb. 19, 1948).
6. Procurement Policy Board, *Action on Report of the Committee to Consider Recommendations for Post War Procurement Policy* (November 20, 1945).
7. President's Air Policy Committee, *op. cit.*, p. 66.

political power, and a decentralization of decision-making.

The first of these policy objectives has at least two important implications for procurement methods. It implies leadership by the services in the development of military weapons. This raises special procurement problems since, as was indicated in Chapter III, there is quite a variety of circumstances in which it is impossible for the services to obtain the necessary items by the formal competitive bid system even in peacetime. These include research and development contracts, some purchases of perishable foodstuffs and other purchases where only the supplier's general reputation gives assurance of quality, and many purchases of proprietary and patented items. In all such cases our military leadership depends upon abandoning in part the system of purchase by advertising for sealed bids in peacetime.

The objective of maintaining a military establishment capable of expansion in time of war also implies the maintenance of a corps of persons in peace who have continuous training and experience in the procurement techniques required in war. This in itself suggests that it is unwise to make a sharp dichotomy between the procurement policies and practices of war and peace.

The second general peacetime policy objective, maintenance of an efficient industrial economy capable of meeting the needs of war, implies use of peacetime procurement to maintain necessary skills and reserve capacity where normal peacetime industry would not do so and to insure a structure and location of industry which will meet the strategic requirements of modern war. A striking example of the problems involved is provided by the recommendations of the President's Air Policy Commission with reference to the procurement of aircraft.[8] The committee recognized the threefold need of the services to keep the aircraft industry geographically dispersed, to provide for reasonable continuity in design, development, and production by each of the major companies, and at the same time to provide incentives to low costs and

8. *Ibid.*, pp. 59–70.

prices. The committee also stressed the need for various policies which would enable a reserve of major aircraft producers to keep together their design, engineering, and production teams. It recommended that so far as possible procurement should be planned in peacetime so that each major producer would have at all times one type of aircraft in production, one in the developmental stage and one in the stage of design. Moreover, it recommended that "in so far as possible aircraft should be produced by the developing company." [9] The formal competitive bid system is clearly not consistent with such procurement policies.

This second objective also implies that military procurement should be undertaken so as to encourage efficiency and eliminate waste in industry.[10] As pointed out in Chapter III, in certain markets competition on government contracts may be ineffective because of the publicity of bids on government contracts in markets characterized otherwise by imperfect price leadership or because of other peculiar conditions surrounding government contracts.

So long as the government was a small buyer in such markets the effects of government procurement could be ignored with impunity. But as the expenditures of our federal government for military and other purposes expand, the effect of such expenditures may be to increase the rigidities of the system, to increase the budgetary costs of a given military program, and to nullify in part the effects of other public expenditures designed to encourage a high level of productive employment. Consequently, in view of the probability that government expenditures will play an increasingly important part in peacetime, it is important to develop procurement

9. *Ibid.*, p. 65.
10. In his message to Congress on January 6, 1947 on the State of the Union President Truman stated, "National security does not consist only of an Army, a Navy, and an Air Force. It rests on a much broader base. It depends on a sound economy of prices and wages, on a prosperous agriculture, on satisfied and productive workers, on a competitive private enterprise free from monopolistic repression, and continued industrial harmony and production, on civil liberties and human freedom—on all the forces which create in our men and women a strong moral fiber and spiritual stamina." *The New York Times,* Jan. 7, 1947, p. 16.

techniques which will foster rather than lessen the competitive elements in the economy.

There are, of course, many forces at work which limit the zeal of those responsible for military procurement in using their procurement powers to break through such industrial pricing practices. Included among these forces are a desire to satisfy requirements before appropriations lapse, a fear of industrial reprisals through pressures on Congress, and a feeling that the policing of industrial practices is the responsibility of other agencies of the government. It is important, however, that our military leaders realize that a positive procurement policy designed to combat monopolistic practices is essential if we are to develop and maintain an efficient industrial machine for wartime production. A contrary policy which reduces business risk by strengthening monopolistic elements is likely on balance to encourage inefficiency and waste, a luxury which we may be able to afford in peace but which might prove disastrous in war.

The third peacetime policy objective, the preservation and strengthening of our democratic institutions, raises serious problems in a crisis society. A continuing large volume of military expenditures in the postwar world may lead to intermittent or continuing inflationary pressures. This will present us with a critical decision. If the services are to be certain of procuring their requirements, it will be necessary either to reduce the inflationary forces through stringent monetary and fiscal policies or to invoke direct controls over production, wages, and prices. The latter is the technique which must generally be used in times of war. But if we are to be faced with continuing or intermittent crisis and are to avoid the extension of centralized controls over our economy, we must plan for the use of the necessary monetary and fiscal policies which will eliminate the forces of inflation and shake loose for the services the volume of resources necessary to satisfy their needs. The wide-spread use of the negotiated contract is compatible with the use either of direct controls or indirect controls in the form of monetary and fiscal policy. However, in the areas in which the negotiated contract must be used the problems of negotiation will be greater if we fail to invoke those monetary and fiscal policies which will promote a stable economy.

The Armed Services Procurement Act

In February, 1948 Congress passed the Armed Services Procurement Act of 1947, designed to give the services greater flexibility in procurement. This bill gave the services the power at their discretion to place contracts by negotiation without advertising in a series of specified situations. While they retain authority to use the traditional system of competitive bidding whenever they believe it desirable, they have the authority to use the alternative techniques of negotiation if:

(1) determined to be necessary in the public interest during the period of a national emergency declared by the President or by the Congress;

(2) the public exigency will not permit of the delay incident to advertising;

(3) the aggregate amount involved does not exceed $1,000;

(4) for personal or professional services;

(5) for any service to be rendered by any university, college, or other educational institution;

(6) the supplies or services are to be procured and used outside the limits of the United States and its possessions;

(7) for medicines or medical supplies;

(8) for supplies purchased for authorized resale;

(9) for perishable subsistence supplies;

(10) for supplies or services for which it is impracticable to secure competition;

(11) the agency head determines that the purchase or contract is for experimental, developmental, or research work, or for the manufacture or furnishing of supplies for experimentation, development, research, or test . . . ;

(12) for supplies or services as to which the agency head determines that the character, ingredients, or components thereof are

such that the purchase or contract should not be publicly disclosed;

(13) for equipment which the agency head determines to be technical equipment, and as to which he determines that the procurement thereof without advertising is necessary in order to assure standardization of equipment and interchangeability of parts and that such standardization and interchangeability is necessary in the public interest;

(14) for supplies of a technical or specialized nature requiring a substantial initial investment or an extended period of preparation for manufacture, as determined by the agency head, when he determines that advertising and competitive bidding may require duplication of investment or preparation already made, or will unduly delay procurement of such supplies;

(15) for supplies or services as to which the agency head determines that the bid prices after advertising therefor are not reasonable or have not been independently arrived at in open competition: *Provided,* That no negotiated purchase or contract may be entered into under this paragraph after the rejection of all bids received unless (A) notification of the intention to negotiate and reasonable opportunity to negotiate shall have been given by the agency head to each responsible bidder, (B) the negotiated price is lower than the lowest rejected bid price of a responsible bidder, as determined by the agency head, and (C) such negotiated price is the lowest negotiated price offered by any responsible supplier;

(16) the agency head determines that it is in the interest of the national defense that any plant, mine, or facility or any producer, manufacturer, or other supplier be made or kept available for furnishing supplies or services in the event of a national emergency, or that the interest either of industrial mobilization in case of such an emergency, or of the national defense in maintaining active engineering, research and development, are otherwise subserved.[11]

These powers of negotiation granted by the act appear to solve the problems pointed out in Chapter III which arose from the traditional purchasing procedures.

The act also provides that in the case of negotiated contracts the services may use any type of contract which they

11. Pub. Law No. 413, 80th Cong., 2d Sess., sec. 2c.

feel will promote the best interests of the government except that the CPPC contract is specifically forbidden. CPFF contracts may be used but the fee cannot exceed 10 per cent of the estimated cost of the contract exclusive of fee, except that in the case of experimental, developmental, or research work the maximum fee may not exceed 15 per cent of the estimated cost exclusive of fee, and in the case of contracts for architectural or engineering services the maximum fee may not exceed 6 per cent of the estimated costs exclusive of fee. The act also makes specific provision that the services may make advance payments on negotiated contracts. The act also provides that it is the policy of Congress "that a fair proportion of the total purchases and contracts for supplies and services for the Government shall be placed with small business concerns." [12]

As the President said in a letter to the Secretary of Defense upon signing the bill, "this bill grants unprecedented freedom from specific procurement restrictions during peacetime . . . To the degree that restrictions have been diminished, therefore, responsibility upon the Defense Establishment has been increased." [13] Procurement regulations have been issued by the armed services which are designed to provide uniform policies and procedures for the various procurement groups operating under the act.

Selection of Sources

One of the serious problems presented by the new powers of negotiation in peacetime is to insure that administrative discretion in the selection of source is used to further the military and economic objectives upon which the procedure is justified rather than to further political or other objectives. The placing of contracts by negotiation does not preclude competition. It precludes only the special formalized procedure required by Section 3709, which procedure often re-

12. *Ibid.*, sec. 2b.
13. *Armed Services Procurement Regulations* (May 19, 1948), p. iii.

duces rather than fosters competitive forces. Of course, the
procedure which is apparently being adopted by the Munitions Board of assigning the productive capacities of various
contractors to specific services in advance of war will reduce
the range of competition to be developed.[14] But such a policy
of assignment or allocation of facilities can and should be consistent with the solicitation of competitive bids. The selection
of a source for a negotiated contract should be made only after
consideration of all possible sources and, wherever practicable,
solicitation of informal bids from and negotiation with several of them. This technique is possible in any case where
formal competitive bidding is technically feasible and in most
other cases as well. A well-administered system of negotiation which makes the maximum use of competition could,
therefore, in many cases increase the degree of competition
over that attainable under Section 3709. Several other steps
are also desirable if the selection of sources is to be well
handled.

A first step, to insure the best possible performance in the
selection of sources, lies in the careful and articulate definition
of the standards to be used in the selection of sources under
various conditions. This problem does not appear to be given
much attention in the Armed Services Procurement Regulations so far issued. In some cases the basis for selecting the
source will be clear. In the purchase of spare parts for a
proprietary item, the source may be clearly indicated by
previous contracts, *e.g.*, the spare parts for the propulsion
machinery of a battleship. In other cases, as in the purchase
of food and clothing, selection may turn, within certain general limits, upon comparative prices.

In many cases, however, the problem is more difficult, *e.g.*,
contracts dictated by considerations of strategic location of
aircraft companies. But a careful definition of the objectives
of the particular procurement program will eliminate some

14. The National Military Establishment, Munitions Board, *Allocation of
Private Industrial Capacity for Procurement Planning of the Armed Services*
(1948).

possible sources; considerations of cost and efficiency will narrow the choice further. In still other cases, such as research and development, there are not objective standards against which performance can be measured. In such cases final reliance must be placed upon the competence, information, and honesty of the technical personnel within the services who designate the sources. Even here, however, much can be done to establish more specific standards to guide the technical and purchasing personnel in their selection of sources and to serve as checks upon their performance.

A second step, which will serve to insure the maximum degree of competition and at the same time promote more effective selection of sources, is through breaking down the barriers between purchase and technical groups in the services and encouraging greater competition in design as well as price. In many cases the functional requirements of the services can be satisfied by various products of different design; an astute buyer will try to take advantage of the competition between sources using different designs, materials, or processes. Changes in technology, in the relative costs of different materials and processes, and in the market conditions of various sources of supply suggest that the competitive picture for certain items may be constantly changing. Recent developments in the field of plastics, synthetic rubbers, and synthetic fibers should offer opportunity to develop new competitive forces through redesign of many conventional items.

A fluidity in specifications and closer cooperation between purchasing and technical personnel are required to exploit such possibilities. Unfortunately the formal competitive bid system has led to a sharp division between the activities of drafting specifications on the one hand and purchasing on the other. More than that, it has meant that in peacetime the services have all too often had highly trained technical personnel responsible for design together with unimaginative groups responsible for purchase. After all, purchase by the competitive bid system required little more than honesty, clerical competence, and general administrative ability. This separation of function, together with the atrophy of the purchasing function in peacetime, must be corrected if procurement is to achieve its greatest effectiveness.

A third step necessary to insure the best possible selection of sources is the development and maintenance of up-to-date lists of potential suppliers and the active use of these lists. Lists of bidders are a familiar device of the formal competitive bid system. Lists are equally necessary when procurement is handled by negotiation. In the case of specialized military items, however, there is a danger that these lists will become unnecessarily limited. The maintenance of useful lists is not a routine job. It requires a high degree of knowledge of technical and market conditions. Improvement in purchasing personnel, which successful negotiation presupposes, together with closer cooperation between them and the technical personnel should serve to improve the development and use of such lists.

Negotiation of Price

Another major problem in the use of negotiation is to make sure that the price and other business aspects of the contracts will be such as to encourage rather than discourage production efficiency and that effort will be directed to securing contractual terms as good as or better than those attainable under the formal competitive bid system. This calls for the development of tools and techniques which are new to peacetime government purchasing.

Wartime policies and procedures are suggestive of what needs to be done, but they are by no means adequate for the peacetime job. During the war industry's attitude was different and the government's powers were greater than can be anticipated in peace. Industry was clearly induced by appeals to its patriotism, by considerations of the government's reserve powers, and by limited opportunities for non-war production to take contracts under conditions and upon terms which it would not willingly accept in times of peace. Moreover, the government possessed powers, both mandatory and otherwise, to induce production and to arrive at reasonable prices which are not compatible with our peacetime traditions. Finally, statutory renegotiation played an important part in this wartime picture.

In peacetime, on the other hand, conditions are not nearly so favorable for the negotiation of reasonable prices. Industry may often find sales to civilians more attractive than sales to the services because the former are not so encumbered with red tape or so vulnerable to changes in the domestic and international political situations. The government, in turn, lacks many wartime powers that facilitated the acquisition of information concerning costs, profits, etc., which is necessary for effective negotiation.

If procurement is to be accomplished by voluntary methods, standards of pricing in peacetime must conform as far as possible to the philosophy and behavior of freely competitive markets. Moreover, if negotiation is to be effective, the services should be prepared to use various types of contractual instruments in addition to the fixed-price contract, such as cost-plus-fixed-fee and incentive contracts. They must also devise tools of analysis and methods of negotiation which are appropriate to peacetime conditions.

Analyzing Costs. The tools of analysis which are available to the services in negotiating peacetime contracts, though less adequate than in time of war, are many. Properly used, they should prove as adequate as those available to industrial purchasers. They include analysis of market trends of items similar to those purchased by the services; analysis of trends of material costs and wage costs for items purchased; analysis of the level and trend of prices on service contracts; development of informal competition between rival sources; cost analysis and cost estimating by the services; and in those limited areas where the services are themselves engaged in manufacture, the use of their own cost experience. As in wartime, the appropriate tools of analysis and contractual instrument will differ with each negotiation.

Although some of the uncertainties of war will be lacking,

the problem of estimating costs may be accentuated in peace by the unwillingness of industry to supply cost information and the lack of power in the government to require it. It must be recognized that in many cases the procurement officer will not be able to get the type of cost data which he would like. This, of course, was often true during the war and is frequently true in the case of industrial purchasers in peacetime.

But there is still much that can be done by the services in estimating costs, particularly if the technical and purchasing personnel will cooperate. Moreover, the skillful procurement officer will often be able to circumvent this difficulty by the use of the appropriate contractual instrument in a specific negotiation to improve his information and thereby his bargaining power in subsequent negotiations. Furthermore, the difficulties of the services in acquiring information will be minimized in the case of major suppliers if the services make arrangements for pooling the price, cost, and profit information which is available in different purchasing offices and if the various procurement officers dealing with a particular contractor will exchange their information and experience and, where appropriate, adopt a united front. In peacetime, when action is less pressing and purchasing is more concentrated geographically, this should be easier to accomplish than in wartime. In this connection company pricing techniques should prove useful in peacetime as well as in wartime.

Pricing Standards. This is not the the place to write a manual on negotiation in peacetime. The Army Service Forces attempted to provide guides to negotiation in wartime.[15] Similar efforts should be undertaken for peacetime. Brief comments on three types of procurement will serve to illustrate some approaches to the task of establishing peacetime standards of good pricing.

Many standard commercial items and items of food and clothing will be purchased in peacetime. Here the standards of reasonable price should be prices arrived at in private trans-

15. ASF Manual, M 601, *Pricing in War Contracts.*

actions in genuinely competitive markets, due consideration being given to differences in the size of the contract and other terms of the sale. In many cases procurement by the formal competitive bid system should yield such prices; but if it does not, recourse may be had to negotiation. In the purchase of such items there is no substitute for intimate knowledge of the markets in question and for a careful comparison of the level and trend of prices on government contracts with those of commercial markets.

At the other extreme are research and development contracts. Here there can be no adequate standards of good pricing. In such cases cost-plus-fixed-fee or maximum-price contracts are probably required. Skillful use of such contracts may yield cost and other information which will be useful in the negotiation of subsequent production contracts.

In the case of production contracts for military items the problems of negotiating prices are most difficult and the dangers of abuse greatest. Such negotiations call for skill and ingenuity in using information acquired as an incident to previous negotiations, analyzing cost trends, estimating costs on fragmentary data, developing rival bidders, and capitalizing on the proceedings at the negotiation table. Such procurements frequently require contracts specially tailored to provide incentives for efficiency or to relieve the contractor of certain risks over which he has no control, in return for which he will accept a price that brings a substantial saving to the government. Thus, if the contractor faces the risk of a patent infringement suit which the services think is unfounded, they may agree to assume the risk. Or if the contractor is asked to take a long-run contract in a period of rising material costs, the government may find it more advantageous to provide for some sort of price-adjustment feature than to negotiate a fixed price with a heavy contingency charge.

The problem of estimating costs on many production contracts, particularly on initial production contracts, will of course be great. In some cases this problem may prove insuperable. It is possible, however, that much can be done by analysis of past cost experience to develop learning curves for various broad classes of products, *e.g.*, radar or air frames, which when applied to cost data for developmental production of new items in the same general class will serve as a guide to the future cost of these items as they move into mass production.

Profit Policy

The Renegotiation Act of 1948 [16] passed by Congress in June and the revival of the profit limitations of the Vinson-Trammell Act [17] raise vividly the question of appropriate policy to be adopted with reference to profits on military contracts in peacetime. In the preceding section it has been argued that prices of military goods in peacetime should conform to the requirements of freely competitive markets. This is particularly necessary if we are to rely on our market pricing mechanism as the instrument for allocating resources as between various uses including the satisfaction of the services' requirements. This means inevitably that there will be significant inequalities in the rate of profit as between different firms and different industries and in some cases even large rates of profits on government contracts are to be expected.

This does not mean that there will be no need for a conscious profit policy on the part of the services. In the negotiation of some contracts, to be sure, profit considerations *per se* need not enter. This is obviously true of contracts negotiated with non-profit-seeking institutions, such as universities. It is equally true of purchases of standard commercial articles negotiated in competitive markets, where the test of a competitively determined price should be adequate. In many other cases where the items purchased do not have exact civilian counterparts, reference to the price and profit policies of the suppliers of similar types of articles sold in competitive markets may offer a reasonable guide to the price and profit policies

16. Pub. Law No. 547, 8oth Cong., 2d Sess. (May 21, 1948) and Pub. Law No. 785, 8oth Cong., 2d Sess. (June 25, 1948).

17. See above, p. 169.

to be followed on military purchases. This might be true, for example, of clothing items, electrical switches, or radio tubes especially designed for military use.

There will remain at least two types of situations in which the test of price and profit policies in competitive markets will not serve as a guide. The first of these involves products where even the civilian markets do not satisfy the tests of competition. The only adequate solution for this situation is a combination of public policies which will make these markets competitive, whether it be antitrust action or other action. In such a program, government procurement policy may play a part. To the extent that monopolistic controls remain, the best the services can do is to use their ingenuity to develop equally good substitute items through redesign or, failing that, to seek prices at least as good as those given comparable industrial purchasers.

The test of a freely competitive market will also fail for certain military items where purchases by the services constitute a predominant share of the industry's output. Aircraft and naval vessels may be cases in point. Because the services' purchasing policy will inevitably be the principal determinant of the price and profit policies of such industries, market experience cannot serve as a guide. Moreover, because the services are particularly vulnerable to public criticism for unreasonable pricing in those areas, they have a special interest in watching carefully the profitability and efficiency of such industries. There is, of course, a minimum supply price to the services for production by such firms. In peacetime this may be low, particularly if there is a large amount of unused capacity which is not required by the military programs and is not readily convertible to other peacetime uses. Under such conditions the services should be prepared, like industrial buyers, to take advantage of such conditions in negotiating their contracts so long as this policy does not conflict with other objectives, such as the maintenance of reserve capacity.

The Renegotiation Act of 1948, however, makes the immediate problem of the services much more difficult. This act provides that the Secretary of Defense may subject both prime contractors and subcontractors whose total annual sales for the end use of the military establishment are $100,000 or more to renegotiation. The procedures are to conform to those used during wartime so far as the conditions and the procedures then used are pertinent. The Secretary of Defense has broad discretion, however, to determine what contracts shall be subject to the act.

Incorporation of this act in several appropriation bills by the Eightieth Congress is indication of the continued public concern with profits on military contracts. It indicates clearly that in all purchasing programs in the immediate future the question of excessive profits must be considered carefully. If renegotiation is extended, however, to a large part of the prime contracts and subcontracts, its effects in peacetime may be extremely unfortunate. In Chapter XI we have seen that it is extremely difficult to negotiate contracts with appropriate incentives to efficient production so long as there is in the background a scheme for recouping excessive profits such as renegotiation. This difficulty remains and becomes intensified in peacetime when patriotic motives for efficiency are inevitably weaker. The extension of renegotiation to peacetime operations threatens to weaken the incentives to efficient production, thereby promoting waste of resources and unnecessary increases in budgetary expenditures.

But renegotiation in peacetime may have equally unfortunate effects upon the pricing mechanism as an instrument for the allocation of resources. If we are to depend upon the pricing mechanism to determine the allocation of resources as between military and civilian demand, it is necessary that the profit prospects from military contracts should be equal to or greater than the profit prospects from non-military production. It is necessary therefore either to allow wide variations in profits as between different contractors and different industries based primarily upon the profitability of alternatives or to impose in peacetime direct controls over the flow of materials and labor and the use of productive facilities. If the former alternative is followed renegotiation is unnecessary. It becomes merely a cumbersome administrative mechanism for doing what the market will do. Moreover, it is very doubtful whether the renegotiation authorities or the public would countenance an administered structure of profits based on these standards. The second alternative means the imposition in peacetime of administered controls over our economy. It appears therefore that peacetime renegotiation will interfere with the incentives to efficient production and with the operation of the price mechanism as a device for allocating resources. These consequences are to be avoided if possible.

The immediate problem of the services is to face the challenge presented by the Renegotiation Act of 1948 to demonstrate their capacity to negotiate reasonable prices on military contracts without the device of recouping profits after they have been received. If the services can eliminate by improved purchasing techniques excessive profits arising from increased volume of business, from poor negotiation, and from the activities of willful minorities seeking to take advantage of the government, while leaving profits based upon greater efficiency or the need to compete for resources with civilian uses, they might convince Congress of the desirability of repealing this legislation. If they should fail to so convince Congress, they might, as an alternative, grant exemptions from renegotiation on a wide scale. The present situation offers an opportunity for the services to see whether under relatively stable conditions they can negotiate reasonable prices free from the extremes of "unconscionable profits." Unfortunately renegotiation is a procedure with considerable appeal. To Congress and the public it appears as a way for recouping expenditures and disciplining greedy contractors. To timid procurement officials and to contractors keenly aware of their public relations it offers a refuge from public criticism. It is to be hoped, however, that the services will accept the challenge presented by the threat of continuing renegotiation in peacetime to demonstrate their capacity to negotiate close initial prices.

Purchasing Personnel

The success of the proposals to develop more business-like purchasing will depend in large part on the calibre and authority of the purchasing officers. Improvement upon prewar procurement practice can be effected only by development of a team of technical experts including engineers, cost analysts, market analysts, lawyers, etc. centered around the purchasing officer. The latter must be a skilled negotiator and must have authority to participate in proposed procurements from their inception. In turn, if competent men are to be recruited as purchasing officers, if will be necessary to establish definite careers in purchasing for which special training and recognized opportunities for advancement are provided.

As part of the training program for such personnel, provision should be made for tours of duty in the purchasing departments of industrial companies. The purpose of this aspect of a training program should not be primarily to acquaint procurement officers with the problems of suppliers of military goods, but rather to acquaint them with purchasing techniques of firms selling in highly competitive markets and depending to a considerable extent for their success upon aggressiveness and skill in purchasing a wide variety of items. Mail order houses, department stores, and chain stores might be included, as well as manufacturing concerns in fields such as the automotive, electrical, and radio industries. Training programs should also provide for the training of technical personnel on the business aspects of design. In fact, technical personnel might also be placed in industry, particularly in firms where the functions of design and purchasing have been closely integrated.

Controlling the Use of Negotiation

Despite such a program to develop competent personnel, there is of course danger that the powers of negotiation will be abused. It should be recognized, however, that the formal competitive bid system itself is not free from abuse. Specifications can often be rigged, especially on technical items, so as to limit the number of responsible bidders. Low bids can be dishonestly rejected on the grounds that the bidder is not responsible. Indeed, one of the merits of proposals to allow the services wider discretion to negotiate contracts is that they place the responsibility squarely upon the services for the selection of the source and the business aspects of each deal. The services cannot hide behind the rigid formalities of an ostensibly impersonal system.

In order to protect the services from abuse by personnel in the lower echelons and unwarranted criticism from outside, there should be at the top level a continuous review of the policies and procedures of the services in the exercise of these powers. This review should include the compilation and analysis of data on prices, costs, and profits on military purchases and comparison with the past record of the services and with appropriate trends in civilian markets. Several steps in this direction were taken during the war, including the preparation of indexes of contract prices for military purchases.

More than this, the prior approval of the Secretary of the Army, Air Forces, or Navy, or of some designated official at top level, should be required on all major proposals prior to the award. During the war similar approval was required first by the WPB and later by appropriate officials in the Office of the Under Secretary of War or the Under Secretary of the Navy.[18] At least in the later stages of the war the emphasis in this review was upon the business aspects of the proposal other than the selection of source. Such prior approval should be based on a carefully written record of the negotiations undertaken on the proposed award, including the alternative sources considered, the various bids received, cost estimates and the way they were arrived at, and the justification for the final source selected and for the business aspects of the proposal. The Comptroller General, of course, would perform a fiscal review upon the completion of every contract to insure that

18. See above, pp. 53, 57–60.

the contract conformed with the letter of the law and that it had been performed faithfully.

Besides the danger of abuse from within the services there is the possibility that unsuccessful suppliers or their communities will seek to influence the decision on the selection of a source or even on the business aspects of the contract. These pressures may prove effective particularly if exerted through Congress. The danger exists that this will lead to the placement of contracts on political rather than on military or economic grounds. The location of veterans' hospitals and tariff legislation stand as horrible examples of such pressures at work.

While Congressional influences of this sort are to be avoided, it should be recognized that Congressional review of the placement of contracts may also be healthy. Ultimately the best protection against outside pressures is the development of enforceable standards and procedures which will not only serve the objectives of the services but also bear Congressional scrutiny. Moreover, the development of a policy of frankness and openness between the appropriate Congressional committees and the services with reference both to general policies and to specific contracts should reduce materially the dangers from this source.

Although Congressional review will always stand as an important check on the more flagrant cases of abuse, it is not sufficient if only because it is not systematic and is itself not always free from political purposes. In addition there is need for a continuous over-all review of the efficiency of the services in the business management of their procurement activities. Such a review would serve not only to allay the fears which are typically aroused by proposals to give the services additional discretion in matters of procurement but also to insure their most effective use. The type of review visualized could perhaps be best performed by the Bureau of the Budget, which, along with its responsibilities for preparation of the budget, is charged with studying the relation of budget policy to economic trends and with the study of ways to insure greater economy and efficiency in the management of the executive departments.[19] The purpose would be to assess the over-all policies and procedures of the services and other government procurement agencies and to determine the effects of these policies and procedures on the placement of contracts, prices, costs, etc.

Because failure to use authority to negotiate may be as serious as abuse of the power, the review should consider decisions to continue procurement by formal competitive bidding as well as decisions to procure by negotiation. Such an outside body might also serve as an impartial forum to which industry and others could take their complaints concerning particular contracts. In this capacity the review body would not be concerned with upsetting the particular contract but rather with determining the merits of the complaint and, where appropriate, making recommendations designed to improve future procurements.

Conclusion

Traditional purchasing procedures were devised when government purchases were small and the direct responsibilities of the government for the functioning of the economy were limited. The principal appeal of the formal competitive bid system was that it reduced the possibilities of fraud and favoritism in the placement of contracts and insured to all industry an equal opportunity to participate in government business. Budgetary economy was a secondary consideration. The increasing magnitude of government purchases and the recent tendency to undertake government expenditures for the explicit purpose of influencing the functioning of the economy suggest the need to reconsider the problem of the methods of government purchasing, by the services and other government procurement agencies alike, in terms of their impact on the price and production policies in our markets. With improvement in the administrative capacities of our bureaucracy and in techniques for selecting sources and for negotiat-

19. Harold D. Smith, *The Management of Your Government* (1945), chap. v.

ing the business aspects of contracts, the former considerations which favored the formal competitive bid system weigh less heavily and the economic considerations take on greater importance.

There are persuasive reasons for giving the services, which are responsible for a good share of current government purchasing, authority to place contracts by negotiation rather than by the formal competitive bid system when in their judgment this is necessary in the interest of national security or to promote active competition and budgetary economy. Such authority rightly includes the power to use various types of contractual instruments other than the traditional fixed-price contract. It is clear that the services are prepared to place contracts by negotiation where military considerations so dictate. Although many contracts will, of course, continue to be placed by the competitive bid system, it is to be hoped that the interest of the services in budgetary economy and in promoting active competition for military contracts will lead them to give increasing attention to the use of negotiation as an instrument to promote competition.

Clearly enough, to secure efficient administration the calibre and training of procurement personnel will need to be improved, and the performance of such personnel will require objective review. Moreover, even with the best administration the services will face many serious problems in using their powers of negotiation. In particular, it must be realized that in many cases the information available for negotiating prices will be insufficient to do a wholly satisfactory job. Often, too, a reluctant seller who has a monopolistic position in the market may still be able to dictate his terms as he has done under the formal competitive bid system. Even industrial purchasers are faced with these situations.

Negotiation is no cure-all. It is at best an additional tool, to be used with discretion in limited circumstances where it appears likely to give better results.

XV

RECOMMENDATIONS

IT IS important to reconsider at this time the purchasing policies of the armed services in both war and peace in the light of our experiences during World War II and the changed position of the United States in world politics. The traditional policies followed by the services before the war did not provide sufficient flexibility to insure fulfillment of the requirements of the services under present conditions without unnecessary waste of our resources. The recommendations for military purchasing below are designed to allow flexibility in policies and procedures in view of the different types of goods and services purchased, varying conditions of supply in different industries, variations in the state of the national economy, and changes in the types and degrees of economic controls. They seek to accomplish this by making it possible to adapt to military purchasing many practices which have already proven their usefulness to industry.

The following recommendations are based upon several assumptions concerning the fundamental objectives of national policy.[1] I assume:

(1) that the overriding objective is to insure to the armed services their requirements of the necessary quality and quantity and at the proper time;

(2) that to insure maximum military effectiveness and economy in the use of labor and materials these requirements should be carefully screened and limited by a group at the highest policy level representative of the major parties interested in mobilization;

(3) that to insure (1) above we must have in peacetime an efficient industrial economy capable of rapid expansion and conversion to the requirements of crisis or war;

1. See above, Chap. I, for a more detailed discussion of these assumptions.

(4) that incentives to efficiency in production must continue in time of war;

(5) that we must develop techniques in both war and peace which will allocate to the services the goods and resources necessary to fulfill their requirements;

(6) that purchasing policies should be designed to promote unity of purpose;

(7) that so far as possible purchasing policies should contribute to the preservation and strengthening of our democratic institutions by insuring respect of the individual, widespread sharing of economic and political power, and a decentralization of decision-making.

I believe that in peacetime these objectives can be best achieved if in military purchasing we make maximum use of the price system working through freely competitive markets. This is the mechanism of our normal peacetime economy for allocating resources as between alternative uses, such as military and civilian, and for providing incentives to efficient production. While I believe that government action may be necessary in peacetime to insure economic stability and to provide certain goods and services which cannot be well supplied by private enterprise, I believe that the pricing mechanism is the appropriate device for organizing economic activity within the sphere of private enterprise. It is within this sphere of our economy that most of the production of goods necessary to the armed services should be undertaken.

In the event of a major war I recognize that many controls must be imposed upon the economic system including controls over the use of materials, facilities, manpower, wages, and prices. It is clear that in the case of war the price system cannot be relied upon as the primary device for allocating resources or as the sole device to insure efficiency in the use of scarce labor and materials. However, the wartime price system will have important effects, for either the good or bad, in allocating resources and providing incentives. It is important that we adopt purchasing policies and procedures which will facilitate the allocation of economic resources to the produc-

tion of goods required by the armed services rather than interfere with this allocation. It is equally important that we adopt
purchasing policies which will provide positive incentives to
economy in the use of scarce labor and materials rather than
policies providing positive incentives to be wasteful in their
use.

In a crisis economy with a high level of employment such
as the present a large volume of military expenditures raises
difficult problems. In such circumstances it will be possible,
however, to place primary reliance upon the price system as
an allocative and incentive device provided we adopt monetary and fiscal policies which will promote stability and avoid
inflationary tendencies. If, however, such monetary and fiscal
policies are not adopted, the impact of large military expenditures upon our economy may make it difficult to insure the
allocation of necessary resources to the production of the
services' requirements without a substantial inflation of prices
in the military goods area, which will seriously accentuate inflation of prices of civilian goods. In such a case the alternative
to either failure to supply the services with their requirements
or continued inflation is the adoption of direct controls over
production, prices, and wages. The following recommendations are made on the assumption that we wish to avoid the
alternatives of continuing inflation, an inadequate military
establishment, or an economy subjected to continuing direct
controls over production, prices, and wages, and that we will
therefore adopt the necessary monetary and fiscal policies to
insure stability. The policies recommended below for use of
the negotiated contract, however, should make it possible to
insure the fulfillment of the services' requirements even
though we fail to provide stability.

It is increasingly clear that the sharp dichotomy which has
existed in the past between procurement policies in peace and
war will not be appropriate for the visible future. Traditional
peacetime procedures were defensible on the assumption that
we needed only a small token military establishment and could
afford to postpone the building of an effective military force

until an emergency was upon us. This assumption is no longer realistic. The appropriate procurement policies in peace and war are becoming increasingly similar.

As a result of this growing similarity between wartime and peacetime policies, peacetime procurement operations can serve increasingly as a testing ground for wartime plans. Moreover, peacetime operations will serve to train personnel more effectively in the duties which they will be called upon to perform in war. It is reasonable, therefore, that the suggestions for future policy with respect to pricing military procurements in war, crisis, and peace should be merged.

The following suggestions are made with a realization that in the field of economic mobilization all suggestions must be tentative. Price policy on military procurements is only one part of the over-all mobilization plan, the various parts of which must be coordinated. Moreover, critical decisions with respect to the internal organization of the Department of Defense may affect the feasibility of alternative policies. Finally, it is one of the basic arguments of the preceding chapters that there are many unsettled issues particularly in respect to the theory of incentive pricing which deserve much more careful study. Despite these limitations I believe there are certain guiding principles which deserve consideration and which are compatible with the foreseeable alternatives with respect to the over-all mobilization plan and organization within the Department of Defense.

Recommendations

1. *The negotiated contract should be used as an instrument of procurement in times of war, crisis, and peace.* The grant of discretionary power to the armed services to procure either by the traditional competitive bid system or by negotiation will provide the necessary flexibility for the adaptation of purchasing procedures to different types of products, to the conditions of various industries, and to varying conditions within the economy. In peacetime, procurement may be made

under the traditional competitive bid system where it is feasible and economical to stabilize and circularize specifications and where markets are actively competitive. But many peacetime contracts should be placed by negotiation. These include research and development contracts; secret contracts; contracts for other items where quality cannot be insured by specifications; production contracts where it is desirable that the contract should be placed with the contractor responsible for developmental work; contracts which must be placed in the light of strategic considerations such as dispersion of industrial capacity; and contracts in markets which are not effectively competitive because of restraints upon competition, the existence of a sole source, or patent monopoly. In time of war or wide-spread mobilization when inflationary pressures are great the negotiated contract should be used for all procurement.

2. *The services should develop specific criteria to guide their procurement officers in selecting sources for the placement of various types of negotiated contracts.* The purpose of such criteria is to serve as a guide to procurement officers and to insure that all contractors will have an opportunity to participate in military contracts so far as this is consistent with the over-all mobilization plan and considerations of economy. Such a policy will minimize the very real dangers of developing favored contractors through fraud or inertia. The criteria will differ for various classes of negotiated procurements. In some cases the emphasis will be on comparative prices and in others upon the contractor's reputation, know-how, location, etc. The criteria will change with time as did the criteria for placing contracts under WPB Directive No. 2 in World War II. It should be emphasized that negotiation does not preclude the informal solicitation of bids from several sources wherever this is feasible. In fact solicitation of bids from several sources should be an established part of approved procedures.

3. *The services should develop closer cooperation between technical personnel and the purchase groups.* Traditional methods of purchasing by circulating rigid specifications have

led to a separation of the functions of purchase and design. As a result specifications have often become unnecessarily rigid and the potential sources of supply unnecessarily limited. With the increasing use of the negotiated contract the logic of the separation of these functions disappears. Much more efficient purchasing can be effected by developing closer co-operation and a greater appreciation on the part of each group of the problems and points of view of the other.

4. *The services should sponsor and adapt their policies to an effective plan of economic stabilization to be put into effect promptly in the event of war or a major mobilization.* Every effort should be made to avoid the inflation of prices which threatens in the wake of a major mobilization program. The maximum possible use should be made of monetary and fiscal policies designed to reduce consumers' disposable income and unnecessary private investment. It is particularly important that these methods should be used rather than direct controls over prices and wages in a society threatened with intermittent crisis. But a major war or mobilization will inevitably require direct controls over wages and prices as well. The rate at which such controls should be imposed will depend upon the economic conditions when mobilization begins.

Economic stabilization contributes to the maintenance of morale within the armed forces and on the civilian front. It is also a prerequisite to successful procurement, for which the services must bear ultimate responsibility. By stabilizing costs economic stabilization reduces uncertainties and thereby facilitates the production and pricing of military goods. It will also constitute a valuable contribution to the services through its control over the prices of many materials and goods purchased on subcontracts. Moreover, the stabilization of prices and profit prospects in the civilian goods area will place the services in a preferential position to bid for industrial resources. Although the over-all allocation of resources will of necessity be determined by direct allocations, priorities, etc., the placing of the services in such a preferential position will facilitate the allocation of resources to specific uses with a minimum use of orders directed at individuals.

5. *The prices of specialized military goods should be the responsibility of the services.* In time of emergency or war the civilian price agency should be responsible for controlling the prices of basic materials and of those manufactured goods a large proportion of which go to the civilian economy. The services can develop more adequate techniques for controlling prices and profits on specialized military goods. Some division of responsibility similar to that worked out by agreement between OPA and the services during World War II should serve as a pattern. But if in an industry subject to price control the ceiling prices appear generally excessive for sales for military use because of increased wartime volume, consideration should be given to industry-wide price action designed to reduce these prices rather than to renegotiation and repricing on an individual company basis.

6. *The services' pricing policies should provide for tailoring prices and other contractual arrangements to varying conditions of procurement.* This should permit a distinction between contracts of such different types as research and development on the one hand and production contracts on the other. It should also permit distinction in purchasing policies and procedures between specialized military goods and items which are the same or similar to those sold in civilian markets. Furthermore, it should permit the adaptation of purchasing policies and procedures to changes in market conditions and changes in the context of economic controls. Finally, this should permit flexibility in purchasing to give consideration to the peculiarities of each contractor including his productive facilities, his efficiency, his financial needs, his accounting system, etc.

7. *A distinction should be made between those risks which are outside of a contractor's control and those which are within his control, and so far as possible the contractor should be relieved from the former.* This calls for various policies

such as government-financed facilities, government guarantee of loans, accelerated amortization, and escalation of prices by negotiation in the event of changes in costs outside the contractor's control.

8. *Every effort should be made to encourage maximum efficiency in the use of labor and materials by producers of military goods.* This may be done in three ways: (1) the development of contractual arrangements which provide price incentives to efficiency; (2) the development of other incentives to efficiency; and (3) the direct control of contractors' efficiency. The first two are more consistent with our traditions of appropriate relations between industry and government and are more likely to encourage cooperation of industry.

There is the danger in military purchasing that contractual arrangements will be adopted which provide positive incentives to inefficiency. It is important that such contractual arrangements be avoided and that contracts be devised that provide incentives to cost reduction and the efficient use of labor and materials. It must be recognized, however, that in time of war with high excess profit taxes and perhaps renegotiation the magnitude of price incentives will necessarily be limited. It is therefore important that appeals be made to other incentives of industry such as its patriotism, its pride in a job well done, and its desire to maintain an efficient organization for the postwar period.

Direct controls over contractors' efficiency are feasible only in the case of major contractors who are producing a limited number of products. In the case of such contractors, however, especially those operating under CPFF contracts, it is important that such direct controls be developed.

The services should study carefully the relative efficiency of various contractual devices and other devices used in World War II to insure efficiency. It may develop that the effectiveness of various devices in inducing efficiency varies with the type of product, size of contractor, or his conditions of production. Since the problem of efficiency bulks so large in case of war, the services should undertake careful study of the various methods for administering CPFF contracts in order to determine the best methods to be used in this area in case of another major mobilization.

9. *An over-all company approach to the problem of pricing should be adopted in order to facilitate incentive pricing and to avoid the inevitable dangers of decentralized purchasing operations.* An effective pricing program with emphasis on incentive pricing on a company basis might be developed along the following lines. Contractors might be divided into two groups: (1) those producing under one or a few prime contracts with a single purchasing office and (2) those producing under a larger number of contracts with several purchasing offices or under subcontracts. The first group might be handled in the conventional way. The cognizant purchasing office would seek by use of various devices outlined in Chapters IX and X to effect close prices on each individual contract or, where cost systems are inadequate, on the group of contracts. Since the cognizant office administers the contracts covering all or nearly all the contractor's war production, it would in fact be able to approach the pricing problem on an over-all company basis.

The other group of contractors would present a more difficult administrative problem. With such firms master pricing agreements might be negotiated in advance of mobilization specifying pricing policies and procedures to be followed on all prime contracts and subcontracts for the end use of the services. Each initial prime contract would be placed by the negotiation of the best possible price based on comparative prices or past cost data, if available. Maximum effort would be made to arrive at close prices consistent with the further objective of minimizing expensive studies and paper work on small contracts. Such contracts would not include specific redetermination or periodic adjustment clauses but would be subject to periodic repricing under the terms of the master company pricing agreement. Pricing of subcontracts would be the responsibility of the contractor in accordance with the master agreement.

This program would call for an over-all review of the prices and pricing policies of each company at periodic intervals in close cooperation with the cognizant renegotiation board. The periodic review would lead to appropriate adjustments on existing contracts and agreement on prices or pricing policies on future contracts. One purpose of such a procedure would be to encourage the development of adequate cost-estimating systems where feasible and the use of resulting cost data in original pricing as well as in repricing. An important advantage of this system to the contractor would be the reduction in the frequency and variety of requests for cost data and other information and in the number of different negotiations for redetermination or price adjustment. From the point of view of the services the program would stimulate more effective coordination of procurement policies, which is important in view of the inevitable decentralization of purchasing operations.

10. *Procedures should be developed in peacetime and expanded in wartime to provide the flow of information on costs, prices, profits, and over-all operations of major war contractors necessary for effective negotiation of prices.* Procedures should provide for systematic and expeditious exchange of information between all interested parties so as to aid in effective procurement and to reduce duplicate requests to industry for information.

11. *The services should intensify their efforts to develop more effective methods for analyzing costs and prices in both war and peace.* This should include an analysis of the record of cost and price changes on past and current procurements and also serve to develop patterns of learning curves for various classes of procurement which may be applicable to new products in the same class. They should also study the techniques used by progressive purchasing groups in industry in order that innovations in industrial purchasing, wherever

applicable, may be adapted to government use. A manual summarizing typical examples of cost and price experience within the services and within industry would provide a useful vehicle for training purchasing officers.

12. *The services should review the experience with various contractual devices in use since 1939 in order to determine the effectiveness of various contractual arrangements and procedures for various classes of procurements.* This should include a comparative study of the experience of various bureaus and technical services. Such a review might best be undertaken as a cooperative venture of the services and representatives of industry and should include a review of industry's experiences under those arrangements as well as the experiences of the services.

13. *The services should develop a program of appropriate control over prices on subcontracts in both wartime and peace.* This involves the development of programs and incentives to encourage prime contractors to negotiate close prices on their subcontract purchases, the direct review of subcontract purchases as in the case of some CPFF contractors during the war, and the use of the company pricing technique to cover subcontract purchases and sales. Comparative study should be made of the methods used by the various bureaus and services to cope with the subcontract problem and their relative effectiveness.

14. *As an aid to controlling and rewarding efficiency more effectively the services should provide roving teams of production and management engineers which would serve in an advisory capacity to industry and the services.* These groups would serve as a clearing house of information on the best industrial practices and might serve a dual function of making suggestions to management for improving internal operations and reporting to procurement and renegotiation officials concerning contractors' efficiency. These functions might be performed by existing groups concerned with other aspects of, production, inspection, and industrial cooperation.

15. *Renegotiation is a useful device in time of war but its*

administration must be modified substantially if it is not to impair incentives to industrial efficiency. Renegotiation serves principally as one element in the economic stabilization program designed to promote harmony and unity of purpose. Its function is not primarily economic. It serves to establish a pattern of the level and structure of allowable profits in time of war and to recoup excessive profits arising from errors of judgment, inadequate personnel, and the efforts of a willful minority to profit unreasonably from the war effort. Properly administered it may serve as one device to reward efficiency. Renegotiation has a tendency, however, as administered during World War II to interfere with incentives to efficiency in production and with good purchasing practices by the armed services and contractors alike.

Renegotiation is a useful power to be used (1) against the willful minority who seek unreasonable profits and (2) during the period of rapid mobilization to eliminate unanticipated excessive profits arising from inadequately trained personnel and errors of judgment incident to the uncertainties concerning costs. To be successful the policies and administration of renegotiation should be closely associated with procurement and in particular with the efforts at company pricing (Recommendation 9 p. 253). More adequate tests of the efficiency and contribution of contractors must be devised through improved cost and price analysis and direct inspection (Recommendations 11 and 14 pp. 254 and 255). With more adequate tests of efficiency it should be possible to provide a greater range of allowable profits than in the past so that significant contributions or superior efficiency can be rewarded sufficiently to make the risks involved worth while.

16. *Much wider use should be made of the privilege of granting exemption from renegotiation.* Exemption should be granted in the case of contracts and contractors where there is reason to believe that such exemption will provide incentives to efficiency, the contractor and government have reasonably accurate knowledge of costs, and the contractor gives evidence of a desire to cooperate in reasonable pricing. More

liberal use of the exemption privilege, particularly after the initial adjustment to wartime production, should provide a strong incentive to cost control and reasonable prices. Emphasis on the over-all company approach to pricing should reduce the difficulties experienced in the past in granting such exemptions by minimizing the accounting problems involved.

17. *Renegotiation should not be a normal part of peacetime procurement policy.* If the services are to fill their requirements in times of peace or intermittent crisis, either controls must be imposed on production, prices, and wages or the services must hold forth the prospect of profits equivalent to those offered contractors in civilian markets. If renegotiation is carried over into peacetime and controls are not imposed, it will be necessary to administer renegotiation so as to reflect the prospective profit opportunities as determined in freely competitive markets. Such an administration accomplishes little and poses serious problems of public policy.

18. *Mandatory filing of price and cost information in peacetime should be required of certain industries the level of profits of which are determined primarily by the services' purchasing policies.* In certain areas such as the production of air frames and ships the services are themselves responsible for the going level of profits. In these areas the services should be able to control profits adequately by contractual arrangements if they pursue vigorous programs of cost and price analysis. In such areas it will be sufficient to provide for the mandatory filing of the cost and price information requisite to reasonable prices.

19. *Steps should be taken to insure that policies of the technical services and bureaus are coordinated and that the powers of negotiation are not abused.* Uniform purchasing policies and procedures should be established at the level of the Munitions Board or higher. Major proposals to contract should be reviewed prior to award at the level of Assistant Secretary or Under Secretary in each of the services. There should also be review of the services' policies and operations by some outside civilian agency such as the Bureau of the Budget

in time of peace and the National Security Resources Board in time of war.

20. *Training in the objectives of purchasing and pricing policies should be extended to all personnel whose activities impinge closely on procurement.* Such training should be given to those responsible for drafting specifications, production, and renegotiation as well as to purchasing personnel.

21. *The services should provide definite careers in procurement for military personnel for which special training and opportunities for advancement are provided.* The training program should include tours of duty in the purchasing departments of companies whose success depends significantly upon aggressive purchasing as well as tours of duty with regular suppliers of the services.

22. *Reserve officer personnel for procurement should be selected with due regard for the various functions involved and the types of experience and temperament which will best qualify for each of these functions.* Such personnel should be trained specifically in procurement policies and procedures by the Industrial College of the Armed Forces during both wartime and peacetime. In the event of mobilization intensified refresher courses should be provided for personnel as it is called up to procurement duty. Case materials on negotiation, price and cost analysis, and contractual arrangements should be prepared for these training programs.

23. *The services should pursue a continuous program of cooperation with industry in the development and operation of purchasing policies and procedures.* This should include consultation in the formulation of major policies and procedures and the explanation of the policies and procedures finally adopted to top-level management in industry and to operating personnel in industry who are closely associated with negotiating and administering military contracts.

XVI

REPORT OF CONFERENCE ON PRICING OF MILITARY PROCUREMENTS [1]

Henry E. Hansen, Rapporteur

THE basic premises and assumptions underlying Miller's conclusions and arguments, as well as his recommendations, generally were agreed to or endorsed by members of the conference. Some significant differences of opinion developed, however, with respect to the role of renegotiation in wartime procurement. Certain shifts in emphasis and increased analysis of some phases of procurement and pricing were suggested. Every effort, it was agreed, should be made to utilize the price mechanism to obtain maximum efficiency in war pro-

1. Summary of a round table discussion of "Pricing of Military Procurements," held at the Yale Club, New York on June 23, 1948 under the auspices of the Committee on National Policy at Yale. The basis of discussion was an earlier draft of the present volume. The participants in this conference were: Kent T. Healy, Chairman, Professor Economics, Yale University; Robert Beach, Director of Contract Administration and Assistant Secretary, United Aircraft Corporation; Rear Admiral James D. Boyle, Assistant Chief of Naval Material, USN; Brigadier General E. M. Brannon, Assistant Judge Advocate General, USA; John W. Gardner, Executive Associate, Carnegie Corporation, New York; Henry E. Hansen, National Industrial Conference Board; John Hewlett, Comptroller, Fairchild Camera and Instrument Corporation; Lt. Commander L. G. Honey, Industrial College of the Armed Forces; James W. Hook, Chairman of the Board of Directors, United Illuminating Company, New Haven, Conn.; Harry E. Howell, Comptroller, UNRRA; F. O. Mavis, Geometric Tool Company; John P. Miller, Associate Professor of Economics, Yale University; Max F. Millikan, Research Associate in Economics, Yale University; John A. Moffit, President, Connecticut Hard Rubber Company; William H. Moore, Office of Assistant Secretary of the Navy; Edwin Pugsley, Vice-President, Winchester Repeating Arms Company; Eugene V. Rostow, Professor of Law, Yale University; Revere G. Sanders, Assistant Vice-President, Fairchild Camera and Instrument Corporation; Gustav Seidler, Assistant Chief, Procurement Planning Branch, Logistics Division, USA; Colonel Phillips W. Smith, Special Assistant to Deputy Chief of Staff, Materiel, USAF; John P. Stevens, President, J. P. Stevens Co., Inc.; J. W. G. Tenney, Attorney, Westinghouse Electric Corporation; George F. Titterton, Assistant Chief Engineer and Military Contract Negotiator, Grumman Aircraft Engineering Corporation; E. Clinton Towl, Vice-President, Grumman Aircraft Engineering Corporation.

duction and to provide incentives which would make it advantageous for producers constantly to seek lower costs and thereby conserve scarce labor and materials. Moreover, it was felt that various types of contractual arrangements and agreements should be developed which would serve these objectives in the wide variety of situations confronting procurement agencies in wartime. It was stressed that the problems of different industries vary greatly and that flexibility is essential. Planning in peacetime and constant study and analysis of the accomplishments and failures of the last war were highly recommended. Finally, it was suggested that more emphasis should be placed on non-monetary incentives. It was felt that these were often overlooked in the formulation of policy.

Controlled vs. Free Market Prices

While it was agreed that the free-enterprise price system should be permitted to function to the maximum degree possible, members of the conference generally approved Miller's recommendation that a high degree of stability of wages, prices of consumer goods, and prices of basic materials is desirable to facilitate procurement and industrial production in wartime. It was emphasized, however, that stabilization must not be carried to a point where incentives to maximum effort are removed. As incentives are impaired, production will suffer. One of the members of the armed forces observed that the initial objective in any war is to obtain as quickly as possible all of the materiel required to win that war. This would undoubtedly mean the use of many controls over prices and production. Consequently prices would not be permitted to serve as the primary devices for mobilization. But price and its effect on production should not be forgotten.

Diversion of Resources

Recognizing the role which price can be made to play in diverting goods from civilian to war production, Miller argues that the services should be placed in a preferential position with military items less vigorously controlled than nonessential civilian goods. Acceptance of such a general principle in advance of another war, it was contended, would save valuable time such as was lost in the controversy between the civilian price control agency and the military in the last war before the issue was finally settled.

Experiences of the last war were cited as supporting Miller's position. It was necessary to grant the military exemptions from price ceilings for products which also were used in the civilian economy. One member of the conference, however, expressed the opinion that price alone cannot be trusted to allocate properly and fairly the nation's resources in time of war. If the military were given too free a hand, it might bid away resources which are absolutely essential to the civilian economy. It was argued that some outside civilian control agency, not the military since it is a claimant agency, should determine allocations and then control the distribution of these goods.

Priorities. The need for priorities and allocative schemes in war was generally taken for granted. One reason advanced for their need was that the price mechanism alone cannot bring about adjustments quickly and speedily enough to divert resources into the channels required. In this connection one of the members believed that Miller should place greater emphasis on the difficulty, if not impossibility, of finding a perfect solution to military pricing in times of war. Any form of control in a free-enterprise system, it was observed, is an inconsistency. But since experience has shown controls to be necessary, the goal in wartime, it was argued, should be the best compromise possible between two systems based on fundamentally different principles.

A minimum of interference with the normal economy in times of war was advocated. One member observed that plans to fight a war while at the same time carrying on "business as usual," to provide both "guns and butter," and to draft manpower while imposing no restrictions on the components of free enterprise are understandable objectives. However, they can only be attained if the type of war permits. The fear was expressed that in the event of a war in the future more stringent controls would be required than in the last war. Advance planning through which mobilization programs are worked out with industry and understood by industry might considerably reduce the need for arbitrary controls. Certainly, it was argued, such planning would permit speedier mobilization and attention was directed to the Munitions Board's current work in developing a program for the allocation of facilities in time of emergency.

Mandatory Orders. Mandatory orders, it was agreed, should be used only after all other methods have been completely exploited. In the last war a few situations occurred where they were undoubtedly necessary, but in others Miller's view was sustained that with better negotiations and more patience resort to mandatory powers would have been unnecessary. One member who had experience in the application of mandatory powers did not regard them as very useful. He observed further that the administration of them required elaborate fact-finding, cost studies, accounting compilations, and other time-consuming mechanisms. Any plans that provided for the existence of such powers in the event of another conflict should carefully consider the administrative problems which arise when these powers are used. He suggested two methods which might simplify these problems. One method would be to take over a plant with its entire staff as a military establishment, compensation for taking the plant to be determined by a court after the period of emergency. The other would be for the contractor to act as a trustee for the government with all of the requirements of this fiduciary relationship.

Scope of Civilian Price Control Agency

No decisive answer was obtained to the question of the extent to which a civilian price agency should control prices of civilian goods when sold on military contracts. A multitude of items used in the civilian economy are identical to those required by the military. A partial answer to the question was given earlier when it was noted that in the last war the military had to give exemptions from ceilings to obtain the necessary quantities of certain items. For many other items, it was contended, control such as OPA exercised in the last war considerably eased the task of the procurement agencies of the military services.

OPA's Role. Cases were cited where OPA's activities were regarded as constructive and others where they were destructive to the interests of maximum production and sound pricing. One member believed that the task of military procurement would have been insuperable if civilian goods used in military production had not been controlled. "There was a very substantial underpinning provided by ceiling prices and controls of all standard components. It was hard enough to handle the problem of price on something that was specially made for war purposes." He also was of the opinion that the relaxation of OPA controls over standard commercial items was unfortunate.

A textile producer, on the other hand, observed that "there was great difficulty in the textile business because of the methods used by the OPA. The price at which you happened to have sold an article in March, 1942, made it purely an accidental ceiling." He further contended that renegotiation killed incentives and that the stimulus to production rested upon patriotic motives.

Another disadvantage of OPA control over items used in military production was that the ceilings established also became floors since they had official approval. Consequently the services had difficulty in obtaining price concessions when large procurements might indicate that discounts were in order. However, one member felt that the net result of OPA's contribution was on the plus side because of the "underpinning provided" on materials and subcontracted items. As a result of OPA's activities thousands of items which prime contractors included in costs required no argument regarding price.

One suggestion advanced was that it probably would have been enough if OPA could have held the line on peacetime volume levels and if the services had had a repricing contract which could have recouped to them the savings arising out of the added volume. It was believed that in many instances no great difficulty would have been experienced in negotiating special discounts which would have been passed on to prime contractors and reflected in lower prices on end items. Such discounts could have been subject to revision from time to time.

Reviewing the problems of the subcontractor, a representative of a firm which acted in this capacity during the last war observed that many subcontractors could not determine whether their products were being used for war work. In fact, he said, their customers often did not know. This was one of the great difficulties encountered in renegotiation; it was almost impossible at times to decide the allocation between renegotiable and non-renegotiable business. Furthermore, he was strongly opposed to a double price system believing that it would do more harm than good. If excessive profits developed, he thought certain revisions in tax laws might be made to take care of that problem.

Negotiation vs. Formal Competitive Bidding

Military procurement agencies should not be forced to place contracts by formal competitive bidding. It was the unanimous opinion of the conference that this should be the case both in war and in peace. Miller's recommendation in this respect was completely endorsed. The criteria, it was felt, should be good purchasing. Whichever method results in the soundest buying in any particular situation should be utilized. An examination of the record of the last war showed that formal competitive bidding quickly broke down and that market conditions were such that the only satisfactory method for obtaining the necessary materiel was through negotiated contracts. One member was of the opinion that "either in war or peace, competitive bids are the shield under which price leader schemes operate. While the method is generally supported by contracting officers of the services, such support seems to be based upon the single argument that it spares them trouble with Congressmen who want to know why some constituent did not get the business."

While negotiated prices are a tremendously important influence in sound procurement, it is clear that the techniques are more difficult and time-consuming than competitive bidding. What is needed, it was said, is discretionary power for the services to use either the competitive bid system or negotiation. By the judicious use of the right method at the right time the procurement agencies could insure freely competitive prices. One member observed that there is nothing wrong with the sealed bid system provided that it is freely competitive. However, negotiation should be permitted even after sealed bids have been opened. The procurement agencies should not be put into a position of being forced to buy from the lowest bid contractor when that contractor does not know his costs and may not be able to complete his contract either because he fails to understand his scope or may go bankrupt. The importance of the procurement function and procurement officers must be given proper recognition such as is accorded in private industry.

Pricing Negotiated Contracts

The desirability and feasibility of devising contractual arrangements under wartime conditions which will provide incentives to efficient production, as Miller recommends, was not questioned. But it was the consensus of opinion that any pricing arrangements or principles must be viewed in the light of whether or not renegotiation is in the picture. If after procurement officers have agreed on a fair and reasonable price with contractors, an outside agency reviews these arrangements and in effect alters them, then little hope is held out for sound and scientific pricing. Consequently, it was felt that the question of sound pricing of contracts could not be divorced from that of the role of renegotiation in any future emergency or war.

The problems of assuring sound prices for subcontracted items were recognized as quite different from those of the prime contractor. In part these have already been touched upon. For example, a double price system was opposed, partly because of the difficulty of differentiating between war and civilian business. A suggestion was made that if prime contractors were provided with a real incentive to do the best possible buying, their efforts would result in sound pricing for subcontracted items. Renegotiation was regarded as destroying that incentive.

Renegotiation in War and Peace

The major difference of opinion between Miller's views and those of the conference developed with respect to the recommendation that "renegotiation should be used in wartime as an aid to procurement and a method of recouping excessive profits." [2] The majority felt that they could not endorse this recommendation and that the record of the last war indicated that renegotiation as administered and sound procurement were incompatible. A few kind words were said for renegotiation, however, by the representatives of two aircraft companies.

The question of the role of renegotiation in peacetime was quickly disposed of. No excuse or reason could be seen for its use or existence. It was agreed that only unfavorable results can be expected from the two renegotiation laws passed by the last Congress. They will not aid procurement but will instead subject many manufacturers to additional costs and time-consuming paper work and negotiations. In addition, they may at times hamper the armed forces in the placing of

2. From earlier draft of manuscript submitted for discussion at Conference. For recommendations on renegotiation as revised since the Conference, see above, pp. 255–257.

contracts. There are, moreover, strong prospects that future appropriations will make similar provisions unless the complete story of the effects of renegotiation are made clear to legislators and the public.

Many of the contractors now subject to renegotiation, it was observed, are also subject to the profit-limitation provisions of the Vinson-Trammell Act. That act was suspended during the war but is now again in effect. A representative of an aircraft company commented: "It is the uniform opinion of our industry, and I am sure also of the shipbuilding industry, that the profit-limitation provisions of the Vinson-Trammell Act are not only patently discriminatory, but in addition they impose a heavy burden of administrative work on both prime contractors and subcontractors. We think that these provisions should be repealed immediately. I doubt very much that these profit-limiting provisions ever produced any significant revenue for the government during the period when they have been in effect."

Effect on Incentives. Among the most serious accusations leveled against renegotiation was that it destroyed incentives. Efficient producers, it was contended, often were penalized. For example, a ten per cent profit allowed to a high-cost producer obviously resulted in a greater dollar profit than when the same percentage was allowed a low cost manufacturer. In this respect it was subject to the same criticism as a "cost-plus-percentage-of-cost" arrangement. It was suggested that a wider range of allowable profits was desirable. If that had been the case, more adequate rewards for efficiency might have been possible, although the difficulty of accurately measuring and comparing efficiency among contractors was recognized.

Insecurity and Uncertainty. Another major defect of renegotiation listed was the long period of time during which the contractor did not know the full extent of his earnings and income. Consequently many important policy decisions had to be held partially in abeyance. Generally a settlement was not reached until many months after the close of a calendar or fiscal year and long after deliveries on a particular contract had been completed. This uncertainty was regarded as one of the most aggravating and destructive features of renegotiation. Normal business practice is for the producer to enter a negotiation, come to an agreement on terms and then return to his plant and do his best. He has every incentive to reduce costs to the lowest possible level. And he knows at the outset roughly where he stands.

Price Consciousness of Procurement Officers. Another result of renegotiation, it was said, was an adverse effect on the price consciousness of procurement officers. With renegotiation in the background, second guessing and acting as a backstop, there was less incentive for officers to carry through as tough a negotiation on price as otherwise. An industry representative observed that renegotiation also had some effect on his thinking as he entered contract negotiations. Frequently, it seems, a "what is the use" attitude developed. Thus the absence of closer pricing in contract negotiations did not necessarily reflect poor pricing methods or principles.

Renegotiation Divorced from Procurement. If renegotiation has any justification, it was contended by several members, it is only as an aid to procurement. Renegotiation was at first part of purchasing, but it was later divorced and developed into a technique for "skimming off profits." Miller recommends the "closest possible coordination of procurement and renegotiation," but it was felt that this point should be emphasized even more, assuming that renegotiation is not entirely dispensed with which many believe desirable. As a profit skimming operation renegotiation failed to provide the incentives and pressures to keep costs down. Even the information collected often came too late to be of any particular help to contract pricing. For these reasons and because of the uncertainty and insecurity it caused, one member of the conference who was active in procurement during the war stated: "I have very definitely come to the conclusion that renegotiation is a great bar to the type of contracting that the services will have to do in peace and war."

Subcontract Pricing. Some difference of opinion existed in regard to the effect which renegotiation had on the pricing policies of subcontractors. One view was that since subcontractors knew that "excessive" profits would be taken away, they were more willing to make price concessions to their customers, the prime contractors. Another member took an entirely opposite point of view. He felt that renegotiation prevented sounder pricing at the subcontract level.

In Support of Renegotiation. Some representatives of the aircraft industry stated that their experiences with renegotiation were satisfactory. They were not opposed to it in principle as were other industry representatives although they thought its administration might be improved. The aircraft industry was constantly being called upon to produce new items or to change existing items radically. Tremendous numbers of engineering change orders were being issued and volume of production was subject to wide and sudden variations. Under these conditions cost estimates, despite the best of intentions, were often found to be wide of the mark. Unintended excessive profits were earned at times and renegotiation simplified the legal problems of a corporate management in making refunds. Some criticism of the methods of administration, however, is found in the following statement by one of the aircraft industry representatives: "I found renegotiation during the war extremely fair, with one exception. There was a basic percentage in the back of everyone's mind conducting renegotiation." Obviously, if this percentage was the same for a low cost as for a high cost producer, the latter received the larger aggregate profits for his efforts. Another member of the industry observed that under the conditions which prevailed during the last war and with government business accounting for nearly all of his company's total production, renegotiation "on the whole, was a pretty good formula and mechanism."

Political Reasons for Renegotiation. While not advanced as an argument in favor of renegotiation, it was recognized that some strong political reasons existed for its establishment. Following World War I Congressional investigations resulted in the country becoming very "war-profiteering" conscious. Renegotiation in part, therefore, was regarded as insurance against situations developing where it might be said that profiteering had occurred while men were giving their lives in defense of the country.

Changes Suggested. Recognizing the difficulty of making reasonably accurate cost estimates in industries subject to constant change, as was true for aircraft in the last war, some members were of the opinion that careful analysis of various industries contributing to war production, either directly or indirectly, would reveal many cases where accurate costing and good pricing is possible. Where sound contract pricing is possible, exemptions from renegotiation, possibly by broad classes, should be granted. A subcontractor believed that such exemptions were particularly appropriate in the case of subcontractors for standard products or materials. This would also eliminate the problem of determining the proportion of renegotiable and nonrenegotiable business. One member felt that even in instances where accurate costing is not possible in advance of production, a good repricing contract clause would be much more desirable than renegotiation. It would do everything that renegotiation could do without incurring the disadvantages of renegotiation.

Another suggestion made was that prime contracts provide for a minimum which will be allowed after renegotiation. Then some of the uncertainty would be removed. If the contractor turned in an outstanding performance, he would be allowed a larger return than the minimum. It was further suggested that the development of techniques for evaluating the efficiency of contractors would be desirable, although some members doubted that this could be done satisfactorily. If efficiency could be measured reasonably accurately, then a wide range of renegotiation allowances would be necessary.

If renegotiation is simply a device for "skimming off" profits, some members suggested that this function could be better performed by the tax laws and the Internal Revenue Bureau. People are accustomed to having that agency take money away from them. The entire process of diverting so-called excessive profits to the Treasury could be performed at a much lower cost. One member questioned whether the profits taken under renegotiation had been worth the great effort. It was suggested that after proper allowance was made for the extra time and cost to industry and government which renegotiation entailed, little, if any, savings resulted.

Some opposition was registered to a suggestion that a 100 per cent excess profits tax be imposed in wartime in place of renegotiation. It was contended that, because of differences in the invested capital of companies, such a tax might prove more unfair in some cases than renegotiation. It would moreover, remove all incentive to efficiency and would "encourage the building up of costs" instead.

Efficient Procurement and Pricing

Efficient procurement and pricing depends upon a wide variety of factors. As the discussion brought out, true incentives must be provided. Certain controls are necessary in wartime but the normal price and market mechanism must not be excessively hampered. One of the essentials to good buying, of course, is the development of terms and conditions of contract which will result in the attainment of the objectives of sound purchasing policy. Much of the remainder of the conference was devoted to a discussion of various types of contracts. Some other essentials to good buying, however, also were touched upon.

Miller's recommendation that the "Services should develop closer cooperation between technical personnel and the purchase groups" was endorsed. Purchasing has been hampered, it was observed, by the rigid separation of the functions of design and purchase. One member with experience in both government and industry purchasing noted that the military purchasing function is performed in a formalistic manner with no scope for initiative or negotiation for cost reductions by minor and unimportant design changes. In turn, specifications are written without any reference to cost and without real consideration given to the efficient use of labor, materials, and machinery. Government, it was felt, could learn much from studying and adopting certain principles of organization and methods of progressive purchasing departments in private industry. Military buying, it was said, was also hurt by the failure to coordinate and consolidate all requirements and to keep them under constant survey.

Use of Management Engineers. As an aid to good buying, Miller recommends that the government use management engineers to evaluate a contractor's efficiency and to assist in the development of more efficient production methods. Upon request, these engineers could help a producer to solve a particular production problem. The principal objection to this suggestion was that it would be difficult to obtain competent engineers in time of war. All of them would be required by industry. In the last war, it was observed, skilled and technical personnel were at a premium. In view of that situation the question was raised whether selective service should not give greater recognition to industry's manpower problems. The military was aware of these problems, it was said, but also had to consider the morale aspects of deferments. It was suggested, however, that during the early stages of a war, when the problem of producing materiel is more formidable than that of obtaining men, deferments might be more liberally granted to key men in industry.

Types of Contracts. One of the basic facts that developed from this discussion is that no single type of contract can be devised to take care effectively of every situation. The problems of the aircraft industry are very different from those of textile producers. Procurement officers and contractors should not be forced to use a designated type of contract if it is not appropriate. One of the great contributions which planning groups can make during peacetime is the development of various contract clauses which will result in maximum efficiency in buying and production in the wide variety of situations which will confront contracting officers in time of war.

Tracing the development of some of the contracts used in the last war, one of the representatives of the services noted that prewar planning had been influenced by the criticism which was directed against excessive profits in war contracts during World War I. The intent of these earlier efforts was to provide incentives for keeping costs down. Consideration was given at the outset of the last war to combining the cost-plus-fixed-fee contract with a target price contract. One of the major difficulties was that with fees limited to a maximum of 7 per cent of estimated cost the reward which could be given a very efficient contractor was small. It was also recognized that in many instances products would be subject to constant change or that contractors would be called upon to make entirely new items. Thus costs could not be accurately estimated and constant adjustments in estimates would be required. Revisions would also be necessary if costs of labor and material increased through no fault of the contractor.

With the experience of the last war as a background, however, it was felt that appropriate types of contracts could be put into use which would provide incentives and sound prices. Some were of the opinion that contractual arrangements could be worked out which would make it safe and desirable to dispense with renegotiation. Attention was repeatedly called to the danger that all efforts to provide incentives in contracts might be nullified by the actions of a renegotiation board.

Target Contracts. Representatives of the aircraft industry commented favorably on their experience with the incentive or target-cost contract used by the Navy Department. These did not generally provide for exemption from renegotiation, but several members were of the opinion that the possibility of providing such exemption in the future should be carefully studied. Such a development would hold out real hope of providing true incentives to maximum efficiency. Under the target-cost contract, contractors share in cost reductions below the target while cost increases result in reduced profits. As Miller observes, the major problem is to negotiate a satisfactory target, which is very difficult or impossible to do for completely new items or those subject to constant engineering changes. The conference agreed, however, that there are many situations where this type of contract would be very helpful and that serious effort should be made to explore its full possibilities.

Redetermination Clauses. Further careful study of the use of redetermination clauses, particularly in cases where costs cannot be accurately estimated at the outset, was recommended. A considerable record of experience in the use of these clauses, their shortcomings, and the areas in which they are most suitable was accumulated during the last war.

One variation in the redetermination type of contract suggested would provide for the negotiation of the profit margin after 25 per cent of the articles called for under the contract had been produced. This type might prove useful in some cases where costs cannot be estimated prior to some production. It might also incorporate an incentive feature in order to make it worthwhile for a contractor to reduce costs as much as possible on the remaining 75 per cent of production. In the case of small contracts, where it "isn't worth while to set targets and reset them," a downward revision clause may prove practical. In addition it was suggested that consideration be given to simplifying the operation and administration of redetermination clauses used during the last war.

Opposition to redetermination provisions was registered by one producer because of the paper work and accounting problems involved. He felt that the influence of T.D. 5000 had been particularly bad. The clauses would be much more acceptable if costs as shown on the company's books were accepted. Attention was called by another member to the lack of uniformity in accounting policy. Policies of the contractor, the procurement agencies, and the General Accounting Office differ considerably. It was further contended that a clarification of accounting policy is essential in order that a basic rule for determining costs can be established. A representative of the military noted that work was progressing in that direction. Another member suggested that too much reliance had been placed throughout the last war on cost-accounting and audit procedures, particularly as they related to individual contracts. He also observed that very simple devices could be written into contracts concerning the key information required to assure proper control. This approach has special merit in master contracts or company pricing, as discussed later.

Cost-Plus-Fixed-Fee. Opinion was divided as to the desirability and value of using cost-plus-fixed-fee contracts in war procurement, especially for production items. It was generally conceded that there are situations, particularly when research and development is involved, where a CPFF contract is about the only type of existing contract which can be used. A representative of the aircraft industry summed up his company's views as follows: "The general belief of our corporation has been that it is an insidious thing to get into the habit of operating under CPFF contracts. You can't help letting it be known that you have a CPFF contract, and the general tendency of management and I think of everybody else is to relax a little."

Evidence of efficient operations under well administered CPFF contracts were cited. The incentive in such cases, however, was not provided in the contract but instead reflected management's fear that bad habits acquired in wartime would be a serious liability in peacetime civilian production. One industry representative favored CPFF contracts if they "could be finalized with the services." He objected to the General Accounting Office getting into the picture unless there was evidence of fraud. It was observed that some of the accounting problems of the CPFF contract had been eased by the adoption of a fixed-overhead type in which overhead can be periodically reset when important changes occur in the volume of production.

Attention was also directed to another variation of the CPFF contract, called the cost evaluation contract. Under this contract, which has never been authorized, the performance of the contractor would be evaluated upon completion on the basis of certain factors specified in advance, such as efficiency in the handling of materials and labor, financing, etc. This evaluation would determine whether the contractor was entitled to any fee in addition to the minimum provided in the contract. A representative of the Army stated that it did not seem that this type of contract would be attractive to industry because of the uncertainty regarding the evaluation of efficiency. He thought, however, that this approach merited additional study.

Company Pricing. Members of the conference familiar with the company pricing program developed near the close of the last war were in agreement with Miller's analysis and recommendation of this technique. Many procurement problems could be solved or eased by using the total company approach particularly for large contractors almost wholly engaged in war work. As one member put it: "The inability to measure the profit outcome on any individual contract; the tremendous mass of cost and accounting work required and the arguments over principles of overhead and cost allocation entailed; the need of a progressive and cumulative review of the contractor's position—all of these make company pricing a logical plan. It is also one which the manufacturer is willing to accept after it has been explained to him." Under the program considerable advance planning would be possible and many details of pricing policy could be analyzed and accepted prior to the actual placing of contracts. Because of the late date on which it was inaugurated in the last war, the record of experience is limited but deserving of intensive study.

The record of accomplishment of the company pricing program was not very impressive, partly because in and out of the services it was regarded as competing with or supplementary to renegotiation. In its short life, however, it was contended that it demonstrated its value in coping with the problem of overabsorption of fixed charges. Such overabsorption was a frequent cause of excessive and unexpected profits. Company pricing provided a mechanism for making continuous adjustments in overhead rates.

One recommendation growing out of this discussion was the use of blanket or master contracts for producers almost entirely engaged in war work. The pricing clause in such a contract would only involve a statement of the company pricing scheme. The requirements of the contract would be that the company produce various items as specified from time to time and that for each of these items a cost estimate would be prepared to provide a basis for tentative billing. Such estimates, of course, would be examined and, if proper, accepted by the procurement officer. Thus instead of a mass of contracts with each concern, there would be a single contract tentatively priced. The final price, however, would be determined under the contract in accordance with company pricing principles. The administration of such contracts would be in the hands of procurement officers who would have the power to recognize efficiency and provide incentives. Another benefit ascribed to a master contract is that many of the accounting problems encountered under individual contracts would be avoided. There would be no need to spend many hours in trying to allocate overhead items among individual contracts. The cost factors which can best be reviewed on an over-all basis would be treated accordingly.

Non-financial Incentives to Efficiency

Reviewing the afternoon's discussion, one member with long experience in industry and government service observed that emphasis had been placed primarily on the profit incentive as a means of assuring low costs and maximum production. He noted, however, that profit may reflect undesirable practices and policies and that the type to be encouraged arises when a manufacturer makes a careful estimate by looking ahead and forecasting his position as to volume and cost, sets himself a tight goal in the price, and proceeds to beat it through efficient methods. Such contractors not only make a contribution by saving the nation's resources but establish a usable standard against which other performances can be evaluated.

The impact of other incentives, non-financial in character, should not be overlooked or unrecognized. It was observed that there are many additional incentives aside from profits, "that people work because they want to do a first-class job and they want to keep their shops running right. It is my opinion that the men who almost killed themselves during the war didn't do so for a few more dollars." Mention of these incentives in Miller's study was suggested. Pride of workmanship, pride of accomplishment, pride of smooth running and efficient organizations, and pride in contributing to the winning of the war were among the non-financial incentives cited. These incentives, another member noted, were the basis of good morale and were hard hit by renegotiation.

APPENDIX A

TABLE IX

EXPENDITURES FOR WAR ACTIVITIES

Quarterly, July 1940–June 1946 *
(Millions of Dollars)

Quarter Ending	Total	War Dept.	Navy Dept.	Maritime Comm.	War Shipping Admin.	Dept. of Agric.	Treasury	Other
1940								
September	663	252	353	25	—	—	8	25
December	1,199	633	511	10	—	—	4	41
1941								
March	1,968	1,306	600	-10	—	—	5	67
June	2,471	1,487	848	26	—	2	8	100
September	3,430	1,860	1,227	81	—	61	32	169
December	4,835	2,677	1,535	170	—	150	105	198
1942								
March	7,121	4,083	2,102	302	18	221	140	255
June	10,627	5,451	3,717	378	114	264	245	458
September	14,766	9,255	3,773	536	266	245	307	384
December	17,348	10,725	4,454	595	323	505	274	472
1943								
March	18,461	11,277	5,329	839	248	47	277	444
June	21,535	11,008	7,333	806	270	1,214	343	561
September	20,616	12,063	5,844	1,046	354	431	327	551
December	21,248	12,156	6,139	1,052	528	553	319	501
1944								
March	22,382	12,423	7,120	1,025	500	512	349	453
June	22,792	12,600	7,434	688	641	648	436	345
September	21,770	11,920	7,388	837	430	358	378	459
December	22,383	12,263	7,664	936	480	270	352	418
1945								
March	22,745	12,844	7,690	671	535	334	367	304
June	23,132	13,310	7,305	782	597	235	366	537
September	19,091	11,079	6,069	446	512	226	240	519
December	13,597	8,004	3,819	199	446	570	234	325
1946								
March	8,669	4,589	3,183	-22	262	101	135	421
June	7,184	4,127	2,088	71	147	144	87	520
Total	330,033	187,392	103,525	11,489	6,671	7,091	5,338	8,527

* Does not include net outlays by government corporations.

Source: United States Treasury, *Bulletin*.

APPENDIX B

MAJOR WAR SUPPLY CONTRACTS AND FACILITY PROJECTS

April 1940–December 1944

Data in Table X and Charts II and III on supply contracts and facility projects are taken from *Summary of War Supply and Facility Contracts by State, Industrial Area and County*, June 4, 1945, published by War Production Board, Program and Statistics Bureau. WPB gives the following explanation of the data:

The total of Federal war supply and facility projects reported is net, reflecting all decreases due to contract cancellations and reductions that have been reported to the War Production Board.

The value . . . shown for supply contracts is the total of individual contracts awarded by the Army, Navy, Maritime Commission, Treasury Procurement Division, and foreign purchasing missions reported to the War Production Board in the period June 1940 through March 1945. Defense aid awards are included (Treasury contracts include only such awards). Army, Navy, and Maritime Commission contracts cover awards since June 1940; Treasury contracts, since March 1941; foreign contracts, since September 1939. Contracts having a value of less than $50,000 and all awards for foodstuffs and food processing are excluded.

The value . . . shown for facility projects represents the total of the latest estimates of final cost of each project for which a contract has been awarded or a letter of intent or project order issued of $25,000 or more as reported to the War Production Board in the period June 1940 through February 1945. Costs such as land purchase, architectural and engineering fees, construction materials, construction work, and manufacturing and maintenance facilities financed by the Army, Navy, Maritime Commission, Defense Plant Corporation, Reconstruction Finance Corporation, and British Empire governments are included. Facilities financed with private funds are excluded.

The . . . total of water supply and facility contracts is substantially below the total commitments as reported through March for these agencies. An important factor accounting for this difference is the lag between the commitment of funds and the award of contracts and the further lag between the award of contracts and reporting of information on individual contracts. Project orders account for another part of this difference, and contracts having a value of less than $50,000 and awards for foodstuffs and food processing aggregate a substantial sum. In addition, the $225 billion does not include revisions in the estimated final cost of products under cost-plus-a-fixed-fee contracts or under contracts containing an escalator clause with respect to wage rates and material prices.

The category "Aircraft" includes contracts for airframes; airplane engines, propellers, and other parts, including starters, generators, carburetors, etc. and certain related equipment, such as parachutes and aircraft pontoons. Armament, such as gun turrets and bomb racks, is included but instruments and communication equipment are excluded. The category "Ships" includes contracts for the construction of new vessels of all kinds; the purchase of used vessels; ship conversion, recommissioning, and repair; and the purchase of marine engines and propulsion equipment. Armor, armament, navigation and radio equipment, parts, and materials are excluded. The category "Ordnance" includes guns, gun mounts, and fire control equipment; ammunition, shells and bombs; explosives, and ammunition loading; and motorized combat and non-combat vehicles. Armament for vessels is included in this category. The category "Communication Equipment" includes contracts for radio, telegraph and telephone sets, parts, and equipment; sound detection equipment; and other related electronic devices including tubes and parts.

Table X

MAJOR WAR SUPPLY CONTRACTS AND FACILITY PROJECTS BY MAJOR OBJECT

Quarterly, April 1940–December 1944

(Millions of Dollars)

Quarter Ending	Total	Supply Contracts						Facility Projects		
		Total	Aircraft	Ships	Ordnance	Communication Equipment	All Other	Total	Military	Industrial
Total Reported	216,210	186,083	59,503	27,648	47,652	9,128	42,152	30,127	13,171	16,956
1940—Total	13,774	10,875	3,823	3,167	2,483	172	1,230	2,899	1,554	1,345
June	1,641	1,641	1,024	87	250	66	214	—		
September	6,366	4,846	1,264	2,336	885	27	334	1,520	949	571
December	5,767	4,388	1,535	744	1,348	79	682	1,379	605	774
1941—Total	25,792	19,070	6,255	2,715	6,028	580	3,492	6,722	2,651	4,071
March	3,093	2,045	271	546	672	53	503	1,048	515	533
June	7,611	6,129	2,707	836	1,559	168	859	1,482	684	798
September	5,999	3,947	923	530	1,563	30	901	2,052	483	1,569
December	9,089	6,949	2,354	803	2,234	329	1,229	2,140	969	1,171
1942—Total	80,949	65,865	19,912	10,757	19,323	2,622	13,251	15,084	6,213	8,871
March	28,186	21,832	7,222	3,577	7,816	423	2,794	6,354	2,441	3,913
June	20,432	15,388	3,396	2,979	4,703	989	3,321	5,044	1,952	3,092
September	18,617	16,368	6,093	2,692	4,286	517	2,780	2,249	1,081	1,168
December	13,714	12,277	3,201	1,509	2,518	693	4,356	1,437	739	698
1943—Total	53,512	49,615	16,178	7,701	9,984	3,570	12,182	3,897	1,891	2,006
March	11,578	9,990	3,082	1,065	2,156	915	2,772	1,588	855	733
June	19,794	18,943	6,941	3,834	3,333	1,174	3,661	851	488	363
September	11,337	10,420	3,333	1,537	2,000	516	3,034	917	375	542
December	10,803	10,262	2,822	1,265	2,495	965	2,715	541	173	368
1944—Total	42,183	40,658	13,335	3,308	9,834	2,184	11,997	1,525	862	663
March	11,753	11,283	5,716	564	2,025	684	2,294	470	287	183
June	14,414	13,923	4,588	1,456	3,553	743	3,583	491	276	215
September	7,845	7,527	1,031	917	1,836	346	3,397	318	176	142
December	8,171	7,925	2,000	371	2,420	411	2,723	246	123	123

Source: WPB, Program and Statistics Bureau.

APPENDIX C

TABLE XI

INDEXES OF CONTRACT PRICE CHANGES: WAR DEPARTMENT

January 1942–August 1945

(October 1942 = 100)

Month	War Dept.	Army Air Forces	Ordnance	Signal Corps	Corps of Engineers	Chemical Warfare Service	Medical Dept.	Quarter-master Corps	Trans-portation Corps
1942									
January	108.6	112.1	107.1	119.4	102.2	104.4	114.2	94.9	99.3
February	108.1	111.5	106.2	119.5	102.2	104.1	114.8	95.3	102.1
March	108.1	111.3	106.3	119.6	102.2	104.1	115.0	95.7	102.1
April	107.8	110.7	105.6	119.5	102.0	104.2	114.0	98.0	101.6
May	106.4	109.4	105.3	107.9	102.0	103.5	111.9	98.1	101.5
June	104.6	106.8	104.3	101.5	101.8	103.3	110.9	98.1	101.7
July	103.1	105.3	102.1	101.1	101.6	101.4	110.2	98.5	101.4
August	101.3	102.9	100.2	100.6	101.5	100.9	105.9	98.9	100.6
September	100.4	101.3	99.6	100.2	99.7	100.7	104.1	99.6	100.3
October	100.0	100.0	100.0	100.0	100.0	100.0	100.0	100.0	100.0
November	99.3	98.9	99.4	99.9	100.2	99.7	99.1	100.6	99.9
December	98.4	97.2	99.0	96.2	100.1	99.6	98.3	101.7	99.9
1943									
January	97.9	96.5	98.6	95.9	100.1	98.7	97.9	101.7	99.9
February	97.5	96.1	98.0	95.2	99.4	98.4	97.8	101.9	99.7
March	97.0	96.0	97.2	92.6	99.5	98.2	97.5	102.5	99.6
April	96.6	95.8	96.5	89.1	99.4	97.3	97.1	102.9	99.8
May	95.7	94.5	95.7	88.2	99.4	97.1	96.4	104.1	98.7
June	94.8	94.1	94.3	86.8	99.1	96.6	96.3	103.6	98.9
July	94.3	93.7	93.6	86.3	97.9	96.5	96.1	102.5	99.0
August	93.7	92.9	93.1	85.4	97.0	96.6	95.8	102.5	99.0
September	92.9	91.6	92.3	85.5	97.0	96.5	95.9	103.0	98.8
October	92.3	90.9	91.7	84.7	96.3	96.5	95.6	103.1	98.9
November	91.5	89.5	90.9	84.1	96.0	96.0	95.5	103.9	99.0
December	91.1	89.0	90.6	83.9	95.5	95.8	95.4	104.0	99.1

TABLE XI (cont.)

INDEXES OF CONTRACT PRICE CHANGES: WAR DEPARTMENT

January 1942–August 1945

(October 1942 = 100)

Month	War Dept.	Army Air Forces	Ordnance	Signal Corps	Corps of Engineers	Chemical Warfare Service	Medical Dept.	Quarter-master Corps	Trans-portation Corps
1944									
January	90.4	88.0	90.3	83.8	95.4	95.6	88.0	103.7	99.1
February	88.2	83.7	89.7	83.8	95.4	94.8	86.5	102.4	98.8
March	87.7	83.0	89.4	83.3	95.4	93.5	83.7	102.3	98.7
April	86.9	82.3	88.6	82.1	95.0	92.7	82.0	102.1	98.5
May	85.6	81.0	87.0	79.7	94.9	91.5	79.5	101.9	98.3
June	84.5	79.0	86.3	79.7	94.3	90.9	77.9	102.1	98.3
July	83.1	77.0	83.8	79.2	93.8	90.0	76.2	103.0	98.0
August	82.7	76.1	83.6	79.2	93.6	88.7	74.4	103.8	97.9
September	81.3	73.7	83.2	78.1	93.7	88.3	71.9	104.3	97.9
October	81.1	73.4	82.7	78.0	93.7	88.2	70.0	104.4	98.0
November	80.9	73.4	82.4	76.8	94.2	87.9	69.0	104.8	97.9
December	80.5	72.9	81.9	76.3	94.3	86.7	67.7	105.0	97.5
1945									
January	79.6	71.2	81.6	76.2	93.9	85.4	65.8	105.5	96.2
February	79.4	71.0	81.4	75.7	94.2	84.4	64.1	105.5	95.6
March	79.1	70.8	80.9	74.0	94.3	84.1	63.6	105.7	95.2
April	77.4	67.8	80.6	73.0	94.5	83.0	61.9	106.3	94.9
May	76.2	65.5	80.3	72.7	94.5	81.2	60.4	107.5	94.2
June	75.5	64.3	80.2	73.1	94.6	80.7	58.9	107.3	93.7
July	75.5	64.1	80.3	72.7	94.4	80.3	58.6	107.8	94.1
August	75.4	64.0	80.3	72.7	94.5	80.3	57.8	107.5	94.1

Source: War Department, Purchases Division, Headquarters, ASF, *Indexes of Contract Price Changes*, July 1945. Corrected data for June, July, and August 1945, from files of Current Procurement Branch, Logistics Division, General Staff, United States Army.

APPENDIX D

TABLE XII

INDEXES OF CONTRACT PRICE CHANGES NAVY DEPARTMENT

January 1942–August 1945

(October 1942 = 100)

Month	Navy Dept.	Bureau of Aeronautics	Bureau of Ordnance	Bureau of Ships Shipbuilding Division	Bureau of Ships Electronics Divison	Bureau of Supplies and Accounts	Bureau of Medicine and Surgery
1942							
Jan.	106.0	113.6	102.3	103.9	104.4	98.3	108.6
Feb.	106.2	114.4	102.6	103.9	104.2	98.3	108.6
Mar.	106.1	113.5	102.5	104.2	104.2	98.4	108.6
Apr.	104.5	109.5	100.4	104.0	103.8	99.0	108.6
May	104.2	109.0	100.4	103.7	103.4	99.7	108.6
June	102.8	106.7	100.6	101.3	101.8	100.5	105.6
July	103.7	110.1	100.6	101.1	101.6	101.1	104.7
Aug.	102.2	105.7	100.2	100.7	101.5	100.7	102.3
Sept.	100.5	100.7	100.2	100.7	100.8	99.9	101.6
Oct.	100.0	100.0	100.0	100.0	100.0	100.0	100.0
Nov.	98.8	100.4	98.4	98.2	96.3	100.0	99.6
Dec.	98.5	100.2	98.2	98.0	94.7	99.9	99.2
1943							
Jan.	98.1	99.8	98.0	97.8	92.5	100.6	98.3
Feb.	97.9	99.6	97.9	97.6	92.7	100.5	98.0
Mar.	97.5	99.4	97.7	97.1	91.1	100.8	96.5
Apr.	96.9	99.9	96.2	96.4	89.7	100.3	95.7
May	96.7	99.4	95.8	96.3	89.6	100.8	95.0
June	95.6	98.9	94.8	94.0	87.8	103.5	92.4
July	93.2	91.4	94.1	93.5	87.7	103.7	92.4
Aug.	92.1	89.3	93.1	93.0	86.2	103.6	91.6
Sept.	89.5	83.0	92.7	92.2	82.5	103.6	91.7
Oct.	89.0	83.1	91.5	91.5	81.6	103.8	89.5
Nov.	88.5	82.4	90.4	91.4	81.2	104.0	88.8
Dec.	87.7	82.3	89.3	90.0	80.3	103.6	88.1
1944							
Jan.	86.4	79.6	87.6	89.8	79.8	103.6	88.1
Feb.	85.8	78.0	86.8	89.8	79.7	103.7	88.0
Mar.	84.7	75.3	86.3	89.5	78.6	103.6	88.0
Apr.	85.4	77.9	86.2	89.4	78.4	103.7	85.7
May	84.8	77.0	85.3	89.4	77.6	103.7	85.3
June	84.5	77.0	85.1	89.3	75.6	103.6	84.2
July	84.1	76.8	84.4	89.2	73.9	103.8	85.8
Aug.	83.6	76.0	84.1	89.1	72.2	104.1	84.8
Sept.	82.9	75.2	83.3	89.0	69.7	104.2	84.8

TABLE XII (cont.)

INDEXES OF CONTRACT PRICE CHANGES NAVY DEPARTMENT

January 1942–August 1945

(October 1942 = 100)

Month	Navy Dept.	Bureau of Aeronautics	Bureau of Ordnance	Bureau of Ships Shipbuilding Division	Bureau of Ships Electronics Divison	Bureau of Supplies and Accounts	Bureau of Medicine and Surgery
1944							
Oct.	82.2	73.8	83.0	89.0	68.5	104.1	84.7
Nov.	81.5	73.0	82.4	88.1	67.7	104.1	84.4
Dec.	81.1	73.1	81.5	87.4	66.7	104.2	84.3
1945							
Jan.	80.4	71.5	80.9	87.4	65.4	104.1	85.7
Feb.	80.2	70.8	79.9	88.0	64.8	104.2	85.8
Mar.	79.9	71.0	79.3	87.8	63.9	104.0	84.5
Apr.	79.8	71.2	78.9	87.6	63.6	104.0	85.3
May	78.6	68.0	78.7	86.4	63.3	104.2	85.5
June	78.4	68.0	77.6	86.4	62.8	104.3	85.9
July	78.2	67.5	77.4	86.4	62.6	104.4	85.9
Aug.	78.1	67.3	77.3	86.4	62.4	104.3	85.9

Source: Navy Department, Price Analysis Division, OP&M, *Indexes of Navy Contract Prices.*

INDEX

Council of National Defense, 48–49, 168
Crisis society, meaning of, 15
Crowell, J. Franklin, 38 n., 124 n.

DANN, ROBERT R., 173 n., 178 n.
Davis, Chester C., 48
Defense Plant Corporation (DPC), reduction of risks, 117–118; renegotiation, 172
Developmental contracts, 31, 70, 128, 131, 227, 249
Division of Contract Distribution, establishment of, 51–52
Draper, Col. W. H., Jr., 62 n., 63 n.

ECONOMIC MOBILIZATION, Canada, 24; Great Britain, 24; impact of, 17; importance of, 1; Japan, 24; purpose, 2; U. S., 24
Economic stabilization, 11–13, 79–82; recommendation, 250–251. *See also* Office of Price Administration
Educational Order Act of 1938, 28, 85 n.
Elliott, Harriet, 48
Emergency plant facility contract, 116–117
Emergency Price Control Act of 1942, 68–70; extension in 1944, 78. *See also* Office of Price Administration
Emergency Purchases, 70
Escalation clauses, material and labor costs, 135–137, 252
Excess Profits Tax, Act of 1940, 169; effects on incentives, 184–185
Executive Order 9001, negotiated contract, 52; advance and progress payments, 118–119

FACILITIES EXPANSION, accelerated amortization, 114–116; methods of financing, 113–120; public financing, 116–118
Ferrand, G. M., 173 n.
First War Powers Act, advance and progress payments, 118–119; CPPC and CPFF contracts, 124; negotiated contracts, 52, 89; relief under, 96, 139 n.
Fisher, Allan G. B., 9 n.
Fixed-price contracts, 95, 133–146; escalation clauses, 135–137; incentive

contract, 144–146; maximum price contract, 137–139; simple, 134; War Department price adjustment clauses, 139–144
Folsom, Frank, 53, 55, 61
Forrestal, James V., 54, 55 n., 67 n., 68 n., 72 n., 74 n.
Forrestal War Labor Board Clause, 137 n.
Freiberg, Albert M., 30 n., 32 n., 33 n.
Friedrich, C. J., 30 n.
Furlong, Admiral, 168 n.

GALBRAITH, J. K., 73 n., 75 n., 76 n.
General Accounting Office, 29; CPFF contract, 125–126
General Maximum Price Regulation (GMPR), 69–71
Ginsburg, David, 114 n.
Goldsmith, R. W., 93, 94 n.
Goubeau, Vincent deP., 96 n.
Government-owned-contractor-operated (GOCO) plants, 129, 131

HANSEN, HENRY E., report of conference, 259–278
Hardy, Charles O., 38 n.
Harris, Seymour E., 9 n., 98 n.
Hart, Albert G., 16 n.
Henderson, Leon, 48, 66 n., 67, 68 n., 72 n., 74 n.
Hensel, H. Struve, 40 n., 89 n., 124 n., 164 n., 165 n., 171 n.
Herring, Pendleton, 39 n., 44 n., 45 n., 46 n.
Hill, A. C. C., Jr., 50 n.
Hillman, Sidney, 48, 52 n.
House Naval Affairs Committee, 170–171

IDENTICAL BIDS, 35
Incentive contract, 144–146
Incentives to efficiency, conference report on, 271–278; in peacetime, 7–8; recommendations, 252–253, 255; use of price system, 246–248; in wartime, 11. *See also* Incentive pricing
Incentive pricing, company pricing program, 200; discretionary exemption from renegotiation, 185–187; effects of excess profits tax on, 184–185; effects of renegotiation, 181–185, 220; problems in future pricing,

Date Due

NOV 21 1969

RESERVE

OFF RES.